SCIENCE TEACHER'S INSTANT LABS KIT

Michael F. Fleming

Illustrated by Michael F. Fleming,
nephew of the author.

THE CENTER FOR APPLIED
RESEARCH IN EDUCATION
West Nyack, New York 10995

Library of Congress Cataloging-in-Publication Data

Fleming, Michael F., 1938–
   Science teacher's instant labs kit / Michael F. Fleming;
illustrated by Michael F. Fleming.
       p.   cm.
     ISBN 0-87628-861-1
       1. Physical sciences—Technique—Study and teaching (Secondary)
     2. Biology—Technique—Study and teaching (Secondary)
     3. Laboratories—Technique—Study and teaching (Secondary)
     I. Title.
     Q182.5.F57   1991
     507.8—dc20   91–28832
                                                                      CIP

ISBN   0-87628-861-1

**THE CENTER FOR APPLIED
RESEARCH IN EDUCATION**
West Nyack, New York 10995

Dedication

To Max P. Gannon and Dr. Samuel M. Long,
both of whom played major roles in
my success and happiness as a teacher.

Acknowledgments

Sincere thanks and appreciation to Sandra Hutchison, whose generous editorial help was always available and invaluable . . .

to Zsuzsa Neff, Production Editor, whose assistance was invaluable in the fine tuning of the final manuscript . . .

to my students, who over the years provided me with feedback for my classroom innovations, and played a major role in my longevity as a teacher . . .

and to my nephew, Michael F. Fleming, whose artwork is excellent and a major contribution to the book.

About the Author

For more than 30 years, Michael F. Fleming has taught biology, anatomy and physiology, microbiology, and behavioral science in the Council Rock School System of Newtown, Pennsylvania. He earned his M.Ed. and Ed.D. degrees at The Pennsylvania State University. He has participated in curriculum development and is vitally interested in new and novel approaches in motivating students to experience learning as an ongoing and enjoyable process. He has been awarded National Science Foundation summer grants and research grants from the Heart Association of Southeastern Pennsylvania. Dr. Fleming has presented papers at conventions of the National Association of Biology Teachers and has published articles in *The American Biology Teacher* and *Focus.* He is the author of *Life Science Labs Kit,* also published by The Center for Applied Research in Education.

Michael F. Fleming, nephew of the author and artist for the activities, is a graduate of The John Herrow School of Art at I.U.P.U.I. in Indianapolis, Indiana.

About This Resource

The *Science Teacher's Instant Labs Kit* offers you more than 40 fully developed, classroom-tested laboratory investigations in the physical and biological sciences for students in grades 7 through 12.

Part I, Content Area Investigations, features 26 activities in astronomy, chemistry, physics, biology, microbiology, genetics, anatomy, nutrition, classification, and more. Part II, Basic Science Process Lessons and Activities, contains 18 investigations you can use sequentially or as needed to teach vital science process skills. It covers specific laboratory techniques, various methods of research, and graphing and simple statistics—all in the context of active investigations. Depending on the abilities of your students, you may actually prefer to begin in Part II.

All 44 activities carefully develop students' understanding with step-by-step procedures and many opportunities for hands-on learning. To make the investigations easy to use, they include:

- lists of the easy-to-obtain materials required
- achievements expected of the students
- fully-illustrated, step-by-step directions to help you guide student learning
- reproducible worksheets that actively involve students in investigating, recording data, and analyzing results
- reproducible crossword puzzles, message squares, library research questions, and evaluation activities
- complete answer keys.

Read each activity before using it with your students and modify it as necessary to meet your particular needs. Make sure that both you and your students are aware of any pertinent safety precautions suggested by the text or by your classroom situation. In addition, be certain that you are familiar with your school district's safety guidelines for laboratory activities and that your classroom has proper safety equipment for all emergencies.

The investigations in the *Science Teacher's Instant Labs Kit* will introduce your students to a full range of scientific disciplines while they equip them with the skills and techniques they need to experience the excitement of real scientific inquiry.

—**Michael F. Fleming**

Contents

Unit 7: Graphing and Simple Statistics   **250**

Activities:

Part I
CONTENT AREA
INVESTIGATIONS

Unit 1
The Physical Sciences

1.1 ACIDS, BASES, AND INDICATORS

You Will Need the Following Materials:

pHydrion paper

red litmus paper

blue litmus paper

Congo red solution

ethyl alcohol

unsweetened grape juice

methyl red solution

red cabbage juice

beakers

glass stirring rods

distilled water

dropper bottles

selection of substances to test, such as dilute acid and base solutions, antacid, white vinegar, household ammonia, baking soda

lab aprons

safety goggles

paper towels

waste containers for used paper towels and paper indicators

Upon Completion of This Activity, Students Will

- Understand the concept of pH and its importance for living organisms.
- Have become familiar with the pH scale and how to interpret it.
- Know, in terms of ions, what differentiates an acid from a base.
- Have discovered the various color changes that indicators undergo in the presence of acids and bases.
- Have tested various materials found around the home for acidity and alkalinity.

1. The Students Are Introduced to the Concept of pH and Its Importance for Living Organisms.

Explain to the students that the p in pH refers to the concentration of hydrogen ($H+$) ions (hydrogen atoms with a positive charge) present in a solution. The greater the concentration of these hydrogen ions, the stronger the acid. Conversely, the lesser the concentration of the hydrogen ions, the weaker the acid. A base, on the other hand, is determined by the concentration of hydroxyl ($OH-$) ions (OH atoms with a negative charge) in a solution. The greater the concentration of these hydroxyl atoms, the stronger the base, and the lesser the concentration, the weaker the base.

Write on the chalkboard the formulas for sulfuric acid (H_2SO_4), hydrochloric acid (HCl), nitric acid (HNO_3), sodium hydroxide (NaOH), ammonium hydroxide (NH_4OH), and magnesium hydroxide $Mg(OH)_2$. Ask the students to indicate which are acids and which are bases. (**Answer: The formulas for acids are those with the H, and the formulas for bases are those with the OH.**) The acids contain H+ ions, and the bases contain OH− ions. If a solution has an equal concentration of H+ ions and OH− ions, then that solution is said to be **neutral**; that is, neither acid nor base. An example of a neutral solution is pure water (H_2O or HOH).

Explain to the students that the human body must maintain certain pH levels in order to function properly. For example, the pH of the skin and the gastric juice in the stomach should be in the acid range. The pH of blood tissue should be within the base range of 7.3 to 7.4. Fluid secreted by the pancreas into the duodenum (first section of the small intestine) should have a pH in the base range. Many chemical activities are specific in their need for either an acid or base environment.

2. The Students Are Introduced to the pH Scale.

Write the following scale on the chalkboard for the students to copy:

pH Scale

0 1 2 3 4 5 6 7 8 9 10 11 12 13 14

Have the students circle the number 7. Explain that 7 is considered neutral; that is, the solution has an equal concentration of H+ and OH− ions. Zero through 6 are varying strengths of acid, with 0 being the stronger and 6 the weaker. Eight through 14 are varying strengths of base (another term for base is alkaline), with 8 being weaker and 14 being stronger.

3. The Students Learn the Value of Materials Called Indicators.

Explain that an indicator is a material that when brought into contact with a solution identifies it as an acid or a base by means of a color change. Some indicators identify only whether the solution is an acid or a base, whereas other indicators go a step further and can show the strength or weakness along the pH scale. This latter ability is important when a scientist is preparing an acid or base solution that must be a particular pH.

4. The Students Experience Using Various Indicators and Discover How Their Color Changes Are Related to Acids and Bases.

Set up at six stations around the lab the solutions that the students are going to test. Set up at stations one, two, and three, respectively, the following solutions: (1) a **very weak** acid solution, prepared using a ratio of two drops of hydrochloric acid per 10ml of distilled water (**SAFETY NOTE: Place this at station #1 along with a card indicating that the solution is potentially**

dangerous and can cause skin burns and clothes damage upon contact); (2) a **very weak** base solution, prepared using a ratio of two drops of sodium hydroxide per 10ml of distilled water (**SAFETY NOTE: Place this at station #2 along with a card indicating that the solution is potentially dangerous and can cause skin burns and clothes damage upon contact**); (3) a **very weak** base solution of household bleach, prepared by using a ratio of two drops of household ammonia per 10ml of distilled water (**SAFETY NOTE: Place this at station #3 along with a card indicating that the solution is potentially dangerous and can cause skin burns and clothes damage upon contact**). Continue setting up stations four, five, and six, respectively, with white vinegar, an antacid tablet dissolved in distilled water, and baking soda dissolved in water. (You might wish to substitute materials and/or add materials. If so, have the students make the proper changes on Worksheet 1.1–1 when they are distributed.) At each station place the following indicators, using dropper bottles for the liquids: pHydrion paper, red litmus paper, blue litmus paper, unsweetened grape juice, Congo red solution, methyl red solution, and red cabbage juice.

(The unsweetened grape juice can be used full strength. The Congo red solution is prepared as a 0.1 percent solution of the powder in distilled water. The methyl red solution is prepared by dissolving 0.1 grams of the powder in 300ml of ethyl alcohol and then diluting to 500ml with distilled water. The red cabbage juice is prepared by boiling a few red cabbage leaves in water.)

Also place at each station the following additional materials: a small beaker and glass stirring rod, paper towels, and a waste container for used paper towels and indicator papers.

Distribute copies of Worksheet 1.1–1. Review with the students the instructions and review the indicators that they will be using. Emphasize that caution is to be used at those stations at which you have placed the caution cards; that is, the stations that have the very dilute hydrochloric acid, the very dilute sodium hydroxide solution, and the very dilute household ammonia solution.

Upon completion of Worksheet 1.1–1 discuss the correct answers with the class.

The indicators change color as follows:

The pHydrion paper turns orange to red in acids and light green to very dark green in bases.

The red litmus paper remains red in acids and turns blue in bases.

The blue litmus paper turns red in acids and remains blue in bases.

The Congo red solution turns blue in stronger acids and red in weaker acids. In base solutions it just colors the solution a light red.

The methyl red solution turns red in stronger acids and yellow in weaker acids and bases.

The grape juice turns red in acids and blue to blue-green in bases.

The red cabbage juice turns pink in acids and blue-green in bases.

The solutions tested by the students will give the following results:

> Hydrochloric acid and white vinegar will test out acid. The remaining solutions will test out basic.

5. The Students Test Various Materials at Home for Acid or Base.

Distribute copies of Worksheet 1.1–2 along with a supply of pHydrion papers and instruct the students to test as many of the itemized materials as they can find at home.

Prior to the students taking the worksheet home, have them guess which of the materials will be acid and which will be base. Pool their responses and record for comparing with the actual data results when discussed in class.

6. The Students Learn Some Additional Information About Chemistry.

Distribute copies of Worksheet 1.1–3. **The answers to the Library Research Questions are** 1. Catalyst. 2. Exothermic. 3. Great quantities of heat will be generated. This is not a safe situation. 4. It is very sensitive to H+ and OH− ion concentrations. 5. There are 2 atoms of hydrogen in a molecule of water.

WORKSHEET 1.1–1
EXPLORING THE USE OF ACID AND BASE INDICATORS

Instructions:

1. Put on lab aprons and safety goggles.

2. Proceeding from station to station, test each solution with each of the seven indicators. Use each indicator as follows:

   a. pHydrion paper: Remove a small strip of the indicator paper. Place the strip on a paper towel. Using the glass stirring rod, carefully transfer a drop of the solution to be tested to the indicator paper. Note any color change and match this color with the pH scale on the indicator box. Record the color change and the pH number. Dispose of the paper towel and the indicator strip in the container provided at the station.

   b. Red litmus paper and blue litmus paper: Follow the instructions in part a above. With the litmus papers, there will be no pH scale to use, so all that you record is color change, if any.

   c. Congo red solution, methyl red solution, grape juice, and red cabbage juice: Carefully pour a small amount of the solution to be tested into a beaker. Add a few drops of the indicator solution and carefully stir with a glass stirring rod. Record any color change. Thoroughly rinse the beaker and stirring rod with water, and place back at the station.

   d. **IMPORTANT SAFETY NOTE:** At stations #1, #2, and #3 the solutions to be tested are potentially dangerous and can cause skin burns and clothes damage upon contact. If you get any of these liquids on your skin, immediately rinse your skin with water and notify your teacher. Also, if you get any of these liquids on your clothing, immediately notify your teacher. Contaminated clothing can eventually cause skin burns.

DATA TABLE FOR RECORDING RESULTS						
	Station					
Data	**1**	**2**	**3**	**4**	**5**	**6**
pHydrion color?						
pHydrion pH number?						
Red litmus color?						
Blue litmus color?						
Congo red color?						
Methyl red color?						
Grape juice color?						
Red cabbage juice color?						

Using the data you have collected above, answer the following questions:

1. a. According to your pHydrion data, which solutions tested as acid?

   _____

   b. What is the color change of pHydrion papers in an acid?

   _____

2. a. According to your pHydrion data, which solutions tested as base?

   _____

   b. What is the color change of pHydrion papers in a base?

   _____

Now that you have learned which solutions are acid and which are base using the pHydrion paper, you can deduce the answers to the following questions:

3. What color does blue litmus paper become in an acid? _____

   in a base? _____

4. What color does red litmus paper become in an acid? _____

   in a base? _____

5. What color does Congo red solution become in an acid? _____

   in a base? _____

6. What color does methyl red solution become in an acid? _____

   in a base? _____

7. What color does red cabbage juice become in an acid? _____

   in a base? _____

Name _____ Date _____

WORKSHEET 1.1–2
TESTING MATERIALS AT HOME FOR ACID AND BASE

Instructions: Test each of the following materials, if you have them around the house, with pHydrion paper, recording the information in the following data table:

Material Tested	Color Change	pH #	Acid or Base
grapefruit			
tea			
soft drink			
hand soap			
apple			
yogurt			
jam or jelly			
coffee			
lemon			
dish detergent			
dill pickle			
shampoo			
orange			
saliva			
mouthwash			
toothpaste			
hair spray			
shaving cream			

WORKSHEET 1.1–3
MESSAGE SQUARE ACTIVITY ON CHEMISTRY

Hint: A very important instruction to remember when mixing an acid with water

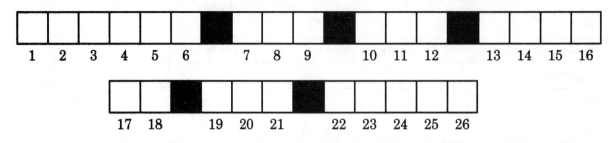

Put: an s in 6

    an a in 1, 4, 7, 13, and 23

    a t in 10, 17, 19, and 24

    a d in 8, 9, and 16

    an e in 12, 21, and 25

    a w in 22 and 3

    an l in 2

    an h in 11 and 20

    an r in 26

    a c in 14

    an i in 15

    an o in 18

    a y in 5

Anticipated Answer

_____

_____

_____

_____

_____

_____

_____

_____

_____

_____

_____

_____

Library Research Questions

Answers   Sources

1. What is the term for a substance that changes the rate of a chemical reaction without itself being used up in the reaction?

2. What is the term for the type of chemical reaction that releases energy?

3. What would happen if you mixed an acid with water in the opposite way from the important instruction above?

4. How does an electronic pH meter detect acids and bases?

5. What does the 2 mean in H_2O?

1.2 CONSTELLATIONS
AND THE CELESTIAL SPHERE

You Will Need the Following Materials:

overhead projector

opaque projector

sheets of opaque construction paper

protractors

paper clip or pin

flashlights

tape

star (constellation) map of
the night sky

red cellophane

Upon Completion of This Activity, Students Will

- Understand what a constellation is.
- Be able to locate Polaris, the North Star, as a starting point in locating constellations.
- Have experienced determining their latitude on Earth by determining the elevation of Polaris above the horizon.
- Understand the concept of the celestial sphere.
- Understand the cause of the apparent motions of the stars through the sky.
- Have learned how to locate selected constellations in the night sky.

1. The Students Are Introduced to the Apparent Motions of the Stars as Viewed from the North Pole.

Measure the image-projecting area of the glass plate on the overhead projector. It is usually 12 inches by 12 inches. Cut a piece of opaque construction paper the size of the image projecting area. Using Teacher Worksheet 1.2–1 as a template, punch pin holes (using the tip of a paper clip or dissection pin) through the construction paper. The first hole punched should be in the center of the paper. This represents Polaris. Placing the construction paper on the overhead projector will allow you to project Polaris (the North Star), the Big Dipper (part of the larger constellation Ursa Major), and the Little Dipper (part of the larger constellation Ursa Minor) on the classroom screen.

Begin by discussing with the students the concept of the constellation. They should realize that a constellation is a group or configuration of stars that have been given a name simply because they represent something to the viewer. For example, the Big and Little Dippers are so named because they look like ladles, or dippers.

The North Star is called Polaris because it is observed directly overhead at the Earth's north pole. Polaris is projected on the center of the screen to represent its being observed directly overhead by an observer standing at the north pole.

Explain that the sky is viewed as, and referred to as, the **celestial sphere**, an imaginary sphere to which the stars are attached. The movement of the stars across the sky is actually caused by the rotation of the Earth. However, we on the Earth are not aware of the Earth's rotation. To us it seems as though the stars move across the sky. It is convenient, therefore, for us to imagine that the stars are attached to the celestial sphere, and as the celestial sphere rotates, it carries the stars with it. The motion of the stars on this imaginary sphere is called **apparent motion**.

Keeping Polaris on the center of the screen and using it as the focal point of rotation, slowly rotate the construction paper so that the Dippers are moving in a counterclockwise direction on the screen. As you continue the rotation, it should be apparent to the students that Polaris remains stationary while the Dippers revolve around it. One complete revolution of the Dippers around Polaris equals one complete daily rotation of the Earth.

2. The Students Observe the Relationship Between Latitude on Earth and the Location of Polaris in the Sky.

Distribute copies of Worksheet 1.2–2. Explain to the students that a map of the Earth shows parallel lines running east-west. These are referred to as **parallels of latitude** and are measured in units called degrees. The equator is zero degrees latitude. The north pole is 90 degrees north latitude, and the south pole is 90 degrees south latitude.

Once again, project Polaris and the Dippers on the screen, with Polaris in the center of the screen. As you now proceed, have the students keep data in the data chart on the worksheet. On the worksheet map, have the students place a #1 at the location they would be standing at to observe Polaris as it is shown on the screen. (The #1 should be placed at the north pole.) How many degrees above the horizon is Polaris in the sky? (90 degrees.) At what degree latitude are you standing? (90 degrees.) Have the students imagine that they have moved their location 10 degrees south of the north pole to #2 on the worksheet at 80 degrees north latitude. Would Polaris remain directly overhead as shown on the screen? (No.) How would the position of Polaris in the sky change? (It would appear to be 10 degrees lower in the sky than it did when you were standing directly at the north pole.) How many degrees above the horizon is Polaris in the sky now? (80 degrees.) At what degree latitude are you standing? (80 degrees.) Show the change in position of Polaris on the screen by lowering the projected image a bit on the screen. Now have the students imagine that they have moved their location 50 degrees south of the north pole to #3 on the worksheet at 40 degrees north latitude. How would the position of Polaris in the sky change? (It would appear to be 50 degrees lower in the sky than it did when you stood directly at the north pole.) How many degrees above the horizon is Polaris in the sky now? (40 degrees.) At what degree latitude are you standing? (40 degrees.) You can again show the change in position of Polaris on the screen by lowering the projected image on the screen. At what point on Earth would Polaris be on the horizon? (At the equator.)

How many degrees above the horizon would Polaris be? (0 degrees.) At what latitude would you be on the equator? (0 degrees latitude.)

Have the students now examine their data table to determine the relationship between the second column (degrees above the horizon at which Polaris is located) and the third column (degrees of latitude at which you are standing). (The degrees above the horizon at which Polaris is located equals the degree of latitude from which you are observing Polaris from Earth.)

3. The Students Locate Polaris in the Night Sky and Determine Their Own Latitude on Earth.

Distribute copies of Worksheet 1.2–3. Once again project Polaris and the Dippers on the screen. The students have a similar diagram on the top of their worksheet. Have them make notes as you explain how to locate Polaris.

   a. First locate the Big Dipper in the northern section of the sky.
   b. The two stars making up the outer portion of the cup on the Big Dipper can be used as pointer stars in locating Polaris.
   c. Follow a short distance in the direction of the arrows on the worksheet and you will locate Polaris, which is the star at the tip of the handle of the Little Dipper.

Assign students (preferably in pairs to make data collecting easier and more accurate) to follow the directions on the worksheet in determining their latitude. Of course, the assignment depends upon the students' being able to locate an environment conducive to viewing the night sky. Hopefully you will have a few students able to carry out the assignment. Point out to them that there is a space on the worksheet to sketch the relative positions of the Big and Little Dippers as they are observed in the sky. The sketch should be as accurate as possible in terms of the positions of the Dippers, as this information is needed later on. Further, they should record the exact time that they make their sketch. (Later you will be projecting the student sketches on the screen in order to show the relationship between time of evening that the sketch was made and the position of the Dippers relative to Polaris. It might be advantageous to assign specific observation times to specific students. For example, have some prepare their sketches at 9:30 in the evening, some at 10:00, some at 10:30, and so on.)

4. The Students Review Their Understanding of the Apparent Movement of Constellations Through the Night Sky.

Upon completion of Worksheet 1.2–3 project student diagrams on the screen. Project the sketches in sequence from those drawn earliest in the evening to those drawn latest in the evening. Note specifically the relationship between the different times of evening that various drawings were made and the location of the

Dippers relative to Polaris. If the students have been accurate in facing north while preparing their sketches, it will be quite evident that the Dippers revolve counterclockwise around Polaris as the evening hours progress. Ask the students to explain this apparent movement of the two constellations through the night sky. (Recalling previous learning, the students should be able to explain that the apparent movement is due to the rotation of the Earth.)

5. The Students Learn Selected Constellations in the Night Sky.

You are going to introduce the students to three relatively easy-to-locate constellations. First, however, punch holes in pieces of construction paper to represent each of the constellations on Teacher Worksheet 1.2–4.

As you project Cassiopeia on the screen using the overhead, explain to the students that it can be located by starting at the star where the handle and the bowl meet in the Big Dipper. Follow in a straight line from this star to Polaris and continue in a straight line for a short distance and you will observe a very visible M or W described by five of Cassiopeia's six stars. (Include the sixth star and it resembles a chair.) You should now project a star map on the screen and show Cassiopeia in the context of other stars in the night sky.

Projecting Cepheus on the screen, explain that it can be located by starting at the pointer stars of the Big Dipper and following straight through Polaris for a short distance until the star at the tip of Cepheus is sighted. Now project the star map showing Cepheus in the context of the other night sky stars.

Finally, project Draco (the Dragon) on the screen. The star in the tip of Draco can be located approximately one quarter of the distance between the pointer stars of the Big Dipper and Polaris. The single line of stars in the tail of the Dragon swing around the Little Dipper and then double back, ending in a group of four stars forming the head of the Dragon. Once again, project the star map on the screen showing Draco in context.

An interesting project for some students would be to prepare a report on various constellations, including the derivation of their names and what they are supposed to represent.

Teacher Worksheet 1.2-1
Template of Dippers and Polaris

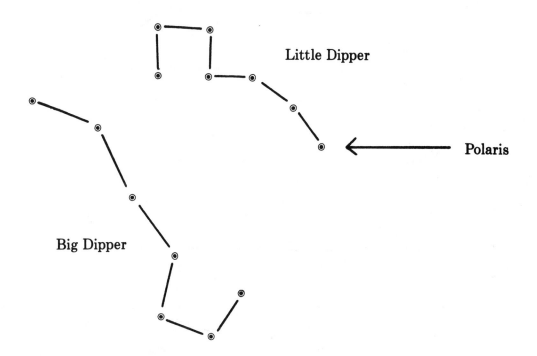

Little Dipper

⟵ Polaris

Big Dipper

Place this sheet over opaque construction paper when punching holes.

WORKSHEET 1.2–2
EXPLORING THE RELATIONSHIP BETWEEN
DEGREES OF ELEVATION OF POLARIS ABOVE THE HORIZON
AND DEGREES OF LATITUDE ON EARTH

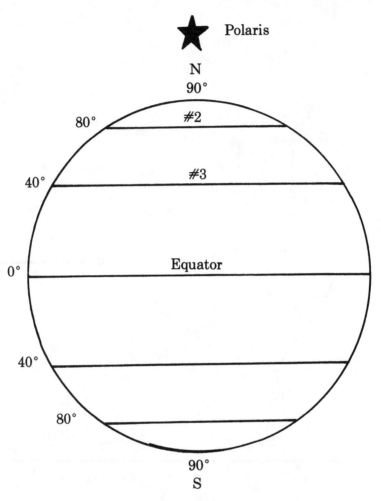

Record data in the following table during class discussion:

Polaris Observation Point	Degrees Above Horizon at Which Polaris Is Located	Degrees of Latitude at Which You Are Standing
1		
2		
3		
Equator		

WORKSHEET 1.2–3 DETERMINING YOUR LATITUDE
ON EARTH BY OBSERVING POLARIS

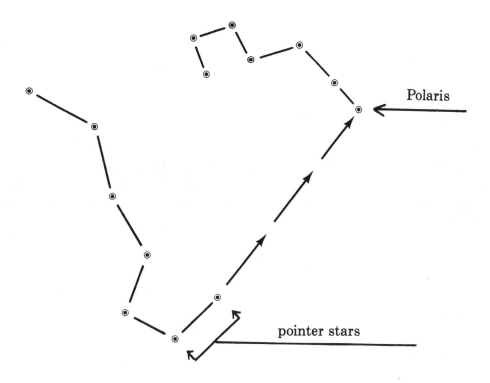

Polaris

pointer stars

Class notes on how to locate Polaris: _____

_____

_____

_____

_____

_____

_____

_____

_____

_____

Directions for determining your latitude on Earth:

1. Working with a classmate makes data collecting much easier and more accurate.
2. Locate an environment that is relatively free from extraneous light from street lamps and so on. Also, make sure that you have an unobstructed view of the northern sky and that the ground you are standing on is level.
3. Once Polaris has been located in the sky, stand facing it with one arm straight out in front of you. The other arm should be elevated until your index finger is pointing directly at Polaris.

4. On a sheet of paper, your classmate sketches the size of the angle between your two arms. See the following illustration:

5. The angle is then measured using a protractor. This angle is equal to your latitude on Earth.

6. In the space below, sketch the actual positions of the Big and Little Dippers as they appear to you as you face north (facing Polaris). To illuminate your paper, use a flashlight with red cellophane taped over the lens. Also record the time at which you made the drawing: _____ _____.

North

West

East

South

The constellation Cassiopeia:

The constellation Cepheus:

Place this sheet over opaque construction paper when punching holes.

The constellation Draco (the Dragon):

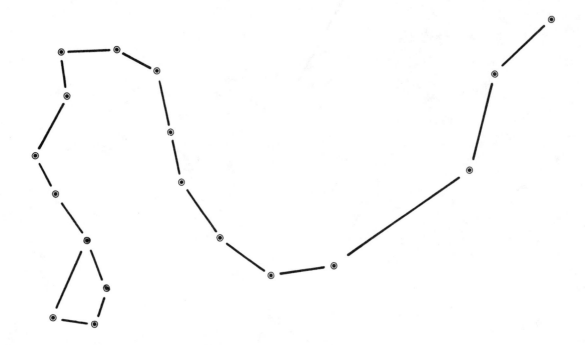

Place this sheet over opaque construction paper when punching holes.

1.3 STUDYING THE MOON USING BINOCULARS

You Will Need the Following Materials:

binoculars, 7 × 35 or other magnifying
    power (telescope can be used)

light source such as filmstrip
    projector

paper clips

tripod (or substitute)

map of surface features of
    the moon

rulers

white globe

opaque projector

masking tape

Upon Completion of This Activity, Students Will

- Have studied the moon's surface features using binoculars.
- Have prepared drawings of some prominent surface features of the moon.
- Know selected facts about the moon.
- Know the conditions under which the phases of the moon are produced.
- Have determined the path traveled by the moon through space.

1. The Students Assess Their Knowledge of Some Moon Facts.

Pass out copies of Worksheet 1.3–1. Upon completing it, discuss with the students the following correct answers: **1. w; 2. o; 3. h; 4. v; 5. l; 6. c; 7. j; 8. f; 9. m; 10. r; 11. q; 12. b; 13. s; 14. i**

2. The Students Receive Guidelines for Using Binoculars to Study the Moon.

The students should realize that a major concern when using binoculars to study the moon is that of firm support for the binoculars to prevent them from moving. A relatively simple way of achieving firm support is to secure the binoculars on a camera tripod. The binoculars can be secured to the camera platform by using masking tape. The tripod can easily be adjusted for convenient height and viewing angle. In addition, the hands are free for preparing drawings.

Although the best viewing time is considered to be two to four days following the first quarter, and the poorest during the full moon, one will want to view the moon through various phases to get complete drawings. When viewing the moon, the most vivid features are observed along the terminator (the boundary line separating light from darkness). **SAFETY CAUTION: It is strongly advised that you do not attempt to view the moon through binoculars or telescope during daylight hours. Should you accidentally view the sun through the**

binoculars or telescope, it takes only a few seconds for the sun's rays to destroy the retina, resulting in blindness.

Distribute copies of Worksheet 1.3–2. Review with the students the instructions on the worksheet regarding their observations and drawings of moon surface features. Encourage the students to go beyond the surface features indicated on the guide map and add as much detail as they can. Also encourage them not to look at any moon maps or photographs for help in this exercise because their drawings should be based solely on their own abilities of observation.

At the conclusion of this exercise, give the students the names of the moon structures numbered on the Guide Map. You might also wish to obtain a map of the moon's features and project it on the classroom screen, allowing students to compare it to their own drawings. Also project several of the students' drawings on the screen.

Answer key to the numbers on the Guide Map: lc = Tycho Crater; 2c = Copernicus Crater; 3c = Plato Crater; 4p = Mare Imbrium; 5p = Mare Serenity; 6p = Mare Tranquility; 7p = Oceanus Procellarum; 8p = Mare Humorum; 9p = Mare Nubium; 10m = Apennines Mountains; 11p = Mare Crisium.

3. The Students Determine the Path the Moon Travels Through Space.

Review with the students the fact that the moon revolves around the Earth once a month. Now ask a student to go to the chalkboard and draw the path that he or she thinks the moon would make during this revolution. The student will no doubt draw a circle. Explain to the students that a circle would be accurate **if the Earth were stationary in space.** However, the Earth is moving at a great speed through space. Keeping this fact in mind, have other students draw what they think might be the path. You will probably get various configurations, but it is doubtful you will get the accurate one.

Pass out copies of Worksheet 1.3–3 and review the instructions with the students. To do the worksheet takes some motor skills, and the students may need to make several attempts. The path of the moon determined should be

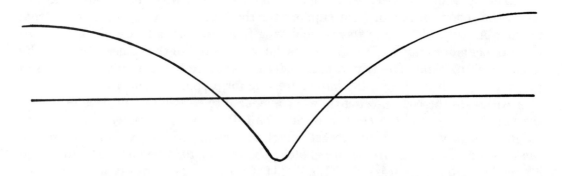

Note: If the pencil on dot #1 is moved too slowly, the results will be

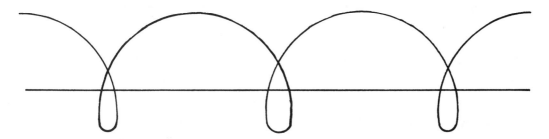

As has been determined, the actual path of the moon through space is not the path one would initially propose, and the actual path usually comes as a surprise to the students.

4. The Students Learn the Conditions Under Which the Phases of the Moon Are Produced.

The following activity can be set up as a demonstration.

Have a student sit facing a filmstrip projector located approximately ten feet from the student. The student's head represents the Earth, and the filmstrip projector represents the sun. Turn the projector on, directing its light not into the student's eyes but just over the top of his/her head.

Turn out the classroom lights. Hold a white globe, representing the moon, in the path of the projector's light between the projector and the student. Ask the student to indicate what portion of the moon's surface is visible from the Earth. **(Answer: None.)** This phase of the moon is called the **new moon**.

Revolve the moon 90 degrees counterclockwise around the student and ask what portion of the moon's surface is now visible from the Earth. **(Answer: One half.)** This phase is called the **first quarter**, meaning that the moon has traveled its first quarter of the distance around the Earth.

Revolve the moon another 90 degrees around the student and question the student. (The student is going to have to turn around in order to make the observation.) **(Answer: The entire surface.)** This phase is the **full moon**.

Finally, revolve the moon another 90 degrees and question the student. **(Answer: One half.)** This phase is the **last quarter**, meaning that the moon is now traveling its last quarter of the distance around the Earth.

The students should realize that new moon, first quarter, full moon, and last quarter together constitute the **monthly phases of the moon.**

5. The Students Work on an Activity Learning Some Additional Information Relating to the Moon.

Pass out copies of Worksheet 1.3–4. **The answers to the Library Research Questions are** 1. July 20th, 1969. 2. Neil Armstrong. 3. Apollo 11. 4. He was teaching the Copernican theory that the Earth revolves around the sun. 5. A refracting telescope is a series of lenses in a tube, and a reflecting telescope employs the use of a mirror.

WORKSHEET 1.3–1
WHAT DO YOU KNOW ABOUT THE MOON?

Instructions: Fill in the blanks in the left-hand column with the letters of the proper answers in the right-hand column.

_____ 1. discovered that the moon has craters

_____ 2. full moon

_____ 3. diameter of the moon

_____ 4. gravitational pull of the moon compared to Earth

_____ 5. man in the moon

_____ 6. rotation

_____ 7. lunar eclipse

_____ 8. libration

_____ 9. revolution

_____ 10. rays

_____ 11. new moon

_____ 12. mare

_____ 13. terminator

_____ 14. distance of the moon from Earth

a. Kepler
b. a "sea" on the moon
c. moon turning on its own axis
d. sun passes between Earth and moon
e. Newton
f. moon wobbling on its axis
g. ¾ that of Earth
h. about 2,160 miles
i. about 239,000 miles
j. Earth passes between sun and moon
k. three times that of Earth
l. caused by patterns of mountains and plains
m. moon circling around the Earth
n. moon passes between sun and Earth
o. this phase of the moon is visible
p. about 1,100 miles
q. this phase of the moon is not visible
r. radiate out from some moon craters
s. line separating light from darkness
t. about 550,000 miles
u. about 5,500 miles
v. ⅕ that of the Earth
w. Galileo

© 1992 by The Center for Applied Research in Education

Name _____   Date _____

WORKSHEET 1.3–2   MOON MAPPING

Blank Moon Map:

Guide Map:

Instructions: Each number on the guide map is in the vicinity of a feature on the surface of the moon to be observed and drawn on the blank map above. The letters following the numbers represent the following:

p = plain (large, dark, flat area)

c = crater

m = mountain range

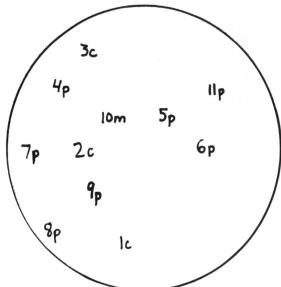

WORKSHEET 1.3–3   PATH OF THE MOON THROUGH SPACE

A

B

Instructions:

1. Tape this worksheet to a solid surface.
2. Using a ruler, draw a line from point A to point B. This line represents the path of the Earth through space.
3. Place a paper clip flat on the worksheet at point A, as shown in the diagram below:

A ————————————————— B

Note the two dots labeled 1 and 2 in the diagram. Two pencils should be held perpendicular to the dots, with each pencil point on a dot.

4. The pencil on dot 1 (representing the Earth) moves directly along the line toward point B. At the same time, revolve the pencil on dot 2 (representing the moon revolving around the Earth) clockwise around dot 1, keeping the paper clip taut.
5. For accurate results, the "moon" should make approximately one revolution around the "Earth" between points A and B.
6. The result of this endeavor is that the pencil on dot 2 will trace a path on the paper representing the path of the moon through space as it revolves around the Earth.

Name _____   Date _____

WORKSHEET 1.3–4
MESSAGE SQUARE ACTIVITY ABOUT THE MOON

A. *Hint:* Invented an astronomical telescope and carried out early observations of the moon

1   2   3   4   5   6   7

Anticipated Answer

Put: an I in 4.   _____
    an A in 2.   _____
    an E in 6.   _____
    an O in 7.   _____
    an L in 3 and 5.   _____
    a G in 1.   _____

B.   Hint: Location on the moon where the first manned mission landed

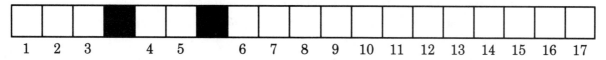

1   2   3   4   5   6   7   8   9   10   11   12   13   14   15   16   17

Anticipated Answer

Put: an S in 1.   _____
    an O in 4.   _____
    a Y in 17.   _____
    an L in 13 and 14.   _____
    an E in 2.   _____
    an F in 5.   _____
    a Q in 10.   _____
    a T in 6 and 16.   _____
    an R in 7.   _____
    an I in 12 and 15.   _____
    a U in 11.   _____
    an A in 3 and 8.   _____
    an N in 9.   _____

Library Research Questions   **Answers**   **Sources**

1. The date that the first manned
    moon mission landed.

2. Name of first man to step on
    moon's surface.

3. Name of the first manned moon
    mission.

4. Why was Galileo put on trial?

5. What is the basic design difference
    between a refracting and a reflecting
    telescope?

1.4 THE SUN

You Will Need the Following Materials:

miniature globe of Earth	light source (filmstrip projector)
large globe of Earth	large glass jar or bottle
thermometer	small telescope (or binoculars)
camera tripod	sheet of white paper
masking tape	

Upon Completion of This Activity, Students Will

- Understand the factors involved in changes of season.
- Realize the significance of solstices and equinoxes.
- Have taken a self-test and become acquainted with many facts about the sun.
- Understand what is meant by the "greenhouse effect."
- Have indirectly observed and tracked the movement of sunspots.

1. The Students Test Their Own Knowledge of Sun Facts.

Pass out copies of Worksheet 1.4–1 and let the students take the self-test. **Upon completion, go over the correct answers, which are** 1. t; 2. e; 3. z; 4. p; 5. m; 6. i; 7. v; 8. y; 9. c; 10. s; 11. j; 12. g; 13. w; 14. u; 15. l; 16. d; 17. q; 18. f; 19. n; 20. o.

2. The Students Learn About the Greenhouse Effect.

Into a large glass jar, place a miniature globe of the Earth and a small thermometer. The jar should be placed in the sunlight (preferably outdoors) with its lid removed. Be sure that the thermometer is located in the shade of the globe so that it is not in direct sunlight.

Explain to the students that the jar represents the atmosphere surrounding the Earth. Short-wave radiant energy waves from the sun pass through the Earth's atmosphere and hit the Earth. This radiant energy is absorbed by the Earth, causing the Earth to warm. This warmth is in turn radiated into the atmosphere in the form of long heat-energy waves. The carbon dioxide in the atmosphere traps these long heat-energy waves and, as a result, the atmosphere heats up. This heating up of the atmosphere is called the **greenhouse effect**. The glass of the jar represents the atmosphere, because like the real atmosphere, it allows the sun's short-wave radiant energy to pass in but tends to prevent the longer heat-energy waves from passing back out. If it were not for the greenhouse effect, we would not have the life-sustaining warmth that we need here on Earth. Now take a temperature reading. Ask the students to comment on what would happen if the carbon dioxide levels in the atmosphere increased. This can be simulated by putting the lid on the jar. Waiting a few minutes and then taking another temperature reading will show that the temperature has increased.

The important point that should be stressed is that some scientists feel that the carbon dioxide in the Earth's atmosphere is increasing to a dangerous level. This they say will cause the Earth's atmosphere to heat to unacceptable levels.

3. The Students Learn the Causes of the Seasons.

Show the students a large globe of the Earth and have them note that its axis of rotation is tilted 23½ degrees. It is because of this tilt that we experience different seasons during the course of a year.

Place a light source (filmstrip projector) in the center of the classroom. This represents the sun. Hold the globe of the Earth in position #1, as illustrated in the following diagram (refer back to this diagram for positions 2, 3, and 4):

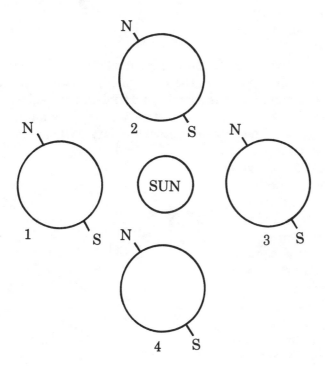

Explain that this represents the relationship between the sun and moon in winter in the Northern Hemisphere. Further, winter in the Northern Hemisphere begins around December 22. This day is referred to as the winter solstice, and it is the shortest day of the year. From this day until the first day of summer, the days will lengthen.

Draw the sketch at the right on the chalkboard. Explain that it shows the relationship between the sun in the sky and the surface of the Earth as winter begins around December 22 in the Northern Hemisphere. On this day the sun's daily arc across the sky is at its lowest. Have the students note that the sun's rays hit the Earth's surface at an angle, thus spreading the sunlight's warming radiant energy over a larger area than occurs in summer, when the sun's rays hit the Earth's surface more directly. Thus, the sun's rays during winter do not heat the Earth as much as they do during summer.

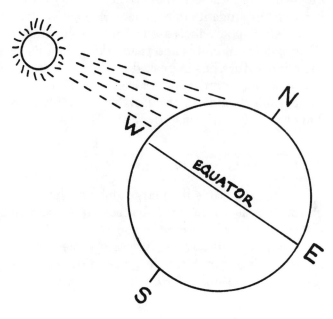

Now hold the globe of the Earth in position #3 (see above diagram). Explain to the students that this represents the relationship between the sun and Earth in summer. Further, summer in the Northern Hemisphere begins around June 21. This day is referred to as the summer solstice, and it is the longest day of the year. From this day until the first day of winter, the days will shorten.

Draw the sketch at the right on the chalkboard. Explain that it shows the relationship between the sun in the sky and the surface of the Earth as summer begins around June 21 in the Northern Hemisphere. On this day the sun's daily arc across the sky is at its highest. Have the students note that the sun's rays hit the Earth much more directly than they do during the winter season. Thus, the sun's rays during summer heat the Earth more than they do during winter.

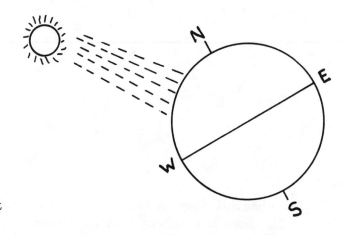

Now hold the globe in position #2 and then #4 (see above diagram). Explain to the students that these two similar positions represent the relationship between the sun and Earth in autumn and spring. Autumn in the Northern Hemisphere begins around September 23, and spring begins around March 20. These dates are referred to as the autumnal and spring equinoxes, respectively. On these dates the sun is directly over the equator, and the lengths of day and night are equal. The sun's arc in the sky is midway between that of summer and that of winter.

4. The Students Learn How to Indirectly Observe and Track the Movement of Sunspots.

Pass out Worksheet 1.4–2 and go over the procedure with the students. **SAFETY CAUTION: Strongly emphasize to the students that at no time should they observe the sun directly through a telescope or binoculars (even for an instant) as it can cause serious damage to the retina of the eye.**

The answer to the question on the worksheet is The sunspots appear to be moving across the surface of the sun from west to east as the sun rotates.

WORKSHEET 1.4–1   THE SUN AND OTHER STARS

Instructions: For each of the following statements, select the correct answer from the list at the bottom and place the appropriate letter in the blank in the left-hand column.

_____ 1. The sun is not classified as a planet but as a what?

_____ 2. The direction in which the sun appears to move across the sky

_____ 3. The season of the year during which the sun is closest to the Earth

_____ 4. The average distance in miles from the Earth to the sun

_____ 5. The cause of a solar eclipse

_____ 6. The oldest form of a time-keeping device

_____ 7. The collective name for the group of constellations that the sun (along with the moon and the planets) appears to move through over the course of a year

_____ 8. Specific details observed on the surface of the sun resulting from turbulence

_____ 9. Visible in the immediate area around the sun at the time of total solar eclipse

_____ 10. The name given to the visible surface of the sun

_____ 11. Breaks down sunlight into bands of different colors

_____ 12. On the first day of winter in the Northern Hemisphere, the sun shines directly on this line of demarcation on the Earth

_____ 13. The type of energy emitted by the sun that has a warming effect on the Earth

_____ 14. An instrument used to measure star positions in the sky

_____ 15. The term used as a relative measure of star brightness

_____ 16. Another name for double stars

_____ 17. Term used for the explosion of a star

_____ 18. The name for the energy-releasing process by the sun

_____ 19. On the first day of summer in the Northern Hemisphere, the sun shines directly on this line of demarcation on the Earth

_____ 20. The most abundant gas comprising the sun

Answer list:

a. Earth moves between sun and moon

b. nitrogen

c. corona

d. binaries

e. east to west

f. thermonuclear fusion

g. Tropic of Capricorn

h. summer

i. sundial

j. prism

k. west to east

l. magnitude

m. moon moves between sun and Earth

n. Tropic of Cancer

o. hydrogen

p. 93 million miles

q. nova

r. sun moves between Earth and moon

s. photosphere

t. star

u. astrolabe

v. zodiac

w. radiant

x. 250 million miles

y. sunspots

z. winter

Name _____   Date _____

WORKSHEET 1.4–2
INDIRECTLY OBSERVING AND TRACKING SUNSPOTS

Sunspots are thought to be storms on the surface of the sun. They persist for weeks to months. According to data collected, sunspots increase to a maximum number in 11-year cycles.

Instructions:

1. **IMPORTANT SAFETY CAUTION: Never observe the sun directly through a telescope or binoculars (even for an instant), as it can cause immediate and permanent serious damage to the eye.**

2. Secure a telescope (or pair of binoculars) to a camera tripod using masking tape.

3. The tripod should support the telescope about two feet above the surface of the ground. A piece of white paper should be positioned on the ground beneath the telescope. Note the following illustration:

4. Through trial and error, line the telescope up with the sun until an image of the sun's disk is projected on the white paper, as illustrated above. **SAFETY NOTE: Once again, do not look through the telescope or binoculars to line them up with the sun. Rely on the indirect method of looking at the sheet of paper for the sun's image.**

5. Once you have the image of the sun's disk on the paper, adjust the focusing knob of the telescope to bring the image into sharp focus. Now look at the image for any black spots. These are sunspots. (If you do not observe any sunspots, wait for a week or so and then try again.)

6. Once sunspots are observed, draw them on the #1 blank sun image circle below. Label with the date of your observation. Then on three or four consecutive days (it is okay if you are interrupted by a couple of cloudy days), follow the same procedure outlined above and prepare further drawings of your indirect observations of the sunspots in the blank sun image circles. After collecting your data, answer the question below.

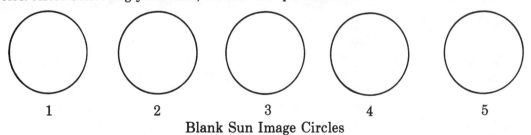

   1   2   3   4   5

Blank Sun Image Circles

Question: What have you determined about the sunspots from your sequence of drawings?

_____

_____

_____

1.5 ELECTRICITY

You Will Need the Following Materials:

paper and pencil

Upon Completion of This Activity, Students Will

- Know what an electric current is.
- Know how to interpret and calculate using Ohm's law.
- Have conducted a home survey of electrical appliances, gathering and interpreting data in terms of relative amounts of current used and cost of operation.
- Know how to define and calculate watts and know their relationship to the amount of electricity used by appliances.
- Know how to calculate kilowatt hours and how they are used in determining the monthly electric bill.

1. The Students Survey Electricity Usage in Their Own Homes.

Distribute copies of Worksheet 1.5–1. Instruct the students to fully inform their parents as to what the activity involves, and have them ask for their permission and help in gathering the data. Apartment-dwelling students will not be able to collect data of their own if the apartment does not have its own electric meter. Have these students help the others in data collecting. Because heating sources must be turned off, this activity might best be used during warm weather.

When discussing the data results with the class, emphasize the following points, which should be supported by their data findings. A. Stereos (cassette and/or compact disk players), radios, and television sets (color as well as black and white) are among appliances that, contrary to popular belief, use relatively small amounts of electricity. B. In contrast, electric stove heating elements and heat pumps operating on internal resistance heating are among the appliances that use relatively large amounts of electricity.

2. The Students Determine the Wattage Requirements of Household Appliances and Discover the Relationship Between Watts and the Amount of Electricity Used.

Distribute copies of Worksheet 1.5–2. Instruct the students to gather data on wattage requirements for as many of the household appliances tested in Worksheet 1.5–1 as possible. Have them ask for their parent's permission and help in gathering the data. The wattage requirements are usually printed somewhere on the appliance. For your information, the wattage requirements for some appliances are listed as follows: can opener = 144; blender = 360; egg beater = 96; iron = 1200;

coffee maker = 840; toaster = 624; popcorn popper = 1200; water heater = 2500. Some appliances do not have the wattage listed on them. In these cases, the students should record the amps and voltage information printed on the appliance. The voltage (with the exception of some large appliances that have higher voltage requirements) can be considered 120. The wattage can be determined by multiplying amps times volts.

Upon completion of this data-gathering activity, have the students compare the order of the appliances listed in Worksheets 1.5–1 (in order from the least to the greatest amount of electricity used) and 1.5–2 (in order from least to greatest wattage requirements). Discuss with the students the relationship between the watts required by an appliance and the amount of electricity used by that appliance. It should be evident that the greater the wattage requirements, the greater the amount of electricity used.

3. The Students Learn How to Use Ohm's Law.

Write the following information on the chalkboard for the students to copy in their notes: One form of Ohm's law

$$V = R \times I$$
$$V = volts; I = amps; R = resistance (ohms)$$

Explain to the students that **the volt is a measurement of the electric force needed to keep an electric current flowing. The amp is a measurement of the amount of electric current flow. The ohm is a measurement of the resistance to the flow of an electric current.** An analogy is a garden hose connected to a faucet. The water flowing through the hose can be considered the amps. The faucet can be considered the voltage. Should one wish to increase the amps, one would open the faucet more, thus forcing more amps through the hose. The resistance of the hose to the flow of water (amps) can be considered the ohms. Two other forms of Ohm's law are

$$R = \frac{V}{I} \quad \text{and} \quad I = \frac{V}{R} \text{ (the law as Ohm expressed it)}$$

Distribute copies of Worksheet 1.5–3, which will allow the students to use the three forms of Ohm's law in calculating some problems. **The answers to the problems are** 4. 1.2; 5. 40; 6. 120; 7. 12; 8. 7; 9.a. 10; b. 6; c. 3; d. decrease; 10.a. 1; b. 2; c. 3; d. increase.

4. The Students Learn How the Kilowatt Is Calculated and Used in Determining a Monthly Electric Bill.

Explain to the students that the watt is a measure of electric power. The formula for calculating the watt is **Watts = I (amps) × V (volts).** The monthly electric bill is based on the number of kilowatts hours of electric power used. A kilowatt hour is the equivalent of 1000 watts of power being used for 1 hour. For example, a 1000-watt light bulb burning for 1 hour equals 1 kilowatt of electric power. A 100-watt bulb would have to burn for 10 hours to use 1 kilowatt of power. The electric company charges a certain fee per kilowatt hour of electric power used. For instance, if an electric company charged 14 cents per kilowatt hour and a home used 715 kilowatt hours of power during the month, the bill would be approximately $100.00.

Have the students refer back to the wattage data gathered for Worksheet 1.5–2. Using this data, have them calculate the cost of using each of the various appliances for one continuous hour based on a fee of 14 cents per kilowatt hour. (If you desire, have the students find out from their parents what they are actually paying per kilowatt hour and use this figure in their calculations.) Instruct them to prepare a list of the appliances, including cost of operation, in the order of least expensive to most expensive.

When discussing the relative cost of operating the various appliances, be certain that the students realize just how inexpensive it is to operate such appliances as color televisions, stereos, and light bulbs. Generate a class discussion dealing with what economy moves a family might initiate in an attempt to significantly lower monthly electric bills. It will be quite obvious that just turning off lights is not an effective way to lower bills significantly.

5. The Students Work on an Activity to Learn More About Electricity.

Distribute copies of Worksheet 1.5–4. **The answers to the Library Research Questions are** 1. Coil wire around an iron rod. When electricity is made to flow through the wire, the rod becomes a magnet. 2. Two or more cells working together to produce a current. 3. It increases or decreases the voltage of alternating current.

Name _____ Date _____

WORKSHEET 1.5–1   A HOME SURVEY OF ELECTRICITY
USED BY HOUSEHOLD APPLIANCES

Important Note: Inform your parents as to what this activity involves. Ask for their permission and help in gathering the data needed.

Part 1: Collecting data on electricity usage of household appliances.

Procedure:

1. Locate the electric meter for your home. Note that the meter has one part that can be seen moving. It is a round aluminum disk called a **rotor disk**. The faster this rotor disk is rotating, the greater the amount of electricity being used by appliances in the home.

2. With your parent's permission and help, unplug or turn off all appliances in the house. After doing this, check the electric meter's rotor disk. It should not be rotating.

3. Note the left-hand column of Data Table #1. It lists an assortment of household appliances. Add any other appliances that you wish to include in your survey.

4. Conduct your survey in the following manner: A. Turn on the appliance. B. Record in the right-hand column of Data Table #1 the number of complete rotations the rotor disk makes in one minute. (The rotor disk is marked, often in black, allowing the detection of motion.) If the rotor disk makes less than one complete rotation in a minute, so note. C. Turn off the appliance and turn on the next one.

5. At the completion of data collecting, make certain that all appliances that should be on are turned back on.

DATA TABLE #1			
Appliances	**Number of Rotor Disk Revolutions per Minute**	**Appliances**	**Number of Rotor Disk Revolutions per Minute**
100-watt lamp		television set (black and white)	
stereo		television set (color)	
clothes dryer		refrigerator	
iron		electric can opener	
hair dryer		popcorn popper	
toaster		microwave oven	
air conditioner		large heating element of electric stove	
heat pump operating on normal mode		heat pump operating on internal resistance mode	
blender		egg beater	
coffee maker		fan	
hot-water heater		vacuum cleaner	
small heating element of electric stove		electric heater	

37

Part 2: In the space below, list the appliances in order from the least amount of electricity used to the greatest amount of electricity used:

1. _____

2. _____

3. _____

4. _____

5. _____

6. _____

7. _____

8. _____

9. _____

10. _____

11. _____

12. _____

13. _____

14. _____

15. _____

16. _____

17. _____

18. _____

19. _____

20. _____

21. _____

22. _____

23. _____

24. _____

WORKSHEET 1.5–2   WATTAGE REQUIREMENTS
FOR HOUSEHOLD APPLIANCES

Procedure:

1. Ask your parents to help you gather the information needed. Some appliances such as refrigerators and heat pumps may not have the information printed in easily accessed locations. In some cases, accompanying service manuals may be needed.

2. Check each appliance that you previously surveyed for electricity usage for the wattage requirements, and record the name of the appliance along with the watts.

3. If the wattage requirements are not printed on the appliance, record the amps and voltage (usually 120 volts) information and use the following formula to determine the watts: Watts = Volts × Amps.

4. Record on a separate sheet of paper the appliances and the wattage requirements. Then record the information below in order of increasing wattage requirements:

Appliance	Watts	Appliance	Watts	Appliance	Watts

5. Compare the order of the appliances in your list above with their order in your list on Worksheet 1.5–1. What relationship do you observe between wattage requirements and the amount of electricity used?

_____

_____

_____

_____

_____

_____

_____

_____

WORKSHEET 1.5–3   CALCULATING USING OHM'S LAW

Instructions: Answer the following questions and show all of your work in the appropriate form of Ohm's law.

1. Write the form of Ohm's law used for calculating amps:

2. Write the form of Ohm's law used for calculating volts:

3. Write the form of Ohm's law used for calculating ohms:

4. A can opener operates on 120 volts and 100 ohm's resistance. The amperage is _____.

5. A blender operates on 120 volts and 3 amps. The resistance is _____.

6. An egg beater uses 0.8 amps and has a resistance of 150 ohms. The voltage is _____.

7. An iron operates on 120 volts and 10 amps. The resistance is _____.

8. A coffee maker operates on 120 volts and 17 ohms. The amperage is _____.

9. Calculate the amps for the following series of problems in which the voltage remains constant but the ohms increase.

   a. volts = 120; ohms = 12; amps = _____

   b. volts = 120; ohms = 20; amps = _____

   c. volts = 120; ohms = 40; amps = _____

   d. With constant voltage, as the resistance increases do the amps increase or decrease?

10. Calculate the amps for the following series of problems in which the ohms remain constant but the voltage increases.

   a. volts = 3; ohms = 3; amps = _____

   b. volts = 6; ohms = 3; amps = _____

   c. volts = 9; ohms = 3; amps = _____

   d. With constant ohms, as the voltage increases do the amps increase or decrease?

© 1992 by The Center for Applied Research in Education

WORKSHEET 1.5–4   MESSAGE SQUARE ACTIVITY ABOUT ELECTRICITY

A. *Hint:* The region within which a magnet can attract an object

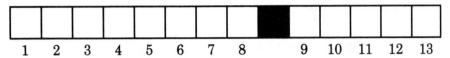

| 1 | 2 | 3 | 4 | 5 | 6 | 7 | 8 | 9 | 10 | 11 | 12 | 13 |

Anticipated Answer

Put: a C in 8   _____
    a D in 13   _____
    a G in 3   _____
    an I in 7 and 10   _____
    an M in 1   _____
    an E in 5 and 11   _____
    an F in 9   _____
    an A in 2   _____
    an L in 12   _____
    an N in 4   _____
    a T in 6   _____

Hint: A charge on the surface of an object caused by electrons

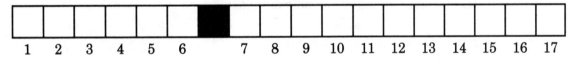

| 1 | 2 | 3 | 4 | 5 | 6 | 7 | 8 | 9 | 10 | 11 | 12 | 13 | 14 | 15 | 16 | 17 |

Anticipated Answer

Put: a T in 2, 4, 11, and 16   _____
    an I in 5, 13, and 15   _____
    a C in 6, 10, and 14   _____
    an S in 1   _____
    a Y in 17   _____
    an L in 8   _____
    an E in 7 and 9   _____
    an A in 3   _____
    an R in 12   _____

Library Research Questions   **Answers**   **Sources**

1. How would you construct an electromagnet?

2. We often refer to a flashlight battery. However, it is really a flashlight cell. What is the definition of a battery?

3. What is the function of a transformer?

1.6 COLOR

You Will Need the Following Materials:

3 slide or filmstrip projectors   glass prism
red, green, and blue cellophane   color wheel
sheets of white paper   aluminum foil
crayons or colored pencils   single-edge razor blade
masking tape   red tomato or apple
green head of lettuce   red and green light bulb
microscope lamps

Upon Completion of This Activity, Students Will

- Know the colors of the visible spectrum.
- Understand the relationship between different wavelengths of light and different colors.
- Have observed additive color mixing of the three primary colors of light.
- Have observed subtractive color mixing of pigments.
- Have prepared and observed examples of color afterimages.
- Understand why certain colors are used in the lighting of vegetable and meat displays in food markets.

1. The Students Observe a Glass Prism Separating White Light into Its Component Colors, and They Learn the Colors of the Visible Spectrum.

Distribute copies of Worksheet 1.6–1.

Using a razor blade, cut a narrow slit approximately one inch long in a piece of aluminum foil. Secure the aluminum foil over the lens of a filmstrip or 35mm slide projector, positioning the slip directly in front of the lens. Holding a glass prism horizontally or vertically in front of the lens and experimenting with its exact position, it is easy to project the visible spectrum on the classroom screen. Have the students note that the colors of the visible spectrum are **red, orange, yellow, green, blue, indigo, and violet.** The glass prism has separated white light into its component colors. Explain that each color has its own specific wavelength, and that the colors of the visible spectrum are arranged in order from the long wavelengths of red to the short wavelengths of violet. Have the students use colored pencils and draw the visible spectrum on their worksheets. (If the students do not have indigo colored pencils, they will have to leave this color out.) Explain that the visible portion of the spectrum is actually a small portion of a larger spectrum of waves referred to as the **electromagnetic spectrum.** Wavelengths longer than red are invisible to the human eye and include infrared waves, microwaves, and radio waves. Wavelengths shorter than violet are also invisible to the human eye and include ultraviolet waves, x-rays, and cosmic rays. Have the students note this information on their worksheets.

2. The Students Learn the Three Primary Colors of Light and Observe How Colors of Light Can Be Mixed Through Additive Color Mixing to Obtain Other Colors of the Visible Spectrum.

Over the lens of one filmstrip projector (or 35mm slide projector), secure a piece of red cellophane. Over the lens of a second projector, secure a piece of blue cellophane. Repeat with a third projector, using green cellophane. Arrange the projectors side by side and project the three colors on the screen as shown in the following diagram:

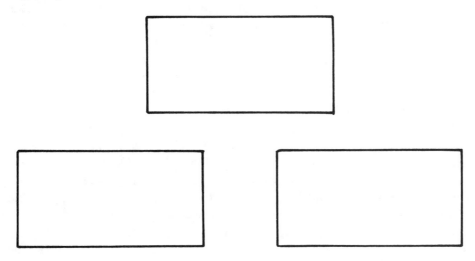

Inform the students that in terms of the colors of light, there are three **primary colors**: red, blue, and green. By mixing these three primary colors, virtually any color of the visible spectrum can be obtained. For example, if one looks closely at the picture on a color television set (especially with the aid of a magnifying glass), one will observe lines or dots of red, blue, and green. The television set mixes these three colors on the screen, thus producing all of the colors you see in the picture. Another example can be found on the retina (light-sensitive layer located on the posterior surface) of the eye. The retina is sensitive to the three primary colors, and from these three, produces all the colors of our color vision.

Ask the students what they think the color of light will be when you mix the projected red and green on the screen. Then superimpose the two colors on the screen to obtain **yellow**. In like manner, superimposing red and blue produces a color called **magenta** (purplish red), and superimposing blue and green produces a color called **cyan** (greenish blue). By varying the amounts (intensities) of colored light mixed (difficult to achieve with the projectors) other colors can be obtained.

Ask the students to predict the result of superimposing all three primary colors on the screen. Superimpose them to illustrate that **white light** results.

Be certain that the students understand that they have observed additive color mixing. For their worksheets, the term means that colors of light are added to and mixed with each other.

3. The Students Observe How Pigment Colors Can Be Mixed to Obtain New Colors and Why It is Referred to as Subtractive Color Mixing.

Explain to the students that when we look at an object, the color of the object that we perceive is the color that that object reflects. For example, a red tomato appears red to us because it reflects primarily the wavelengths of red and absorbs most or all of the other wavelengths of the other colors.

Distribute copies of Worksheet 1.6–2 and have the students use colored pencils and mix yellow with blue in the appropriate space. The result of this color mixing will be **green**. Explain to the students that instead of mixing colors of light (as was illustrated on the screen), colors of pigment from the pencils have been mixed. The results of mixing pigment colors is somewhat different from those obtained from mixing colors of light. In explaining how the color green is derived from mixing yellow and blue pencil pigments it is important to note that pigment colors are usually not pure colors.

Have the students refer to the diagram of subtractive color mixing on their worksheets as you continue your explanation. The yellow pencil pigment, while reflecting primarily the wavelengths of yellow, also reflects some green wavelengths. The blue pencil pigment, while reflecting primarily blue wavelengths, also reflects some green wavelengths. When the two pigments are mixed, the blue pigment absorbs wavelengths of yellow, and the yellow pigment absorbs wavelengths of blue. The only wavelengths of color that both pigments reflect in common is green. Thus green is perceived after mixing. When mixing pigments, the term **subtractive color mixing** is used because the color perceived is the color reflected, not the colors subtracted or absorbed by the pigment. The principle of subtractive color mixing occurs when mixing paints. One might have a particular color in mind for painting a room. Often, the paint store will have to mix various colors of paint to achieve the desired color of the paint pigment.

Another example of relying on subtractive color mixing is in applying eye shadow. Often, various colors of eye shadow pigment are brushed on and mixed until the right color is achieved.

4. The Students Observe a Demonstration That Explains Why Colored Lights Are Often Used for Illuminating Meat and Vegetable Displays at a Food Market.

Illuminate a red tomato or apple with white light and then red light. It should be observed that the tomato or apple appears a more vivid red under red illumination. The explanation is that the red tomato or apple reflects primarily red wavelengths while absorbing the other color wavelengths. Thus, the additional red illumination by the red light bulb allows the tomato or apple to reflect more red and consequently to appear a more vivid red to the observer. The same principle applies to red meats when they are illuminated by a red light bulb.

Illuminate a green head of lettuce with a green light bulb and elicit from the students an explanation of why the lettuce appears a more vivid green.

5. *The Students Observe Examples of Color Afterimages.*

Although the exact visual and perceptual mechanisms responsible for afterimages are being researched, afterimages can easily be experienced. Distribute copies of Worksheet 1.6–3 and allow the students to complete the activity. The answers are 5. green; 7. red; 8. blue; 9. yellow.

6. *The Students Work on an Activity to Learn Some More Facts About Color Vision.*

Distribute copies of Worksheet 1.6–4. **The answers to message square activity = trichromatic. Library Research Questions:** 1. This theory explains human color vision by citing research that indicates that the human retina contains three types of color vision receptors called cones. One type of cone is sensitive to red, a second type to blue, and a third type to green. 2. Recent research indicates that cats may have limited color vision. 3. Dogs probably have very limited color vision because their retinas are composed predominantly of rods with very few cones. 4. Monkeys. 5. Yes. 6. Yes.

WORKSHEET 1.6–1
THE VISIBLE SPECTRUM AND ADDITIVE COLOR MIXING

1. Drawing of the visible spectrum:

Longer
Wavelengths

Shorter
Wavelengths

Longer wavelengths not visible to the human eye include:

 a. _____

 b. _____

 c. _____

Shorter wavelengths not visible to the human eye include:

 a. _____

 b. _____

 c. _____

2. Explanation of the term *additive color mixing:* _____

_____

_____

_____

_____

_____

_____

_____

_____

_____

_____

Name _____   Date _____

WORKSHEET 1.6–2   SUBTRACTIVE COLOR MIXING

1. Using colored pencils, mix yellow and blue pigment in the circle:

What color results? _____

2. Diagram of subtractive color mixing:

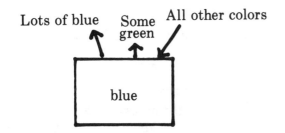

Note that the yellow pigment absorbs **all colors** except yellow and a small amount of **green,** which are reflected.

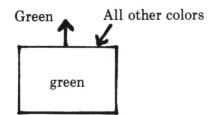

Note that the blue pigment absorbs **all colors** except blue and a small amount of **green, which** are reflected.

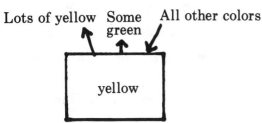

Note that when the yellow and **green pigments** are mixed, all colors are absorbed (subtracted) except that color which they **reflect in common:** green.

3. Explanation of the term *subtractive color mixing:* _____

_____

_____

_____

_____

_____

_____

_____

WORKSHEET 1.6–3 AFTERIMAGES

Materials needed: Colored pencils
Five sheets of plain white paper
Microscope lamp

Procedure:

1. In the center of one sheet of white paper, color an approximate two-inch square red.

2. Repeat #1 above for the colors green, yellow, and blue on three more sheets of paper.

3. Illuminate the red square by placing the microscope lamp very close to it.

4. Stare at the red square from about 5 inches directly over the square. Stare for about 90 seconds, trying not to blink.

5. Quickly place a piece of white paper under the illumination and stare at it. Blinking a few times will help. What color do you see? _____

6. Allow your eyes to "rest" for a few minutes before continuing.

7. Repeat the above procedures for the green square. What color do you see? _____

8. Repeat for the yellow square. What color do you see? _____

9. Repeat for the blue square. What color do you see? _____

10. In the space below, draw a sketch of the American flag using the appropriate colors so that it will produce an afterimage of the flag with its natural colors. (You can omit the individual stars.) Does your sketch produce an accurate afterimage?

WORKSHEET 1.6–4
MESSAGE SQUARE ACTIVITY ON COLOR VISION

Hint: Name of the theory that seeks to explain human color vision

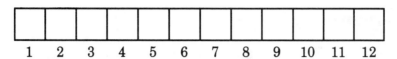

1	2	3	4	5	6	7	8	9	10	11	12

Anticipated Answer

Put: a T in 1 and 10   _____

     a C in 4 and 12   _____

     an R in 2 and 6   _____

     an I in 3 and 11   _____

     an M in 8   _____

     an O in 7   _____

     an H in 5   _____

     an A in 9   _____

Library Research Questions   **Answers**   **Sources**

1. Briefly explain the above theory.

2. Do cats have color vision?

3. Do dogs have color vision?

4. What nonhuman mammals are considered to have the best color vision?

5. Do birds have color vision?

6. Do fish have color vision?

1.7 ELEMENTS, ATOMS, MIXTURES, AND COMPOUNDS

You Will Need the Following Materials:

glucose	stereomicroscopes (or magnifying glasses)
salt	filter paper
small cork pieces	funnels
iodine solution	beakers
sand	nonsoluble starch
silver nitrate solution	Benedict's solution
stirring rod	iron filings
magnet	250ml flask
red food coloring	scoops
paper towels	test tubes
test tube clamps	3″ × 5″ cards
ring stand	ring clamp

Upon Completion of This Activity, Students Will

- Understand the concept of the atom.
- Understand the concept of the element.
- Have learned the symbols for some common elements.
- Understand the concept and characteristics of the compound.
- Understand the concept and characteristics of the mixture.
- Have prepared mixtures and separated them into their substances.
- Have observed a compound being formed.
- Understand the differences between a physical and a chemical change.

1. The Students Are Provided Information About Elements and Atoms.

Explain to the students that an **element** is considered the basic form of all matter. It is the simplest substance and cannot be broken down into simpler substances by chemical or physical changes. There are more than 100 chemical elements, and they are the building blocks for all matter. Our body, for example, could be separated into the various elements of which it is composed—such as hydrogen, oxygen, carbon, and iron, to name a few. Each element has a symbol which represents it. For example, the element hydrogen is represented by the symbol **H**, and the element iron, by the symbol **Fe**.

The smallest part of an element that can exist and have all the properties of that element is called an **atom**. For example, an atom of the element gold is the smallest amount of that element one can have and still have gold. If you separate the gold atom—or any atom for that matter—into its component parts, you will end up with electrons, protons, and neutrons.

Pass out copies of Worksheet 1.7–1 and allow the students to complete it.

2. The Students Prepare, Separate, and Learn Characteristics of a Mixture.

Distribute copies of Worksheet 1.7–2 and allow the students to perform Activity #1. At the conclusion of the activity, have students take notes as you explain to them that a mixture is a physical combination of substances. The substances in a mixture do not undergo a chemical change and they retain their own characteristic properties. Further, a mixture can be separated into its component substances by physical changes. The iron filings can be recovered using a magnet. (The students might suggest putting the mixture in water and letting the iron and sand settle out and then using a magnet to recover the iron.) The salt can be recovered by evaporating the water.

The students can now carry out Activity #2. The students will discover that the sand settles out and the cork pieces float to the top. However, the red food coloring has not been recovered. Demonstrate procedure #5 of this activity for the class by gently boiling a small quantity of water with red food coloring. Continue boiling until the water disappears. **SAFETY CAUTION: Make certain that the students are wearing lab aprons and goggles, as there is always a danger of a beaker overheating and breaking.** They will note that the red food coloring has been recovered and remains on the bottom of the beaker.

The students can now carry out Activity #3. Demonstrate procedure #7 of this activity for the class by adding 5ml of Benedict's solution to 15 or 20ml of the filtrate. Carefully bring the liquid to a boil. A color change to red or green will indicate that sugar (glucose) is present. **SAFETY CAUTION: Make certain that the students are wearing lab aprons and safety goggles in the event of beaker breakage.**

Conclude Activity #3 by engaging the students in a discussion of the results. They should realize that starch, sugar, and salt were all accounted for, thus indicating that none had undergone any chemical changes. In this activity the salt and sugar were not recovered physically (although this could have been accomplished by evaporating the water away), but their physical presence was evidenced indirectly through the use of indicator solutions. The starch was recovered physically through the use of filter paper and verified through the use of an indicator solution. The reason that the starch could be filtered out, and the salt and sugar could not, is due to the starch molecules being too large to pass through the pores of the filter paper. (Actually, the starch forms a suspension, whereas the salt and sugar go into solution. If the liquid were left standing, the starch would settle out, which is characteristic of a suspension.)

3. The Students Observe and Learn Characteristics of a Chemical Change Resulting in a Compound.

You can demonstrate a chemical change for the class by again adding a few drops of silver nitrate solution to a test tube of a solution of salt in water. A milky-white precipitate forms. This precipitate can be isolated by filtering the liquid. Explain to the students that they are observing a chemical change resulting in a new compound. The silver from the silver nitrate solution chemically combines with the chloride from the sodium chloride (salt) to form a new compound called silver chloride. The precipitate is the silver chloride compound. A **compound** is the result of a chemical change whereby two or more elements chemically combine. The compound has different properties from those of the individual elements comprising it. Unlike a mixture, you cannot separate the compound into its individual components by physical means.

4. The Students Learn Some Additional Information Related to Chemistry.

Distribute copies of Worksheet 1.7–3 for the students to work on with the aid of a supplement text.

The answers to the Crossword Activity are 1. lead; 2. density; 3. noble; 4. nitrogen; 5. electron; 6. neutrons; 7. solid; 8. litmus; 9. bonds; 10. saturated.

WORKSHEET 1.7–1
CHEMICAL ELEMENTS AND THEIR SYMBOLS

There are more than 100 chemical elements. They are arranged together in the **periodic table**. The arrangement is not random. Elements with similar properties are grouped together. Each element has its own specific chemical symbol by which it is known. The symbols have wide use in writing chemical formulas and equations.

Listed below are 28 elements taken from the periodic table. Also listed are 28 chemical symbols. For each element, select the correct symbol and write it in the space to the left of the element.

CHEMICAL ELEMENTS

_____	1. sodium	_____	15. nitrogen
_____	2. potassium	_____	16. cobalt
_____	3. hydrogen	_____	17. mercury
_____	4. nickel	_____	18. phosphorus
_____	5. silver	_____	19. tin
_____	6. magnesium	_____	20. carbon
_____	7. calcium	_____	21. neon
_____	8. copper	_____	22. gold
_____	9. radon	_____	23. chlorine
_____	10. lead	_____	24. uranium
_____	11. helium	_____	25. aluminum
_____	12. manganese	_____	26. silicon
_____	13. radium	_____	27. sulfur
_____	14. oxygen	_____	28. zinc

CHEMICAL SYMBOLS

U	Ag
N	Au
P	Na
Ra	Zn
Cu	Al
O	H
Cl	Ne
Mn	K
S	Si
Ni	C
He	Ca
Hg	Mg
Sn	Pb
Co	Rn

The chemical formula for table salt is NaCl. Name the chemical elements: _____

_____

The chemical formula for sulfuric acid is H_2SO_4. Name the chemical elements: _____

_____

Some electric signs use Ne. What is the chemical element? _____

Many people are checking their homes for the presence of Rn. What is the chemical element?

_____

WORKSHEET 1.7–2 MIXTURES AND THEIR CHARACTERISTICS

Activity #1:

1. Observe some salt using a stereomicroscope. Repeat with sand and then iron filings. Note the appearance of each substance.
2. Mix together in a small beaker a scoop of sand, salt, and iron filings.
3. Pour some of the mixture onto a 3″ × 5″ card and observe using the stereomicroscope.
   a. Do the substances appear to have changed in appearance or can you still identify each one?
   b. What procedure might you use to recover the iron filings?
   c. What procedure might you use to recover the sand?
   d. What procedure might you use to recover the salt?

Notes provided by the teacher: _____

_____

_____

_____

_____

_____

Activity #2:

1. Fill a 250ml flask with water and add a drop of red food coloring.
2. Add a scoop of sand and a scoop of small cork pieces to the water.
3. Shake the flask, thoroughly mixing the contents.
4. Set the flask down, observe what happens to its contents, and answer the following questions.
   a. What happens to the sand? _____
   b. What happens to the cork pieces? _____
   c. What happens to the red food coloring? _____
5. Now observe as your teacher boils some water containing red food coloring until the water is evaporated away.
   a. Has the food coloring also disappeared? _____

Activity #3:

1. Fill a 250ml beaker with approximately 200ml of water. Add a scoop of sugar (glucose), a scoop of salt (sodium chloride), and a scoop of corn starch (nonsoluble).
2. Mix the substances in the water using a stirring rod.
3. Support a funnel over a beaker using a ring stand and ring clamp. Place a piece of filter paper in a funnel (if you are not certain how to fold the piece of filter paper, check with your teacher) and filter some of the liquid into a clean beaker, in an attempt to separate by physical means one or more of the substances from the water.

4. Examine the surface of the filter paper, and using a stirring rod, remove a small amount of the residue and place it in a small beaker. To this residue add a drop or two of iodine solution. **If starch is present, it will turn blue-black in the presence of iodine.**

   a. Is starch present in the residue? _____

5. Hold a test tube using a test tube clamp and carefully pour in a small amount of the filtered liquid (filtrate). Carefully add a few drops of iodine solution.

   a. Is starch present in the filtrate? _____

   b. How can you explain the starch being present (or absent) in the filtrate? _____

   _____

6. Again hold a test tube using a test tube clamp and carefully pour in a small amount of the filtrate. Carefully add a few drops of silver nitrate solution. **If salt is present, you will observe a milky-white cloud form.**

   a. Is salt present in the filtrate? _____

7. Your teacher will add 5ml of Benedict's solution to a small amount of the filtrate and bring the liquid to a boil. **If glucose sugar is present, the liquid will turn green or red.**

   a. Is sucrose present in the filtrate? _____

Notes on chemical changes provided by the teacher: _____

_____

_____

_____

_____

_____

_____

_____

_____

_____

_____

_____

_____

_____

_____

_____

_____

WORKSHEET 1.7–3   CROSSWORD ACTIVITY ON CHEMISTRY

Instructions: Fill in the spaces in the crossword puzzle at the bottom of this sheet with the answers to the following.

1. Name of the chemical element that has the symbol Pb

2. The ratio of mass to volume of a substance

3. The elements listed in the far-right column of the periodic table are known as the

   _____ gases

4. Name of the chemical element that has the symbol N

5. A negatively charged particle of an atom

6. Particles found in the nucleus of an atom, which have no charge

7. One of the states of matter

8. A type of indicator paper that is used to test for acids and bases, which comes in red strips as well as blue

9. Atoms are held together by electrical forces called _____

10. What is the name for a solution that has as much of the solute dissolved in it as possible, at a particular temperature?

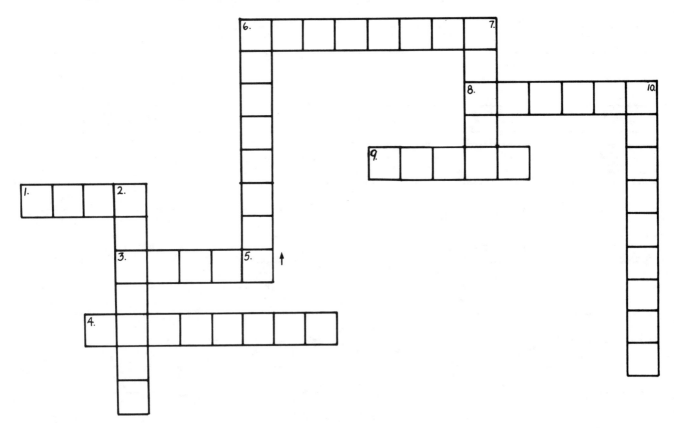

1.8 COMPARING ACID NEUTRALIZATION OF VARIOUS ANTACIDS

You Will Need the Following Materials:

distilled water	mortar and pestle
graduated cylinders	hydrochloric acid
Congo red indicator solution	medicine droppers
beakers	safety goggles
lab aprons	various antacid tablets
baking soda	stirring rod
paper towels	rulers
graph paper	colored pencils

At the Conclusion of This Activity, Students Will

- Have experienced a consumer chemistry type of investigation.
- Have collected and interpreted data and prepared bar graphs.
- Have experienced the use of an indicator solution in gathering data.
- Have learned the necessity of reading labels on medicine containers.

1. The Students are Given Some Preliminary Information Regarding the Need for and the Use of Antacids.

The stomach contains gastric juice, which is essentially a mixture of mucus, digestive enzymes, and hydrochloric acid. To be effective, the digestive enzymes require an acid environment. Occasionally, gastric juice will enter the lower part of the esophagus (that portion of the gastrointestinal tract that carries food from the mouth to the stomach), causing a burning discomfort referred to as heartburn. Antacids are used to neutralize the acid, thus eliminating the burning sensation. Please note that *chronic* heartburn is not a normal condition and provides cause to see a physician.

An interesting investigation is to compare the effectiveness of various antacid tablets in neutralizing hydrochloric acid.

2. The Students Gather Data Relevant to the Acid-Neutralizing Capabilities of Selected Antacids.

Distribute copies of Worksheet 1.8–1. Review the instructions with the students. **SAFETY CAUTION: Emphasize that lab aprons and safety goggles must be worn due to the students' use of hydrochloric acid. The acid is dangerous and can cause burns to the skin and damage to clothes upon** contact. **The student should rinse the skin with water and notify you immediately if he/she comes into contact with the acid.**

To prepare a synthetic gastric juice for the students, use a ratio of 2 drops of hydrochloric acid per 10ml of distilled water.

Prepare baking soda for the students to test using a ratio of ¼ teaspoon of baking soda per 20ml of distilled water. Explain to the students that baking soda is sometimes used as a home remedy for heartburn. **(SAFETY NOTE: Emphasize to the students that they should never use baking soda as a medication unless prescribed by their family physician.)**

Along with a selection of antacid tablets, you might also wish to use some different brands of liquid antacids. These latter antacids can be tested full strength without dilution in 20ml of distilled water.

Upon completion of the activity, discuss the data results with the students. For example, baking soda will probably be found to be the most effective, turning the gastric juice pink with only 1 or 2 drops. Other antacids will test in at less than 15 drops to more than 70 drops.

Inform the students that product testing such as they have carried out is regularly performed by companies, often to obtain a database for advertising their product's speed and/or effectiveness.

3. The Students Prepare Bar Graphs and Summaries of Their Data Results.

Pass out sheets of graph paper, rulers, and colored pencils, and allow the students to follow the instructions on their worksheet in preparing bar graphs.

At the conclusion of the activity, discuss with the students their summary of the data findings. Also discuss other examples of product testing and how such testing might be carried out. Examples range from testing the ability of fiber in cereal in lowering cholesterol to the effectiveness of enzyme stain removers in laundry detergents.

If you have some students interested in product testing, they might wish to write to various companies that make specific claims for their products, asking for the testing procedures used and their data results. Mouthwash companies, for example, are quite receptive to such requests for information.

4. The Students Gather Information from the Antacid Product Labels and Learn the Necessity of Reading Such Labels Carefully Prior to Use.

Have the students complete the final section of the worksheet regarding information on medicine product labels. They can use the library or perhaps in-class resource materials that will provide information regarding the function of active and inactive ingredients.

Conclude with a discussion of the necessity for always checking with their family physician prior to using over-the-counter medicines. And regardless of the medicine used, instructions for use, warnings, and drug interaction precautions should always be completely understood.

WORKSHEET 1.8–1 COMPARING ACID NEUTRALIZATION
OF A SELECTION OF ANTACIDS

SAFETY NOTE: Wear lab aprons and safety goggles during this activity. You will be working with hydrochloric acid, which can cause skin burns and clothes damage upon contact. Should you come into contact with the acid, immediately rinse your skin with water and notify your teacher.

Procedure:

1. Put on lab apron and safety goggles. Cover your working surface with paper towels.

2. Place an antacid tablet into a mortar and add 20ml of distilled water.

3. Using a pestle, thoroughly crush and mix the antacid tablet until completely dissolved.

4. Into a small beaker, carefully put 5 drops of the hydrochloric acid, (synthetic gastric juice) using a clean medicine dropper. (**CAUTION: The hydrochloric acid can burn skin and damage clothes upon contact.**) Immediately rinse the medicine dropper thoroughly.

5. Add 1 drop of the Congo red indicator solution to the hydrochloric acid. The acid should now be blue. (Congo red indicator solution turns blue in acid solutions and light pink in neutral solutions.)

6. Using a clean medicine dropper, begin adding the dissolved antacid one drop at a time. Using the stirring rod, mix it with the hydrochloric acid after each drop.

7. Continue adding the drops and stirring until the hydrochloric acid turns a light pink, indicating that the acid has been neutralized.

8. In the data table below, record the number of drops of antacid solution needed to neutralize the acid.

9. Rinse the equipment that you have used, **being especially careful with the beaker containing the hydrochloric acid**, and repeat steps 2 through 9 for each antacid tested.

DATA TABLE			
Name of the Antacid	**Number of Drops Needed for Neutralization**	**Name of the Antacid**	**Number of Drops Needed for Neutralization**

10. Prepare a bar graph based on the data table results. The vertical axis can be labeled Number of Drops Needed for Neutralization. Along the horizontal axis can be labeled the names of the antacids tested, in order from least effective to most effective, leaving two or three spaces between each. In coloring the bars, use red for the most effective antacid and black for the least effective.

11. Prepare a brief summary of the data findings. (Were there great differences between the effectiveness of the various antacid brands? Was one brand much more effective than the others?)

_____

_____

_____

_____

_____

_____

_____

_____

One should always use caution when using over-the-counter medicines. The best procedure is to always check with your family physician first. And when using the medicine, the instructions should always be read and understood. Often, the directions for use, warnings, and drug-interaction information is overlooked.

Obtain the following information from the product label of an antacid:

1. List the active and inactive ingredients. Using library resource materials, see if you can determine the function of each.

Active Ingredients Function	**Inactive Ingredients Function**
_____	_____
_____	_____
_____	_____
_____	_____

2. List the directions for use: _____

_____

_____

3. List the warnings: _____

_____

_____

_____

4. List the drug-interaction precautions: _____

_____

_____

_____

1.9 COMPARING DISSOLUTION TIMES OF PAIN RELIEVERS

You Will Need the Following Materials:

time-keeping device

100ml beakers

graduated cylinders

glass stirring rod

selection of pain reliever tablets,
    capsules, and caplets (coated
    and uncoated)

thermometer

lab apron

paper towels

rulers

graph paper

Upon Completion of This Activity, Students Will

- Have experienced a consumer chemistry type of investigation.
- Have gained experience in gathering and interpreting data.
- Have gained experience in preparing bar graphs.
- Be aware of the relationship between laboratory investigation and product advertising.

1. Materials Are Prepared Prior to the Classroom Investigation.

Obtain the pain relievers to be tested. You might wish to have the students compare different brands of caplets; or compare caplets, capsules, and tablets; or perhaps compare coated and uncoated tablets.

Each group of students participating will need a 100ml beaker, a graduated cylinder, a glass stirring rod, and paper towels.

Explain to the students that water can be used in this activity instead of hydrochloric acid (found in gastric juice in the stomach) because the dissolution rates of the pain relievers in these two liquids are similar. The water should be warmed to approximately 98.6 degrees F (normal body temperature). For convenience sake, heat the water for the students and dispense from a central location.

2. The Students Are Provided with Some Historical Background Information Relative to the Investigation.

Product testing prior to commercial advertising designed to entice potential consumers to see a need to purchase a product is an ongoing process in laboratories. All major companies have laboratory facilities to carry out these investigations. This investigation deals with an activity in **consumer chemistry**.

A few years ago, pain-reliever advertising stressed the speed at which the pain-relieving substance would dissolve in the stomach, allowing it to then be absorbed into the bloodstream. The advertising emphasis was upon the time it would take to relieve a pain such as a headache. Various companies were endeavoring to persuade the consumer that their pain reliever would "work faster" than any of the others.

A simple classroom investigation will be conducted in an effort to determine, and compare, the time it takes various pain relievers to dissolve in water.

3. The Students Carry out the Investigation.

Distribute copies of Worksheet 1.9–1. Review the investigation procedure with them, and monitor them as they conduct the investigation.

4. The Students Prepare Bar Graphs of the Pooled Class Data Results.

Lead the class in pooling their data.

Pass out graph paper and rulers, and have the students prepare bar graphs according to the instructions on their worksheets.

Involve the class in a discussion of their results. They will probably find considerable differences in the dissolution times of the various pain relievers, ranging from 2 or 3 minutes to more than 15 minutes (in the case of certain coated tablets). Coated tablets are advertised to be "safety coated" to prevent the tablet from dissolving in the stomach, which might cause stomach upset, and allowing it to dissolve after it reaches the small intestine.

Finally, have the students obtain answers to the final portion of the worksheet, and engage them in a discussion involving the widespread use of over-the-counter pain remedies. For example, do we have a real need for them or are we being convinced through advertising that we need them?

Name _____ Date _____

WORKSHEET 1.9–1   COMPARING DISSOLUTION TIMES
OF PAIN RELIEVERS

Procedure:

1. Put on a lab apron.
2. Pour 50ml of distilled water (which has been warmed by your teacher) into a 100ml beaker.
3. Place the pain reliever to be tested in the beaker of water.
4. Every 15 seconds, agitate the solution **very gently** with a glass stirring rod and **very gently** move the pain reliever a bit. Do not crush the pain reliever. You might have to position the pain reliever near the edge of the beaker so that it can still be observed, should the liquid become cloudy. The pain reliever can be considered dissolved when it has completely disintegrated, even though residue will still be visible. (Do not continue beyond 15 minutes per pain reliever.)
5. Record the name of the pain reliever; whether it was a caplet, tablet, or capsule, coated or uncoated; and the dissolving time in the Data Table below.
6. Rinse out the beaker and repeat steps 1 through 4 above for each additional pain reliever tested.

© 1992 by The Center for Applied Research in Education

DATA TABLE			
Name of Pain Reliever	**Caplet, Tablet, or Capsule (coated or uncoated**	**Dissolving Time (in seconds)**	**Class Average Dissolving Time (in seconds)**

Worksheet 1.9–1   (cont'd.)

7. Prepare a bar graph based on the pooled class dissolving time. Label the vertical axis, Dissolution Time in Seconds. Allow each space to equal 30 seconds. The horizontal axis can be labeled Pain Relievers, and their names can be listed (noting whether caplets, tablets, capsules, coated, or uncoated), separating each by two or three spaces. Upon completion of the bar graph, answer the following questions:

a. Which pain reliever dissolved the fastest? _____

b. Which pain reliever dissolved the slowest? _____

c. Write a summary comparing coated and uncoated caplets, tablets, and capsules in terms of dissolution times.

_____

_____

_____

_____

d. Are any differences between dissolving time great enough to persuade you to choose one particular pain reliever over another?

_____

_____

Over-the-counter pain relievers for pain ranging from headache to back pain to muscle aches are popular products. They should not be used on a long-term basis without your family physician's permission.

Obtain the following information from your family members and several friends:

1. How often do you take a pain reliever: a. for headache? _____

                                                  b. for back pain? _____

                                                  c. for muscle ache? _____

2. Do you take any pain reliever more than once every three weeks?

3. Are you taking any pain reliever at the direction of a physician?

4. Have you ever read the directions, warnings, and drug-interaction precautions on the labels of any pain relievers that you take?

© 1992 by The Center for Applied Research in Education

Unit 2
The Biological Sciences

2.1 THE HUMAN IMMUNE SYSTEM

You Will Need the Following Materials:

colored pencils

Upon Completion of This Exercise, Students Will

- Be familiar with some of the body's defense barriers that protect against entry by microorganisms.
- Know a definition for infection.
- Understand what is initiated by the immune response.
- Know some of the major structures of the immune system.
- Know the definition of an antigen.
- Understand the lock-and-key concept regarding antibodies and antigens.
- Know the important developmental stages of lymphocytes.
- Know the roles played by various types of T-cells.
- Understand two ways that antibodies deal with antigens.
- Realize the immune system's role in tissue transplant rejection.
- Learn what specific part of the immune system is destroyed by the virus that causes AIDS.

1. The Students Learn Some of the Body's Defense Barriers That Protect Against Entry by Microorganisms.

Explain to the students, as they take notes, that the body has several barriers that help protect it against unwanted entry by potentially pathogenic (disease-causing) microorganisms. One major barrier is the unbroken **cutaneous membrane (skin)**. Even its surface is adapted to prevent the growth of unwanted microorganisms. The surface is kept acidic due to perspiration, and it has many colonies of normally safe microorganisms. Both of these surface features tend to discourage the establishment of colonies of pathogens.

Both **tears and saliva** contain an enzyme called lysozyme, which inhibits the growth of bacteria. **Stomach acid** provides a chemical barrier against microorganisms entering the digestive tract in food materials.

Small hairlike structures called **cilia** help keep the nasal passages and the respiratory tract free of microorganisms by continually sweeping the surfaces clean.

It is obvious that these barriers are not always 100 percent effective, and when they are not, there is always the possibility of an infection. An infection occurs when pathogenic microorganisms become established in (or on) the body. It is when pathogenic microorganisms have successfully invaded the body and are in the process of causing an infection that the body initiates an **immune response**. This action means the body's immune system is now operating to help the body resist the disease.

2. The Students Learn the Basic Structures and Functions Involved in the Operation of the Immune System.

Distribute copies of Worksheet 2.1–1 along with colored pencils. As you are presenting the following material, the students can take notes and color the appropriate diagrams.

Four important component parts of the immune system are neutrophils, lymphocytes, macrophages, and antibodies. Have the students label "a" *neutrophil,* and then color the three-lobed nucleus purple and the stippled cytoplasm blue. Neutrophils are white blood cells that actually move out of the bloodstream into the surrounding tissues. There they engulf and destroy invading microorganisms. They can now label "b" *lymphocyte* and then color the round nucleus purple and the stippled cytoplasm blue. Lymphocytes deal in antibody production. Next, "c" should be labeled *macrophage.* The nucleus can be colored purple and the stippled cytoplasm blue. The macrophage is a specialized tissue cell that can engulf and destroy invading microorganisms. Now label "d" *antibodies* and color them red. Antibodies are substances produced by immune system cells that are important ammunition in destroying antigens.

Antigens, "e," are specific molecules carried on microorganisms. They identify the microorganism as a foreign invader, to be destroyed by the body.

The *function of the immune system,* "f," is to provide immunity or resistance to disease.

Lymphocytes mature into "g," *B-cells* and "h," *T-cells.*

The role of B-cells is that of coming into contact with a specific antigen which combines with a receptor on the surface of the B-cell. Then these B-cells eventually develop into "i," *plasma cells* and "j," *memory B-cells.* The role of the plasma cell is to immediately produce and release large quantities of antibodies directed against the antigen (and therefore the microorganism). The role of the memory B-cells is to "remember" the antigen and, if a future attack of the microorganism occurs, they become plasma cells and produce antibodies specifically directed against the antigen (and therefore the microorganism).

The role of the T-cell is that of coming into contact with a specific antigen. The T-cell then undergoes many divisions and then "k" seeks out and *combines with specific antigens.* This causes "l," a *chemical released* by the T-cell *to attract macrophages,* special tissue cells, which in turn destroy the antigens (and therefore the microorganisms).

Certain T-cells become "m," *helper T-cells.* The role of the helper T-cells is to stimulate the plasma cells into producing more antibodies.

In summary, "n," the *plasma cells, are crucial in their role of producing antibodies,* and "o," *the helper T-cells, are crucial in stimulating the plasma cells to produce their antibodies.*

3. The Students Learn the Lock-and-Key Concept Regarding Antigens and Antibodies.

The students continue color coding and keeping notes on Worksheet 2.1–1.

Once again, an antigen, "p," is a molecule that is carried on a microorganism. Each different kind of microorganism (be it bacteria, fungus, and so on) carries its own specific antigen. The immune system identifies microorganism type by the specific antigens the microorganism carries. Have students color the stippled bacteria, diagrammed in "q," black and the attached shaded structure, green. The green structure represents the antigen (in reality there are far more than just one antigen per microorganism).

Have students color the antibody "r" red. Note that the configuration of the antibody is such that it can fit itself against the antigen. In space "s," have them draw and color appropriately a combination of figures "q" and "r," showing the antibody fitted into the antigen. This fitting together of specific antibodies with specific antigens is referred to as a *lock-and-key arrangement.*

The immune system is amazing indeed in its ability to produce specific antibodies against specific antigens. Further, the memory B-cells "remember" the specific antigen and are ready to produce the appropriate antibodies should there be a repeat attack of the microorganisms carrying those antigens.

Two ways that antibodies destroy antigens are "t," *the antibody combines with the antigen to render the antigen harmless by interfering with its chemical structure,* and "u," *the attached antibodies cause the antigens to clump together in bunches.* This enables the special tissue cells called macrophages to more efficiently engulf the invading microorganisms, as illustrated in "v." Have students color the stippled macrophage yellow and the bacterial microorganisms being engulfed black.

4. The Students Learn What Part of the Immune System Is Destroyed by the AIDS Virus.

Explain to the students that the full name of AIDS is **acquired** (meaning that the disease can be transmitted) **immune deficiency** (meaning that the body's immune system becomes deficient in "doing its job") **syndrome** (meaning a group of several different symptoms that can characterize the disease).

The cause of AIDS has been traced to the HTLV-3 virus. This virus destroys the helper T-cells in the body. As you will recall, the helper T-cells are crucial in stimulating the plasma cells to produce antibodies. When the human body can no longer produce the needed antibodies to fight microorganisms, it becomes host to a great variety of different diseases, which is exactly what occurs to the victim of AIDS.

WORKSHEET 2.1–1
BASIC STRUCTURES AND FUNCTIONS OF THE IMMUNE SYSTEM

Four important component parts of the immune system:

a. _____   c. _____

b. _____   d. _____

a. _____: _____

                                    _____

                                    _____

                                    Role: _____

                                    _____

b. _____: _____

                                    _____

                                    Role: _____

                                    _____

c. _____: _____

                                    _____

                                    Role: _____

                                    _____

d. _____: _____

                                    _____

                                    Role: _____

                                    _____

e. Antigen: _____

_____

f. Function of the immune system: _____

_____

_____

LYMPHOCYTES
mature into

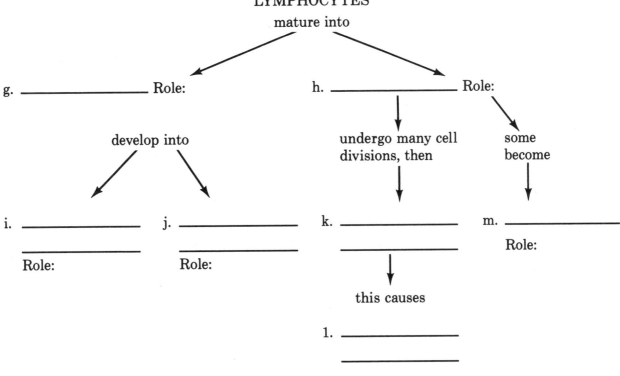

g. _____ Role: h. _____ Role:

develop into   undergo many cell   some
                      divisions, then   become

i. _____   j. _____   k. _____   m. _____
   _____   _____   _____   Role:
   Role: Role:
                                         this causes

                                         1. _____
                                            _____
                                            _____

IN SUMMARY:

n. _____
   _____

o. _____
   _____

THE LOCK-AND-KEY CONCEPT:

p. Antigen: _____
   _____

q. Bacteria with antigen:

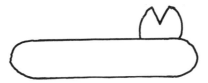

r. Antibody:

s. Antibody fitted into the bacterial antigen:

Two of the ways that antibodies destroy antigens:

t. _____

_____

u. _____

_____

v. Macrophage engulfing clumps of microorganisms:

Notes on AIDS and the immune system:

_____

_____

_____

_____

_____

_____

_____

_____

_____

_____

_____

_____

_____

_____

2.2 DNA AND THE STEPS
IN PROTEIN SYNTHESIS

You Will Need the Following Materials:

scissors
assorted colored pencils or crayons

At the Conclusion of This Activity, Students Will

- Know the structure of the DNA molecule.
- Know the role of DNA in protein synthesis.
- Understand the relationship between DNA and a chromosome.
- Have learned the role of "protein recipes" in the inheritance of traits.
- Know the basic steps involved in the cell's manufacture of protein.
- Know the roles of messenger RNA, transfer RNA, and ribosomes in the manufacture of protein.
- Understand the relationship between amino acids and proteins.

1. The Students Construct a Molecule of DNA and Learn Its Structure and Significance.

Distribute scissors, colored pencils, and copies of Worksheet 2.2–1 to the students. Inform them that two halves of a DNA molecule are diagrammed on the worksheet. Instruct them to leave the top circle of each half white, color the next circle down black, and continue to alternate white and black, proceeding down both halves of the molecule. Put the following symbols on the chalkboard along with the color scheme:

Upon completing the coloring, have them cut out the two halves of the molecule. The two halves can now be "joined together"—the components of the left half having been cut to fit the right half.

Discuss with the students the organizational structure of the DNA molecule. There are six component parts. Two of the parts are **phosphate units** (black) and **sugar units** (white). The remaining four parts, referred to as **nitrogen bases**, are **adenine bases** (red), **thymine bases** (green), **guanine bases** (yellow), and **cytosine bases** (blue). Direct the students into realizing that adenine is always paired with thymine, and guanine is always paired with cytosine.

The following information should now be given to the students:

a. DNA stands for deoxyribonucleic acid.

b. The model assembled represents a very short section of DNA.

c. Chromosomes, which carry genetic traits inherited from parents, are made of DNA. Therefore, the DNA model assembled can be considered a very short section of a chromosome.

d. Genetic traits carried on chromosomes, in the form of genes, are actually **protein recipes** which the cells can use in manufacturing proteins that they need.

e. Traits that are inherited from parents—from hair and eye color to growth hormones—have their start as protein recipes on the DNA of which the chromosome is made.

f. The protein recipes on the DNA molecule are "spelled out" in the sequence of the nitrogen bases.

2. The Students Learn the Basic Component Parts Involved in the Cell's Manufacture of a Protein.

Distribute copies of Worksheet 2.2–2. The ribosomes can be left white. The messenger RNA molecule should be color coded similar to the DNA molecule, but with one exception. RNA molecules have the nitrogen base uracil instead of thymine. Therefore, the nitrogen bases that look like thymine should be colored brown to represent uracil. The same holds true for the color coding of the nitrogen bases on the transfer RNA. All component parts on the worksheet should be carefully cut out. Review the cutout structures with the students, explaining that they are the basic structures involved in protein manufacture (synthesis) by the cell. They are **messenger RNA (mRNA), transfer RNA (tRNA), and amino acids**.

3. The Students Learn, as They Are Directed Through the Process, the Major Steps Involved in the Cell's Manufacture of a Protein From the "Protein Recipe" Located on the Original Chromosome (DNA Molecule).

Refer to Teacher Worksheet 2.2–3 (which corresponds to the steps below, a, b, c, and so on) as you direct the students through the following steps of protein manufacture, providing these essential notes as you proceed:

a. The right and left halves of the DNA molecule move apart.

The students separate the halves of their DNA molecules. The process by which this occurs is known as the **zipper theory**. Actually, the chemical bonds between the component parts of each nitrogen base pair break, thus allowing the two halves of the molecule to separate.

b. The DNA molecule makes a molecule of messenger RNA.

The students represent the DNA molecule making messenger RNA by pairing up their messenger RNA molecule alongside the left half of the DNA molecule. (Actually, the right side of the DNA molecule could be involved, but this activity is designed to use the left side.) In making messenger RNA, the DNA molecule has effectively transferred its protein recipe to the messenger RNA.

c. Messenger RNA moves out of the nucleus of the cell in order to get to structures called ribosomes.

The students can now put the DNA molecule aside, as it is no longer needed (actually, the two halves of the DNA molecule zip back up until once again it will unzip when another protein recipe is needed) and assume that the messenger RNA is now in the cytoplasm of the cell outside the nucleus.

d. The messenger RNA carries its protein recipe to the ribosomes.

The students should line up their three ribosomes side by side horizontally, along the front edge of their desk. The transfer RNAs and the amino acids can be "scattered" about on the desk above the ribosomes.

e. The messenger RNA begins moving across the surface of the first ribosome.

The messenger RNA molecule should be positioned horizontally (with the nitrogen bases pointing up) to the left of the left ribosome. The messenger RNA is then moved to the right until its first three nitrogen bases are on the surface of the first ribosome. Explain to the students that a protein is composed of many amino acids attached (chemically bonded) together in a chain. Each sequence of three nitrogen bases on the messenger RNA molecule spells out a code for a particular amino acid. For example, the three nitrogen bases now on the surface of the first ribosome are cytosine, uracil, and guanine, and they spell out a particular amino acid that is going to become part of a protein.

f. Transfer RNA brings the proper amino acid to the first ribosome.

The students now select the transfer RNA that fits the three-nitrogen base code on the first ribosome. This transfer RNA picks up the appropriate amino acid (one whose cutout configuration allows it to attach to the transfer RNA) and brings it to the ribosome. The amino acid is left at the site of the ribosome, and the transfer RNA moves back out into the cytoplasm of the cell.

g. The messenger RNA now moves to the right until its first three nitrogen bases are on the surface of the second ribosome and its second three nitrogen bases are on the surface of the first ribosome.

Procedure f above is now followed for each of two ribosomes. Upon completion of this step, ribosome #1 has two amino acids at its site and ribosome #2 has one amino acid at its site.

h. **The messenger RNA now moves to the right until its first three nitrogen bases are on the surface of the third ribosome, its second three nitrogen bases are on the surface of the second ribosome, and its final three nitrogen bases are on the surface of the first ribosome.**

Again, procedure f above is followed, this time for all three ribosomes. Upon completion of this step, ribosome #1 has three amino acids, ribosome #2 has two amino acids, and ribosome #3 has one amino acid.

i. **The messenger RNA continues moving to the right until it has completely passed over the three ribosomes.**

Upon completion, there will be three amino acids at each ribosome site. Noting the configurations cut into the amino acids, have the students attach each of the three groups of amino acids into three chains. These three chains each represent a protein, perhaps for hair or eye color. Explain to the students that in reality, far more than three ribosomes are used in the manufacture of proteins, and proteins consist of far greater numbers of amino acids than just three.

Have the students look closely at the three proteins just manufactured. It should be obvious that they are identical in structure. They are, therefore, assembly-line copies of the same protein. The number of ribosomes involved in the manufacture of any one kind of protein depends upon the quantity of that protein needed by the cell.

WORKSHEET 2.2-1   THE DNA MOLECULE

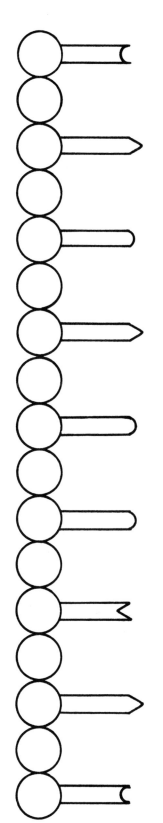

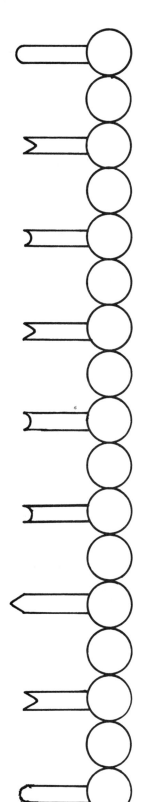

WORKSHEET 2.2–2 RIBOSOMES, MESSENGER RNA, TRANSFER RNA, AND AMINO ACIDS

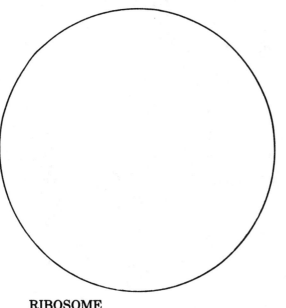

RIBOSOME

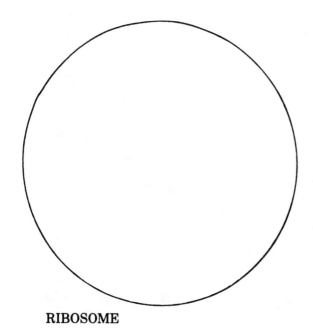

RIBOSOME

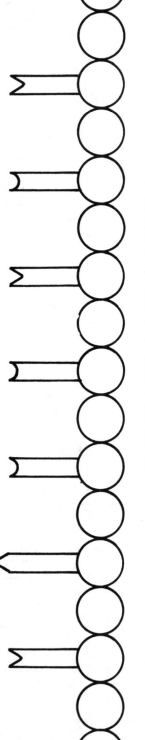

MESSENGER RNA MOLECULE

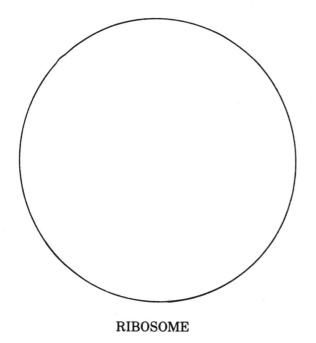

RIBOSOME

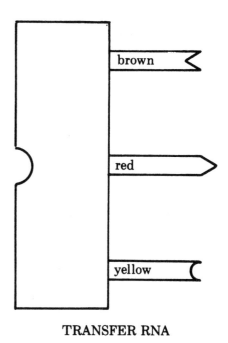

TRANSFER RNA

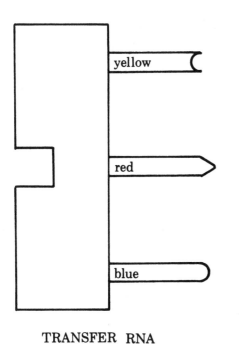

TRANSFER RNA

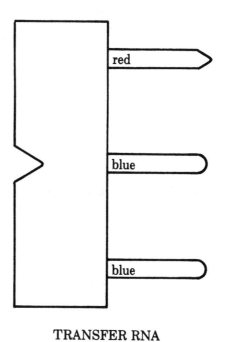

TRANSFER RNA

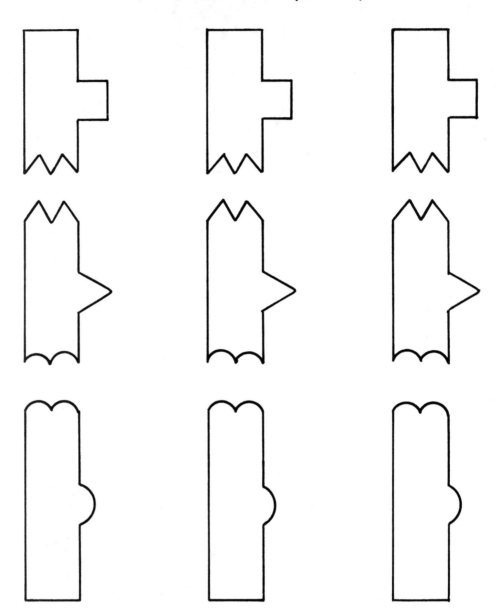

Three each of three different amino acids

Color the top row of amino acids red.
Color the middle row of amino acids blue.
Color the bottom row of amino acids yellow.

Teacher Worksheet 2.2–3
Illustrations of the Steps Involved
in the Cell's Manufacture of a Protein

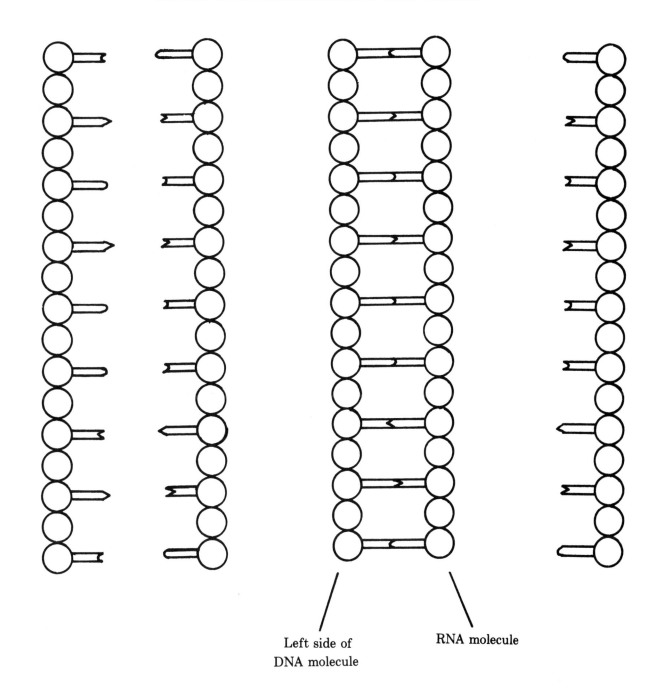

Left side of
DNA molecule

RNA molecule

a. Halves of a separated
   DNA molecule

b. Pairing up of mRNA
   alongside DNA

c. mRNA in the cytoplasm
   of the cell

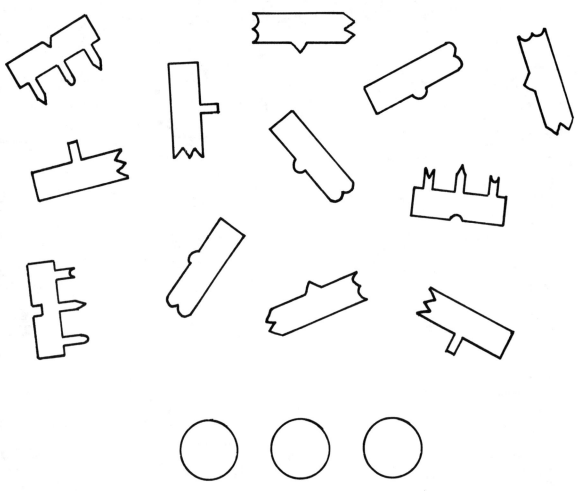

d. Ribosomes lined up and mRNA and tRNA "scattered" in the cytoplasm of the cell

Sequence of three
nitrogen bases

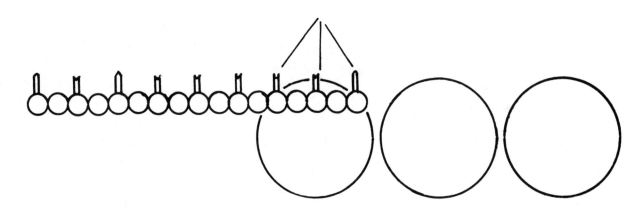

e. Messenger RNA moving across the surface of the first ribosome

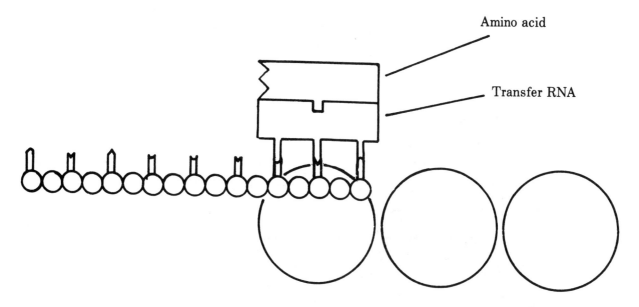

f. Transfer RNA brings the proper amino acid to the first ribosome

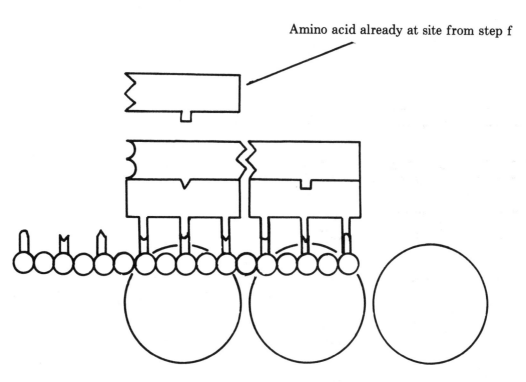

g. Two ribosomes involved in protein synthesis

Amino acids already at site from step g

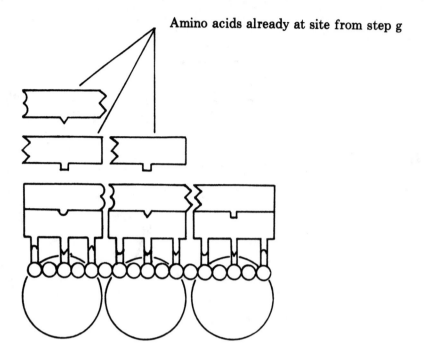

h. All three ribosomes involved in protein synthesis

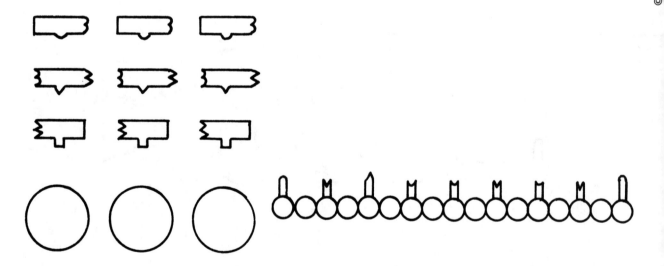

i. Protein synthesis is complete. Each ribosome has three identical amino acids that will bond into three identical proteins.

2.3 TRACING SOME FAMILY TRAITS

You Will Need the Following Materials:

PTC paper, opaque projector
colored pencils or crayons

Upon Completion of This Activity, Students Will

- Have gained experience in tracing some family traits over two or three generations.
- Know what a pedigree is and its value in hereditary research.
- Have analyzed pedigrees.

1. The Students Learn the Concept of a Pedigree.

Distribute two copies of Worksheet 2.3–1 to each student. Tell the students that the six charts on the worksheets are blank **pedigree charts**. Explain that the value of a pedigree chart is that it can be used in tracing a selected trait (genetic or otherwise) through successive generations of a family.

2. The Students Are Provided Instructions for Developing Three Pedigree Charts.

Help the students in setting up the first pedigree chart by giving them the following information. The chart should be given the number 1 and should be titled, Eye Color. The following symbols should be used for the chart: S = self; M = mother; F = father; GF = grandfather; GM = grandmother.

The students should begin putting data in the pedigree chart by coloring the square labeled S (self) with as close a color proximation as possible to the color of their own eyes. Above the square should be written the name of the eye color. They should also record similar data, in the other squares in the first row, for any brothers and/or sisters.

The second and third rows will probably require that the students collect this data at home. Point out that the second row of squares will be for their mother and father as well as for any brothers and/or sisters of their parents. The third row of squares will be for grandparents as well as their brothers and/or sisters. Remind the students to keep information about their grandparents on their father's side (the left side of the pedigree chart) separate from information about their grandparents on their mother's side (the right side of the pedigree chart).

If need be, extra squares can be added to the pedigree chart. Also, a fourth line of squares can be added if some students have access to information about great grandparents.

The second pedigree chart should be numbered 2 and titled, Hair Color. The data-gathering procedure is the same as that for eye color.

The third pedigree chart should be numbered 3 and titled, Handedness. The students should use the following symbols for filling in the squares: L = Predominantly uses the left hand for eating, writing, and so on; R = Predominantly uses the right hand for eating, writing, and so on; A = Ambidextrous (equally proficient at using both hands for eating, writing, and so on).

3. The Students Begin Gathering Data for Pedigree Chart #4.

Before giving the students any information about the nature of PTC, give each one a piece of PTC paper. Have them chew the piece of paper for a few seconds and then dispose of it in a waste container. The students are now asked to describe the taste of the PTC paper. Some will report a bitter taste and others will report no taste at all. Occasionally, one will report a sweet taste. Tell the students that PTC stands for **phenylthiocarbamide**. Upon tasting the PTC paper, approximately 66 percent report a bitter taste and 28 percent report no taste at all. About 6 percent report some other taste, such as sweet.

The students should use the following symbols for filling in the squares of the pedigree chart: B = bitter taste, N = no taste, S = sweet taste. The students can immediately fill in the S (self) square.

Provide the students with enough pieces of PTC paper to take home with them to test family members.

4. The Students Are Provided an Opportunity for Collecting Pedigree Data on Traits of Their Own Choosing.

The two remaining pedigree charts can be used by students who might wish to follow other traits through their family. Such traits might be weight, height, blood type, musical ability, or personality type, such as very outgoing (extrovert) or solitary (introvert).

5. The Students Discuss Their Completed Pedigree Charts.

Using an opaque projector, project completed pedigree charts on the classroom screen while engaging the students in a discussion of the data. Is a particular eye color more prevalent in some families than in others? Do some families have more left-handed members than others? Is a particular hair color more prevalent on one side of the family than the other? Do some families have large numbers of PTC tasters while others do not?

6. The Students Are Given an Opportunity to Explore Topics in Genetics.

Distribute copies of Worksheet 2.3–2 and review the topics with the students. You might wish to make individual and/or small group assignments, and then take the class to the library for research skills practice.

7. The Students Work on an Activity to Learn About Gene Splicing (Genetic Engineering).

Distribute copies of Worksheet 2.3–3. **The answers to the Library Research Questions are** 1. A gene is removed from one chromosome and is placed (or spliced) onto another chromosome. 2. Because the gene removed from the first chromosome is recombined with genes on the second chromosome. 3. Insulin and human growth hormone.

WORKSHEET 2.3–1   BLANK PEDIGREE CHARTS

Chart Number: _____ 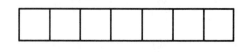 Title: _____

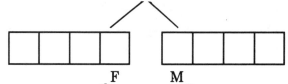

S

F   M

   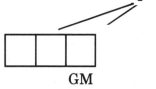   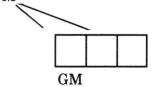   

GF   GM   GM   GF

Chart Number: _____ 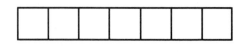 Title: _____

S

F   M

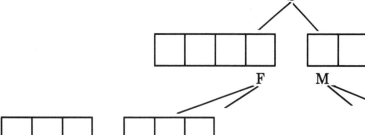

   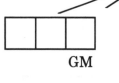   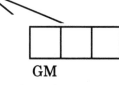   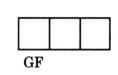

GF   GM   GM   GF

Chart Number: _____ 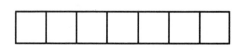 Title: _____

S

F   M

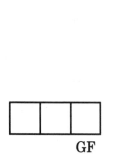   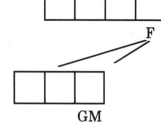   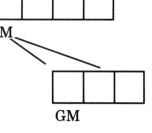

GF   GM   GM   GF

© 1992 by The Center for Applied Research in Education

HANDOUT 2.3-2 SOME GENETIC TOPICS FOR INVESTIGATION

Instructions: The following is a list of several topics related to the field of genetics. Perhaps you will find one or more of them interesting enough to explore using resources available to you in the library.

1. **Genes and chromosomes:** What are they? Where are they found? What are they made of?

2. **Dominant and recessive traits:** What is a dominant gene? What is a gene that is said to be recessive? What are some traits that are known to be dominant and recessive? What are some diseases caused by dominant genes? Recessive genes?

3. **The genetics of colorblindness:** What are the different types of colorblindness? What type of colorblindness is most common? Why is colorblindness most prevalent among males?

4. **The genetics of blood type:** What are the four major blood types, and what are their frequencies among the population? What specific genes carry the blood type traits? Do different ethnic groups have different percentages of the blood types? Why or why not?

5. **Sex-linked genetic diseases:** What are some different sex-linked genetic diseases, and why are they referred to as sex-linked?

6. **The genetics of handedness:** Are there more right-handed or left-handed individuals? Is handedness determined by the genes that you inherit?

7. **The genetics of eye color:** Is your eye color determined by specific genes that you have inherited? What part of the eye gives it its color? Why are some eyes blue when, in fact, there is no blue pigment? Do eyes change color during the day? What color eyes are most babies born with, and why?

8. **The process of meiosis:** What are the steps involved in meiosis? What are the final products of meiosis?

9. **The story of the discovery of the structure of DNA:** What team of scientists has been credited with discovering the structure of DNA? How can you build a model showing the different parts of a DNA molecule? What is the relationship between DNA and chromosomes? Why is DNA referred to as the "code of life"?

10. **The story of Gregor Mendel:** Why is Mendel called the "Father of Genetics"? What are Mendel's Laws of Inheritance? What plants were used by Mendel in conducting his genetic research?

WORKSHEET 2.3–3   MESSAGE SQUARE ACTIVITY ON GENETICS

Hint: Another name for genetic engineering or recombinant DNA

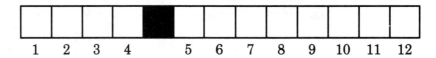

1   2   3   4   5   6   7   8   9   10   11   12

Anticipated Answer

Put: a P in 6
    an E in 2 and 4
    a G in 1 and 12
    an S in 5
    an N in 11
    an I in 8 and 10
    an N in 3
    an L in 7
    a C in 9

_____
_____
_____
_____
_____
_____
_____
_____
_____

Library Research Questions

1. Explain the technique of
    recombinant DNA.

Answers   Sources

2. Why is the technique referred
    to as recombinant DNA?

3. Name two human hormones
    that are being produced using
    recombinant DNA technology.

2.4 STUDY OF ALGAE

You Will Need the Following Materials:

student microscopes	clean microscope slides
microscope lamps	cover slips
lab aprons	medicine droppers
drawing paper	colored pencils
forceps	paper towels
iodine solution	

prepared slides (and/or living cultures) of selected algae such as:
Closterium and other desmids, Spirogyra, diatoms, Oscillatoria, Protococcus

If using living cultures, you will need a guidebook to freshwater algae. (In the spring it is easy to collect living algae from ponds and streams and the bark of trees. A guidebook will allow you to make identification.)

Upon Completion of This Activity, Students Will

- Be able to identify various kinds of algae through the microscope.
- Realize that algae is grouped according to pigment.
- Be able to identify some cell structures of algae and provide their functions.
- Be able to identify some ecological roles of algae.
- Have learned where various kinds of algae are found in nature.

1. The Students Study the Alga Spirogyra.

Distribute drawing paper and colored pencils (students might wish to prepare drawings according to the colors observed on their slides).

Distribute prepared slides of Spirogyra. (If you are using living cultures of algae for this specimen or any of the others, have the students prepare their slides by placing a drop of water on the center of a clean microscope slide. Then, using forceps, place a small quantity of the algae sample in the water and add a cover slip.)

The following sketch can be referred to as a guide in directing the students as to which structures to draw and label. High power is recommended.

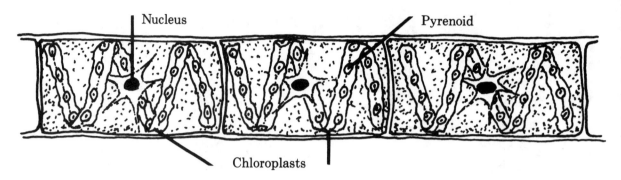

Nucleus   Pyrenoid

Chloroplasts

If living Spirogyra are used, direct the students to lift the edge of the cover slip and add a drop of iodine solution. When observed, the pyrenoids will be stained blue-black. (Pyrenoids contain starch, which stains blue-black in the presence of iodine.)

The following notes are to be given to the students:

Structure	**Function**
Chloroplast:	Carries out photosynthesis (food manufacture)
Pyrenoid:	Food manufactured by photosynthesis stored here in the form of a starch
Nucleus:	Contains the genetic instructions for the cell

a. In terms of pigment, Spirogyra is classified as a green alga.

b. Spirogyra is eaten in some parts of the world; for example, in India.

c. Spirogyra forms "clouds" of growth in quiet waters such as ponds.

d. Spirogyra derives its name from the spiral chloroplasts in its cells.

e. When reeling in their lines, angler may find clumps of Spirogyra attached.

2. The Students Study the Alga Oscillatoria.

After distributing the materials, use the following sketch as a guide in working with the students as they make their observations and drawings. High power is recommended.

The following notes are to be given to the students:

a. In terms of pigment, Oscillatoria is classified as a blue-green alga. (*Note:* Blue-green algae, according to some classification schemes, are classified as cyanobacteria.)

b. Oscillatoria derives its name from the observable oscillating of its tips in living cultures.

c. Anglers may find Oscillatoria tangled around their lines or hooks.

d. Oscillatoria forms "clouds" of growth in ponds and other slow-moving waters.

3. The Students Study the Alga Protococcus.

The following sketch will aid you in helping students with their observations and drawings. High power is recommended.

The following notes are to be given to the students:

a. Protococcus is one of the most common and widely distributed of the algae.

b. In terms of pigment, Protococcus is classified as a green alga. Protococcus gives a greenish surface cover to things like flowerpots, rocks, fence posts, and trees. It grows on the less-lighted sides of objects. For example, in the Northern Hemisphere it grows on the less-lighted north side.

c. Protococcus is a single-celled alga, although at times several cells may comprise a colony.

4. The Students Study Diatoms.

The following sketch will aid in studying diatoms. High power is recommended.

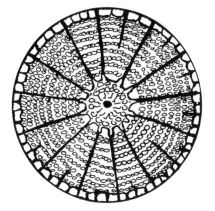 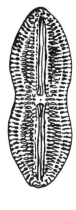 

The following notes should be given to the students:

a. Diatoms are found in a great variety of shapes with beautiful surface detail.

b. In terms of pigment, diatoms are classified as golden-brown algae.

c. Diatoms are a major constituent of plankton, which in turn is a major food source for aquatic life—both in fresh and salt water. The walls of diatoms are made of silica. Thus, diatoms are important economically for such uses as insulating materials, cosmetics, polishing agents, and filters in producing beverages such as fruit juice.

5. The Students Study Desmids.

The following sketch can be used as a guide in studying the desmids. High power is recommended.

The following is an additional sketch of a specific desmid named Closterium. If the students observe living cultures, a drop of iodine solution added to the slide will stain the pyrenoids.

Chloroplast

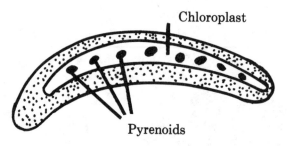

Pyrenoids

The following notes should be given to the students:

a. Each desmid is comprised of two symmetrical halves.

b. In terms of pigment, desmids are classified as green algae.

c. Desmids are an important constituent of plankton as a food source and as a producer of atmospheric oxygen.

6. The Student's Knowledge of and Identification Skills of Algae Are Evaluated.

Prior to the evaluation exercise, set up five microscopes as follows:

a. Pointer on a pyrenoid of either Spirogyra or Closterium.
b. Pointer on a chloroplast of either Spirogyra or Closterium.
c. Focus on desmids.
d. Focus on Oscillatoria.
e. Focus on Spirogyra.

At each microscope place a 3-inch by 5-inch card with the question number and the question on it as follows:

13. Name the structure that the pointer is on.
14. Name the structure that the pointer is on.
15. Provide the name of the alga.
16. Provide the name of the alga.
17. Provide the name of the alga and tell where it is found in nature.

Hand out Worksheet 2.4–1 when you are ready to administer the evaluation.
The answers to the worksheet follow: 1. i; 2. e; 3. a; 4. a, g, h; 5. b; 6. f; 7. e; 8. d, g; 9. a, e; 10. d; 11. h; 12. e; 13. pyrenoid; 14. chloroplast; 15. desmids; 16. Oscillatoria; 17. Spirogyra is found in quiet waters such as a pond.

WORKSHEET 2.4–1   EVALUATION EXERCISE

Fill in the blanks in the left-hand column with the letter of the proper answer from the list of terms below. A letter can be used more than once, and more than one letter can constitute an answer.

_____ 1. Structure that carries out photosynthesis

_____ 2. Walls are made of silica

_____ 3. Important producer of atmospheric oxygen

_____ 4. Kinds of green algae

_____ 5. Food stored here in the form of starch

_____ 6. Name of a specific desmid

_____ 7. Used as insulating material and polishing agents

_____ 8. Forms clouds of growth in quiet waters

_____ 9. Comprises plankton

_____ 10. Derives its name from its tips that move back and forth

_____ 11. Most common and widely distributed in nature

_____ 12. Golden-brown algae

a. desmids   d. Oscillatoria   g. Spirogyra   j. silica
b. pyrenoids   e. diatoms   h. protococcus
c. pigments   f. Closterium   i. chloroplast

Microscope Identification   Answer the questions on the cards located at each microscope.

13. _____.

14. _____.

15. _____.

16. _____.

17. _____.

2.5 DISSECTION OF THE SHEEP'S HEART

You Will Need the Following Materials:

paper towels

lab aprons

stirring-type rods (preferably other than glass)

scalpels or single-edge safety razor blades (such as Treet™)

sheep's hearts (could be obtained from a local abattoir)

dissection trays (or newspaper)

Upon Completion of This Activity, Students Will

- Know the names of basic heart structures.
- Know the pathway of blood through the heart.
- Know the basic functioning of the heart.
- Know the names of basic blood vessels associated with the heart.
- Have developed or improved psychomotor skills associated with dissecting

Important note for teacher: It is recommended that you practice this dissection prio: to class because the students will need help with some of the cutting procedures.

1. The Students Learn Some Introductory Material About the Heart.

Distribute copies of Handout 2.5–1. This handout provides illustrative guides throughout the dissection. Refer the students to Figure #1. This is a simplified cross section of the human heart. It can serve as an anatomical road map during the dissection. Have the students examine it as you give them the following notes:

a. Since structures are similar, a dissection of the sheep's heart is an excellent way to learn about the human heart.

b. The mammalian heart has four chambers.

c. Two chambers of the heart—the right atrium and the left atrium—receive blood from the body and from the lungs, respectively.

d. Two chambers of the heart—the right ventricle and the left ventricle—pump blood to the lungs and to the rest of the body, respectively.

e. The heart itself is composed of cardiac muscle tissue, a type of muscle tissue found only in the heart.

2. The Students Gather the Materials Needed for Dissection.

Each student or group of students will need a sheep's heart, scalpel (or single-edge safety razor blade), dissection tray (or newspapers), and four stirring-type rods (preferably other than glass). Have the students apply a hand lotion prior to dissection, which will act as a partial barrier to skin odors.

3. The Students Become Acquainted with the Exterior of the Heart.

Refer the students to Figure #2 on their handout. Note that the "bottom" rounded portion of the heart is the apex. Note also that vessels carrying blood to and from the heart are located at the "top." The bulk of the heart is cardiac muscle tissue.

4. The Students Dissect Openings into the Right and Left Ventricles of the Heart.

SAFETY CAUTION: Emphasize to the students that the razor blades and scalpels must be handled very carefully. They could easily slip and cause injury to the skin.

Using the scalpel (or single-edge blade), have the students cut about ½ inch off the apex of the heart. The exposed surface should resemble Figure #3. (If it does not, then cut off another ¼ inch or so until it does. The amount cut will vary with the size of the heart.)

The students should realize that the crescent-shaped opening (labeled #1) leads into the heart's right ventricle. The round opening (labeled #2) leads into the heart's left ventricle. The right and left ventricles are the two lower pumping chambers of the heart.

Explain that the heart wall surrounding the round opening is very thick. This is because the left ventricle has the task of pumping blood to all parts of the body (with the exception of the lungs). Thus, it is surrounded with plenty of cardiac muscle to accomplish this task.

On the other hand, the heart wall surrounding the crescent-shaped opening is not nearly as thick. This is because the pumping job of the right ventricle is much easier than that of the left ventricle. The right ventricle has to pump blood only to the lungs (and not to the rest of the body).

5. The Students Explore Structures Located in the Right Ventricle.

Have the students now open the right ventricle. This is achieved by cutting along the sides of the heart from the ends of the crescent, as shown by the dotted lines on Figure #3. Do not cut beyond the dotted lines. They have now created a flap that can be pulled back, exposing the inside of the right ventricle.

The right ventricle should now be fully exposed, as shown in Figure #4. If it is not, have them make further adjusting cuts, slightly widening the flap.

The following notes, based on the structures labeled in Figure #4, should be given to the students:

a. The right ventricle receives blood from the right atrium (not yet dissected).

b. The tricuspid valve consists of three flaps that are attached to the wall of the heart by "stringlike" structures. This valve opens when blood enters the right ventricle from the right atrium. It then closes to prevent blood backflow.

c. The chordae tendinae are "stringlike" structures that attach the flaps of the tricuspid valve to the wall of the heart. They function to stabilize the opening and closing of the valve flaps.

d. Papillary muscles serve to anchor the chordae tendinae to the heart wall.

e. The pulmonary artery carries blood from the right ventricle to the lungs.

6. The Students Locate and Learn the Names of the Blood Vessels Attached to the Right Side of the Heart.

A rod is **gently** pushed through the opening of the tricuspid valve. (**SAFETY CAUTION: If a glass rod is used, it should be pushed very gently, as the rod can easily break and injure a student.**) Since the tricuspid valve is the opening between the right ventricle and the right atrium, the rod is being pushed into the right atrium.

Once in the right atrium, the student continues to push gently on the rod and "probes around," trying to locate an opening leading out of the top of the right atrium. When this opening is located, the tip of the rod will emerge as shown in Figure #5. (The rod is labeled #1.) It is important to realize that what the students have located is one of two vena cava veins that drain blood into the right atrium from all parts of the body (except the lungs).

7. The Students Locate the Pulmonary Artery.

The first rod can be left in place, and a second one now used. The students probe to the right of the tricuspid valve (see Figure #4) while pushing gently on the rod. Eventually, they will locate the pulmonary artery, and the rod can be pushed through it until the tip exits at the top of the heart, as shown in Figure #5. (The rod is labeled #2.) The students should be told that the pulmonary artery carries blood pumped out of the right ventricle to the lungs.

8. The Students Review What Has Been Learned Thus Far About the Flow of Blood Through the Right Side of the Heart.

The following information should be given to the students:

a. The vena cava veins drain blood from all parts of the body (except the lungs) into the right atrium.

b. Blood then flows from the right atrium through the tricuspid valve into the right ventricle.

c. The right ventricle pumps blood through the pulmonary artery to the lungs. As it is doing this, the tricuspid valve is forced closed to prevent blood from backtracking into the atrium.

9. The Students Explore Structures Located in the Left Ventricle.

The two rods can now be removed from the right side of the heart and used again as dissection continues.

To open up the left ventricle, have the students cut along the sides of the heart as shown by the dotted lines in Figure #6. Do not cut farther than the dotted line.

Figure #7 shows the left ventricle exposed. If the ventricle is not fully exposed, have them make further adjusting cuts.

The following information, based on structures labeled in Figure #7, should be given to the students:

a. The left ventricle receives blood from the left atrium.

b. The bicuspid (mitral) valve consists of two flaps attached to the wall of the heart by chordae tendinae. This valve opens when blood enters from the left atrium and then closes to prevent backflow of blood.

c. The chordae tendinae and papillary muscle have been previously explained.

d. The aortic artery carries blood from the left ventricle to all parts of the body except the lungs.

10. The Students Locate the Blood Vessels Attached to the Left Side of the Heart.

The rod is gently pushed through the opening of the bicuspid valve. Since the bicuspid valve is the opening between the left atrium and the left ventricle, the rod is being pushed into the left atrium.

The student continues to gently push on the rod and "probes around," trying to locate an opening leading out of the left atrium. When they locate this opening, the tip of the rod will emerge as shown in Figure #8. (The rod is labeled #1.) The students should realize that they have located the pulmonary vein that carries newly oxygenated blood back to the left atrium from the lungs.

11. The Students Locate the Aortic Artery.

The rod can be left in place and a second one now used. The students will probe the area to the left of the bicuspid valve while gently pushing on the rod. They will eventually locate the aortic artery and be able to push the rod through until the tip exits at the top of the heart, as shown in Figure #8. (The rod is labeled

#2.) Have the students realize that the aortic artery carries newly oxygenated blood from the left ventricle to all parts of the body (except the lungs).

12. The Students Review What Has Been Learned About the Flow of Blood Through the Left Side of the Heart.

Give the students the following information:

a. Blood is carried into the left atrium from the lungs by the pulmonary veins.
b. Blood flows from the left atrium through the bicuspid (mitral) valve into the left ventricle.
c. The left ventricle pumps blood through the aortic artery to all parts of the body (except the lungs). As it is doing this, the bicuspid valve is forced closed, preventing blood from backtracking into the atrium.

13. The Students Dissect Free a Valve Flap for Closer Observation.

Have the students carefully dissect free a flap from either the tricuspid or bicuspid valve. They should do this by cutting free the chordae tendinae attachments to the heart wall. Refer to Figure #7.

14. Two Optional Dissection Exercises Can Be Carried out by the Students.

Using a rod, relocate either the pulmonary artery or the aortic artery. Both of these vessels have a semilunar valve at its point of entry into the heart. The valve resembles an arrangement of three cuplike structures, as shown in Figure #9. The function of the valve is to prevent blood backflow. To reach one of these valves it is necessary to cut open the vessel along its length. The valve is located at the point where the vessel opens into the ventricle.

If some students wish to open an atrium, this can be accomplished simply by carefully cutting beyond the tricuspid or bicuspid valve.

15. The Students Test Their Knowledge of Heart Structure and Function.

Distribute copies of Worksheet 2.5–2. **The answers to the evaluation exercise are** 1. g; 2. f; 3. n; 4. a; 5. l; 6. s; 7. b; 8. m; 9. r; 10. e; 11. p; 12. h; 13. k; 14. d; 15. c.

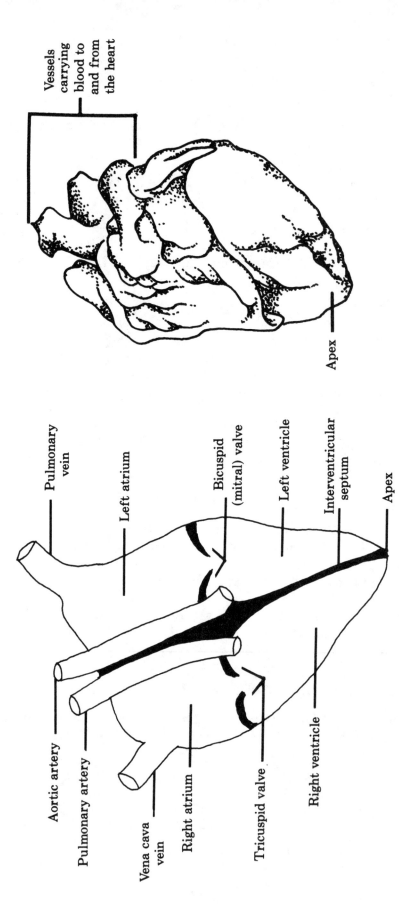

Vessels carrying blood to and from the heart

Apex

Figure 2
Exterior of the Sheep's Heart

Pulmonary vein

Left atrium

Bicuspid (mitral) valve

Left ventricle

Interventricular septum

Apex

Aortic artery

Pulmonary artery

Vena cava vein

Right atrium

Tricuspid valve

Right ventricle

Figure 1
Simplified Cross Section of the Human Heart

HANDOUT 2.5-1   A GUIDE TO DISSECTING THE SHEEP'S HEART

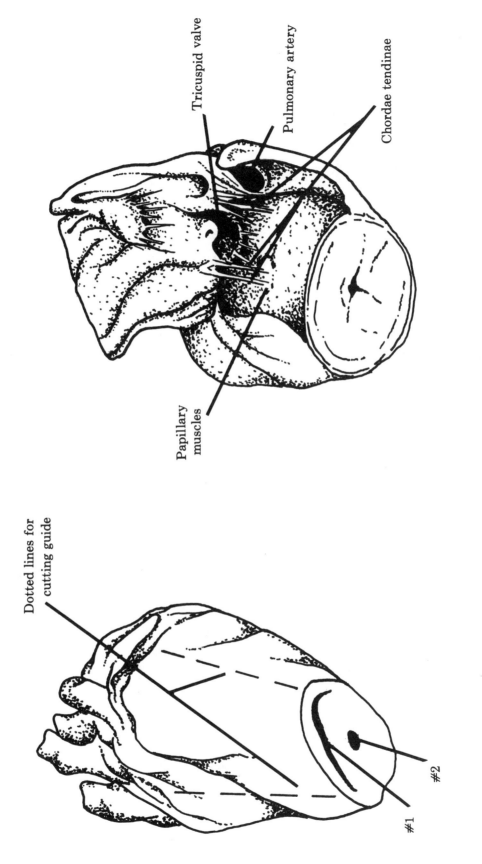

Dotted lines for
cutting guide

#1

#2

Figure 3
Heart With Apex Dissected Away

Tricuspid valve

Pulmonary artery

Chordae tendinae

Papillary
muscles

Figure 4
Heart Showing Open Right Ventricle

101

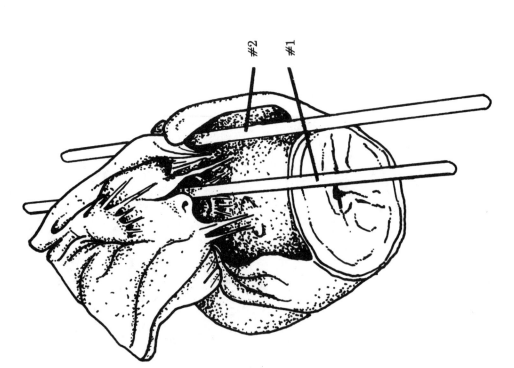

Dotted lines for cutting guide (dotted lines on the side of the heart away from you are not shown)

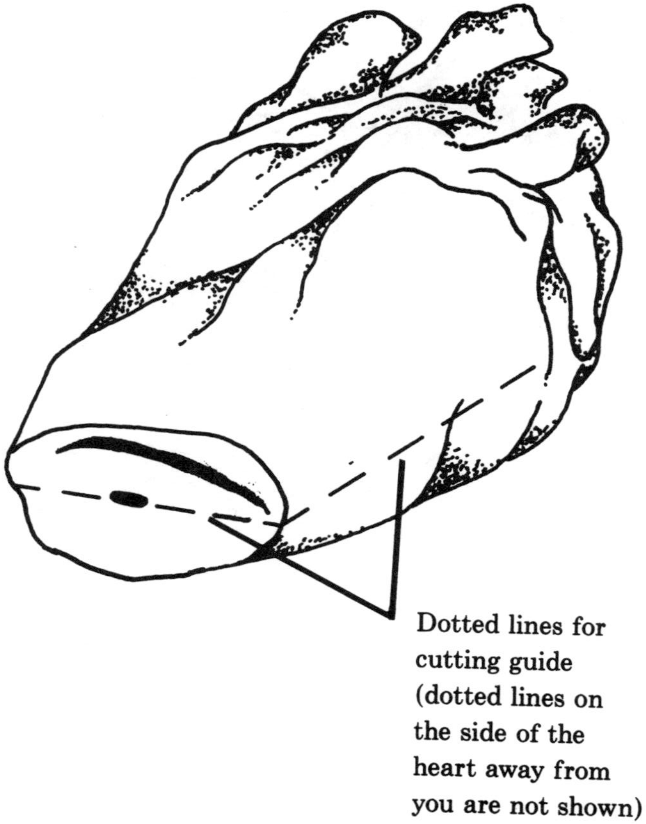

Figure 6
Guide for Opening the Left Ventricle

#2
#1

Figure 5
Rods Passing Through the Vena Cava Vein and the Pulmonary Artery

HANDOUT 2.5–1 A GUIDE TO DISSECTING THE SHEEP'S HEART

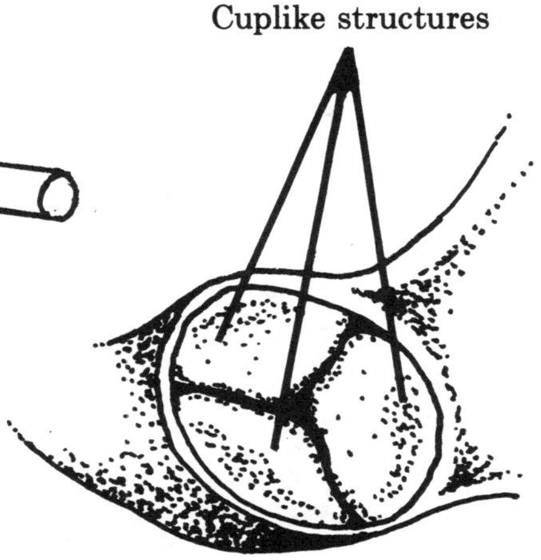

Figure 9
A Semilunar Valve Showing
the Three Cuplike Structures

Cuplike structures

#2

#1

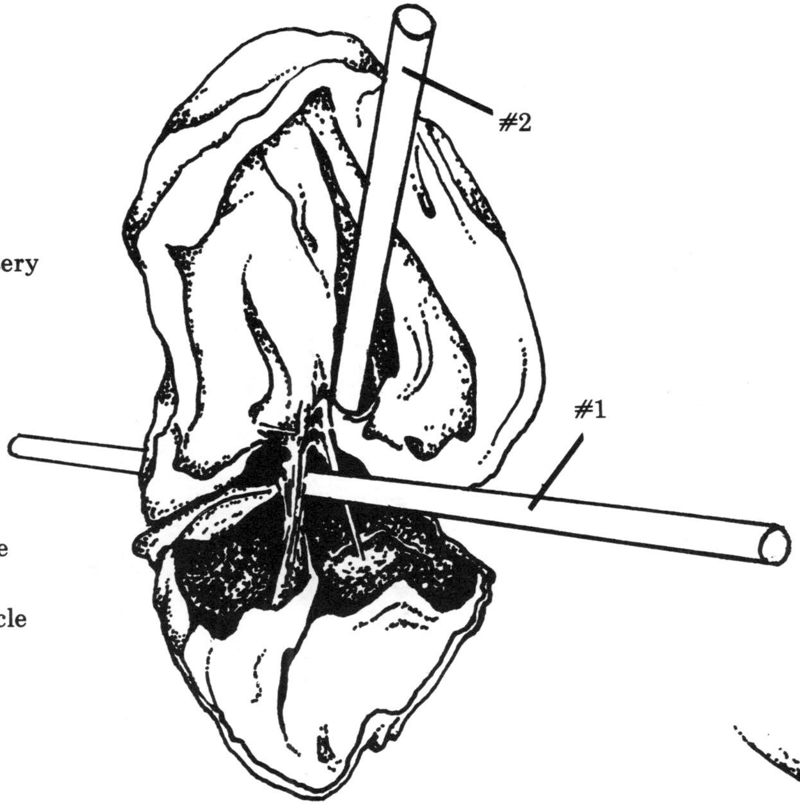

Figure 8
Rods Passing Through Pulmonary
Vein and Aortic Artery

Aortic artery

Bicuspid valve

Chordae tendinae

Papillary muscle

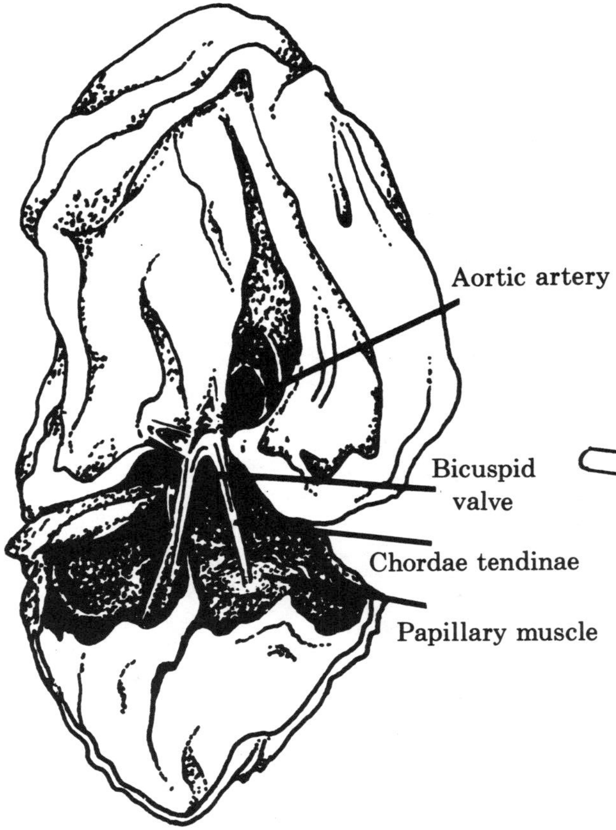

Figure 7
Heart Showing Open
Left Ventricle

WORKSHEET 2.5–2   EVALUATION EXERCISE

Instructions: Place the correct letter of the answer from the right-hand column with the proper question in the left-hand column.

_____ 1. How many chambers does the human heart have?

_____ 2. To where does the right ventricle pump blood?

_____ 3. What vessel carries blood returning to the heart from all parts of the body except the lungs?

_____ 4. What is the name of the valve located between the left atrium and ventricle?

_____ 5. What is the function of the chordae tendinae?

_____ 6. What vessels carry blood to the heart from the lungs?

_____ 7. Which ventricle of the heart has the thickest walls for pumping blood?

_____ 8. Which vessel carries blood from the heart to the lungs?

_____ 9. Which chamber of the heart receives blood from all parts of the body except the lungs?

_____ 10. What vessel carries blood from the heart to all parts of the body except the lungs?

_____ 11. What is the name of the valve located between the right atrium and ventricle?

_____ 12. What two chambers of the heart pump blood?

_____ 13. What is the lower pointed portion of the heart called?

_____ 14. What is the function of the papillary muscle?

_____ 15. What is the function of the valves of the heart?

a. bicuspid (mitral) valve

b. left ventricle

c. to prevent blood from backtracking

d. anchor chordae tendinae to wall of heart

e. aortic artery

f. lungs

g. four

h. left and right ventricles

i. five

j. all parts of the body except lungs

k. apex

l. stabilizes valves

m. pulmonary artery

n. vena cava

o. left and right atria

p. tricuspid

q. two

r. right atrium

s. pulmonary veins

t. three

2.6 A STUDY OF FOOD PRODUCTS IN TERMS OF CHOLESTEROL, FAT, SALT, AND SUGAR

You Will Need the Following Materials:

hand calculator (optional)
product labels containing nutrition information per serving

Upon Completion of This Activity, Students Will

- Know how to read and interpret the nutrition information on food items.
- Know how to calculate the percentage of fat per serving of a food item.
- Know current recommendations for daily amounts of fat, sugar, salt, and cholesterol in the diet.
- Be able to make a prudent selection of food items at a grocery store.
- Know examples of specific types of food nutrition labeling that can be misleading and/or lacking in certain types of information.

1. The Students Are Given Information Regarding Cholesterol, Fat, Salt, and Sugar.

Distribute copies of Worksheet 2.6–1. This worksheet is designed to be filled in as you provide the following information.

A common topic for discussion these days is one's blood serum cholesterol level. Cholesterol has been described as a fatty, waxy substance that can build up on artery walls and eventually block them. Many experts feel that a blood serum cholesterol level for teenagers should not exceed 150mg, and for adults, it should not exceed 200mg. The organ in the body that produces cholesterol for daily needs is the liver. For those who have elevated levels of cholesterol, the sources are often cholesterol and saturated fats in the foods we eat.

It has been recommended that our total daily intake of cholesterol should not exceed **300mg**. Further, it has been recommended that **fat be limited to 30 percent of our daily caloric intake**. There are three basic types of fats in the foods we eat: **polyunsaturated fat (recommended), monounsaturated fat (recommended), and saturated fat (not recommended)**.

It has been recommended that our daily intake of salt (sodium) be no more than **3,000mg**, and that of sugar, a refined carbohydrate without nutritional value, be no more than 3 tablespoons.

2. The Students Learn How to Calculate the Percentage of Calories from Fat Per Serving of Food.

Put the following information on the chalkboard under the heading Nutrition Information per Serving: calories = 100; fat = 1 gram. Explain that you need know only three pieces of information in order to determine the percentage of calories from fat per serving of a food. One is the number of calories per serving, the second is the number of grams of fat per serving, and the third is that 1 gram of fat has 9 calories. With this information, the percentage of calories from fat per serving of a food can be calculated as follows:

$$\frac{\text{Grams of fat per serving} \times 9}{\text{Total calories per serving}} \times 100 = \frac{9}{100} \times 100 = 9\%$$

Thus, we have determined that 9 percent of the total calories per serving is from fat. This is well under our 30 percent guideline limit.

Put the following nutrition information per serving on the chalkboard and let the students calculate the percentage of fat per serving: calories = 200; fat = 10 grams. (Answer: 45 percent. This is over our 30 percent guideline limit.)

3. The Students Learn How to Determine the Amount of Sodium (Salt), Sugar, and Cholesterol in a Serving of Food.

The amount of sodium is indicated in milligrams (mg) under nutrition information per serving. As stated above, the total milligrams per day should not exceed 3,000mg (3 grams). You might want to weigh out 3 grams of salt on the laboratory balance for visual reinforcement.

The amount of sugar per serving is indicated under Carbohydrate Information on the food container. It is usually listed as **Sucrose and Other Sugars**, and it is expressed in grams. It is important to know that 12 grams = 1 tablespoon. Thus, the total daily intake of sugar should not exceed 36 grams (3 tablespoons).

The amount of cholesterol is expressed in milligrams when included along with product nutrition information.

4. The Students Learn Some Specific Examples of How Nutrition Information Labels Can Be Misleading and Lacking in Certain Types of Information.

Give the students the following information:

a. Although increasing numbers of food products now contain nutritional information per serving, many still do not. It can be of value to write to those companies not providing such information suggesting that they include this information on their product packages.

b. The information on sugar content is sometimes "hidden" in the grams of carbohydrate information, rather than listed separately as grams of sugar. For example, on certain candy bars, carbohydrates will be listed as 22 grams, rather than 2 grams of complex carbohydrates and 20 grams of sugar (which is a refined carbohydrate).

c. Fat content will often be listed as, for example, 3 grams, rather than 2 grams of polyunsaturated fat (healthy) and 1 gram of saturated fat (unhealthy).

   d. Portion sizes per serving are often very small, so that the amounts of fat, sugar, sodium, and cholesterol per serving are expressed in lower numbers. When consumed in larger quantities, these substances are, of course, taken into the body in larger quantities.

   e. Many products advertise that they are cholesterol free. This in no way assures that the product is nutritionally sound. These same products may contain large amounts of fat, which can be more harmful than moderate amounts of cholesterol.

   f. A product advertised as low fat may still be providing 30, 40, or more percent of its calories from fat.

5. The Students Practice Examining and Recording Data from Nutritional Information About Various Food Products.

Distribute copies of Worksheet 2.6–2. Check the students' answers to Part 1 to make certain they can interpret the nutrition information given.

For Part 2, in analyzing the "fast-food" meal, the students should obtain the following data:

Total amounts of: Fat (g) 68
                    Sugar (tbsp) 4
                    Sodium (mg) 1,943
                    Cholesterol (mg) . . 166

Total number of calories for the fast-food meal 1,417

Percentage of total daily recommendations for: Sugar . . . . .133 percent
                                                 Sodium. . . . . .65 percent
                                                 Cholesterol . . . . . .55 percent

Percentage of calories from fat for the entire meal . . . . .43 percent

Initiate a discussion of the data results with the class, noting, among other things, that this meal represents just a small portion of the average daily food intake for a teenager.

6. The Students Calculate the Percentage of Calories from Fat for Milk.

Let the students complete Part 3 of their worksheets.

Comparing milk types, the following data should be obtained by the students:

Whole milk   = 48 percent fat
Low-fat milk = 27 percent fat
Skim milk   = 3 percent fat

Point out to the students that even low-fat milk is close to the 30 percent of calories-from-fat guidelines. For someone concerned about fat in the diet, it would be prudent to drink skim milk. (As an optional activity, you might want to run a taste test between the three types of milk. Adding some chocolate syrup to the milk will make differentiation very difficult.)

Also point out that whole milk has over 30mg of cholesterol per serving.

7. The Students Bring in Food Product Nutrition Information and Develop Skills at Selecting Products for Healthy Meals.

This portion of the activity is important for its potential carry-over value outside the classroom.

Instruct the students to bring in as many empty food packages and/or nutrition information labels as they can. Attempt to obtain as diverse a selection as possible. For example, include an assortment of breakfast cereals, breads, soups, desserts, vegetables, meats, beverages, spreads, salad dressings, and so on. Organize these products and/or labels into food categories and place at various locations around the classroom. Allow students to make prudent selections for sandwiches, snacks, and complete meals that are low in fats, cholesterol, salt, and sugar. Upon completion, have students go to the chalkboard and itemize their food selections, noting amounts of cholesterol, fat, salt, and sugar, as well as the percentage of total daily recommendations that they represent.

As an additional activity, you might offer extra credit to students for bringing in foods prepared from nutritionally sound low fat, cholesterol, salt, and sugar recipes.

8. The Students Work on an Activity to Learn More About Cholesterol and Diet.

Pass out copies of Worksheet 2.6–3 for the students to work on. **The answers to the Library Research Questions are** 1. HDL = high-density lipoprotein and LDL = low-density lipoprotein; 2. HDL; 3. colon (large intestine) cancer; 4. triglycerides; 5. A section of vein from the patient's leg is removed and used as a detour around a clogged artery in the patient's heart.

Name _____   Date _____

WORKSHEET 2.6–1
NOTES ON CHOLESTEROL, FAT, SALT, AND SUGAR

Instructions: Fill in this worksheet as your teacher gives you notes.

1. A common topic for discussion these days is _____

2. Provide a description of cholesterol: _____
   _____
   _____

3. Teenage cholesterol levels should not exceed: _____
   Adult cholesterol levels should not exceed: _____

4. What organ in the body produces cholesterol? _____

5. For those who have elevated levels of cholesterol, the sources are often:
   a. _____
   b. _____

6. It has been recommended that the daily intake of cholesterol should not exceed: _____

7. Fats should be limited to what percentage of our daily caloric intake? _____

8. Three types of fats in our diet are
   a. _____
   b. _____
   c. _____
   (Note which fats are recommended and which are not.)

9. What are the suggested daily intake limits for
   a. sodium (salt)? _____
   b. sugar? _____

10. What is the formula to use in determining the percentage of calories from fat in a single serving of a food:
    _____

WORKSHEET 2.6–2
CALCULATING THE AMOUNTS OF FAT, CHOLESTEROL, SUGAR, AND SALT (SODIUM) IN SERVINGS OF FOOD

Part 1:

Instructions: Read each of the following Nutrition Information per Serving for various food products and fill in the information asked for at the right.

Nutrition Information per Serving

Cereal

Serving size..........	½ cup	
Calories	60	Percentage of calories from fat: _____
Protein (g)...........	2	mg of cholesterol: _____
Carbohydrate (g).....	23	mg of sodium: _____
Fat (g)	1	g of sugar: _____
Cholesterol (mg)	0	
Sodium (mg)........	250	
Sugar (g)	0	

Mayonnaise

Serving size..........	1 tbsp	
Calories	100	Percentage of calories from fat: _____
Protein (g)...........	0	mg of cholesterol: _____
Carbohydrate (g).....	0	mg of sodium: _____
Fat (g)	11	
Sodium (mg)........	80	
Cholesterol (mg)	5	

Mayonnaise (reduced calorie)

Serving size..........	1 tbsp	
Calories	40	Percentage of calories from fat: _____
Protein (g)...........	0	mg of cholesterol: _____
Carbohydrate (g).....	1	mg of sodium: _____
Fat (g)	4	
Sodium (mg)........	80	
Cholesterol	0	

Candy bar #1

Serving size..........	1 bar	
Calories	230	Percentage of calories from fat: _____
Protein (g)...........	4	mg of sodium: _____
Carbohydrate (g).....	22	tbsp of sugar: _____
Fat (g)	14	
Sodium (mg)........	35	
Sugar (g)	20	

Candy bar #2

Serving size.........	1 bar
Calories	220
Protein (g)..........	3
Fat (g)	14
Sugar (g)	20
Sodium (mg)........	125

Percentage of calories from fat: _____
mg of sodium: _____
tbsp of sugar: _____

Cream cheese

Serving size.........	1 tbsp
Calories	50
Protein (g)..........	1
Carbohydrate (g).....	0.5
Cholesterol (mg)	15
Fat (g)	5
Sodium (mg)........	42

Percentage of calories from fat: _____
mg of sodium: _____
mg of cholesterol: _____

Chicken pot pie

Serving size.........	1
Calories	730
Protein (g)..........	28
Sugar (g)	8
Fat (g)	39
Sodium (mg)........	1,680

Percentage of calories from fat: _____
mg of sodium: _____

Part 2:

The following information is of a typical fast-food restaurant meal consisting of **a hamburger** with cheese, French fries, a shake, and dessert:

Hamburger with cheese

Serving size.........	1
Calories	525
Protein (g)..........	30
Sugar (g)	0
Fat (g)	32
Sodium (mg)........	1,220
Cholesterol (mg)	107

Percentage of calories from fat: _____
mg of sodium: _____
mg of cholesterol: _____
tbsp of sugar: _____

French fries

Serving size.........	1 order
Calories	280
Protein (g)..........	4
Sugar (g)	0
Fat (g)	14
Sodium (mg)........	95
Cholesterol (mg)	15

Percentage of calories from fat: _____
mg of sodium: _____
mg of cholesterol: _____
tbsp of sugar: _____

Shake

Serving size	10 oz	
Calories	352	Percentage of calories from fat: _____
Protein (g)	9	mg of sodium: _____
Sugar (g)	39	mg of cholesterol: _____
Fat (g)	8	tbsp of sugar: _____
Sodium (mg)	201	
Cholesterol (mg)	31	

Cherry pie

Serving size	1	
Calories	260	Percentage of calories from fat: _____
Protein (g)	2	mg of sodium: _____
Sugar (g)	14	mg of cholesterol: _____
Fat (g)	14	tbsp of sugar: _____
Sodium (mg)	427	
Cholesterol (mg)	13	

Now determine the total amounts of fat, salt, sugar, and cholesterol that would be consumed in the fast-food meal above:

Total amounts of: Fat (g) . . . . _____
Sugar (tbsp) . . . . _____
Sodium (mg) . . . . _____
Cholesterol (mg) . . . . . _____

Total number of calories from the fast-food meal: _____

Now determine the percentages of the total daily recommendations for sugar, sodium, and cholesterol that the above amounts represent:

Percentage of total daily recommendation for: Sugar: _____
Sodium: _____
Cholesterol: _____

Determine the percentage of calories from fat for the entire fast-food meal: _____

Part 3:

Instructions: The following compares the amounts of fat and cholesterol in whole milk, low-fat milk, and skim milk. Calculate the percentage of calories from fat for each kind of milk.

	Calories per 8 oz	Fat (g)	Cholesterol (mg)	Percentage of calories from fat
Whole milk	150	8	33	_____
Low-fat milk	100	3	10	_____
Skim milk	90	0.4	4	_____

WORKSHEET 2.6–3
MESSAGE SQUARE ACTIVITY ON CHOLESTEROL AND DIET

Hint: The two components or types of cholesterol tested for in a blood serum cholesterol analysis

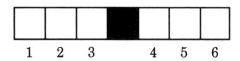

1	2	3		4	5	6

Anticipated Answer

Put: an L in 3 and 6   _____
    an H in 1   _____
    an L in 4   _____
    a D in 2 and 5   _____

Library Research Questions   **Answers**   **Sources**

1. What do the initials in each part
of the answer above stand for?

2. Which of the above two components
is considered to be the "good type"
of cholesterol?

3. What type of cancer seems to be the
result of too little fiber in the diet?

4. What is another type of fat that is
often tested for in blood serum?

5. When cholesterol deposits build up to
a dangerous level in the arteries of
the heart, bypass surgery is often
recommended. What is bypass
surgery?

2.7 CLASSIFICATION OF LIVING ORGANISMS

You Will Need the Following Materials:

scissors

Upon Completion of This Activity, Students Will

- Be able to name and define the two major aspects of taxonomy.
- Know the taxonomic categories used in classification.
- Realize the importance of classification.
- Know the five kingdoms of living organisms.
- Have "classified" geometric designs into categories.
- Know the derivation of an organism's scientific name.

1. The Students Learn the Fundamentals of Classification.

Distribute copies of Worksheet 2.7–1. As you give the students the following information, they can record it on their worksheets.

Have the students give several examples of the classification or categorization of materials in their everyday life. For example, products are grouped together in food stores. Soups are categorized in one section, and laundry products are categorized in another. Records, tapes, and compact disks are each in a separate group in record stores, and each of these groups are further subdivided into type of music and artist. A student might have his or her notebook categorized into subjects. Books are grouped according to subject in a library or a bookstore. Lead the students to realize that classification is absolutely necessary to bring order into our lives.

Taxonomy consists of two major aspects. One is **classification**, which deals with the arranging or grouping of organisms into specific categories. The other is **nomenclature**, which deals with the scientific naming of each organism classified.

The basic classification categories are kingdom, phylum (botanists use the term *division*), class, order, family, genus, and species. The kingdom is the most general category of classification, and the species category is the most specific.

The five kingdoms of living organisms are plant, animal, fungi, protist, and moneran.

A human being is classified as follows: kingdom: animal; phylum: Chordates; class: Mammals; order: primates; family: Hominids; genus: Homo; species: sapiens.

Each classification category is based on specific characteristics shared by all organisms in that category. For example, the human being is classified as a mammal, which means that humans have hair and milk glands. Humans are further classified as hominids, which means, for example, that they have upright posture, large brains, and hands and feet. Having, for example, a spinal column with two major curves is one of several criteria that places humans in the genus Homo; and having certain well-developed facial features places them in the species sapiens.

All classified organisms have what is referred to as a **scientific name.** This is the name by which they are known in the scientific community throughout the world. The scientific name is composed of the genus and species names. The scientific name for a human being is *Homo sapiens.* The scientific name of the dog is *Canis familiaris.* The corn plant is *Zea mays.*

2. The Students Classify Geometric Figures into Categories.

Distribute copies of Worksheet 2.7–2 along with scissors. Instruct the students to cut out the geometric figures and organize them into related categories or groups based on similarities and differences in design. Upon completion of the activity, have some students show their classification scheme and explain how they arrived at it. For example, two main groups could result, one of circles and one of triangles. These can be considered two kingdoms. All members of one kingdom would have the triangle shape in common, and all members of the other kingdom would have the circle shape in common. Continuing with the triangles (and then with the circles), two subgroups can be made: those triangles with a vertical line and those with a horizontal line. These can be considered the phyla. Each phyla can be further subdivided into four groups based on the designs on each side of the lines. These can be considered classes. (The detail on the geometric designs does not allow for going beyond the class category of classification.)

3. The Students Work on an Activity to Learn Some More Facts About Classification.

Pass out copies of Worksheet 2.7–3. **The answers to the Library Research Questions are** 1. Answers will vary. 2. *Quercus.* 3. Paramecium, amoeba, and so on. 4. The genus name is capitalized and both names are underlined or italicized. 5. *Felis domesticus.*

WORKSHEET 2.7–1
NOTES ON THE FUNDAMENTALS OF CLASSIFICATION

Three examples of classification used in everyday life:

1. _____
2. _____
3. _____

The two major aspects of taxonomy and what each deals with:

1. _____
2. _____

The basic classification categories:

1. _____
2. _____
3. _____
4. _____

5. _____
6. _____
7. _____

Which of the above is the most general category of classification? _____

Which of the above is the most specific category of classification? _____

The five kingdoms of living organisms:

1. _____
2. _____
3. _____

4. _____
5. _____

The classification of the human being:

Kingdom = _____

Phylum = _____

Class   = _____

Order   = _____

Family = _____

Genus   = _____

Species = _____

The scientific name for the human being is _____ _____.

Name _____   Date _____

WORKSHEET 2.7–2
CLASSIFICATION OF SOME GEOMETRIC FIGURES

Procedure:

1. Cut out the geometric figures.
2. Arrange the geometric figures into categories or groups based on similarities and differences between the figures.
3. *Note:* The small x on each figure denotes the base of the figure.

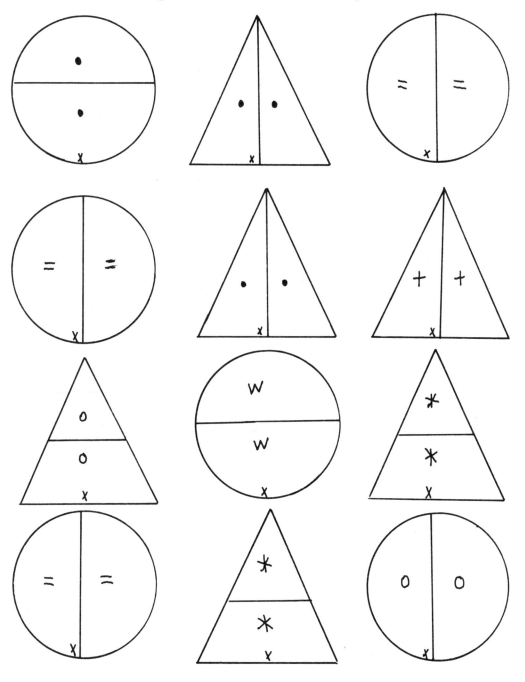

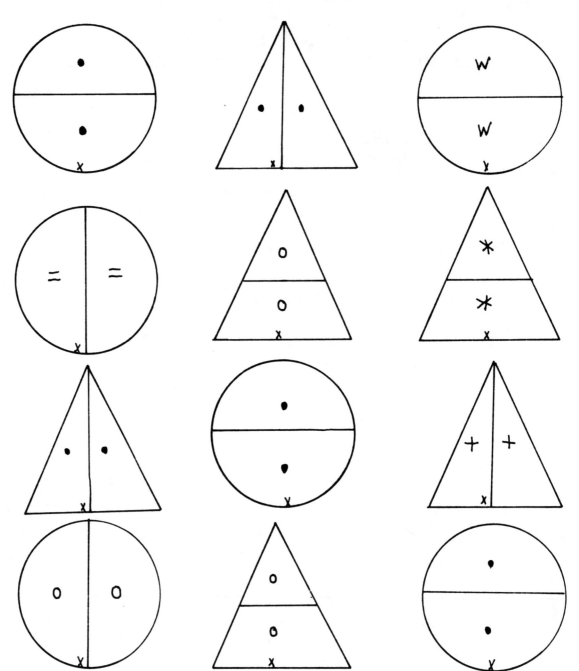

WORKSHEET 2.7–3
MESSAGE SQUARE ACTIVITY ON CLASSIFICATION

Hint: The last name of the man who developed the system now used for classifying organisms

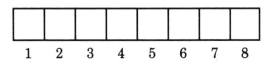

1 2 3 4 5 6 7 8

Anticipated Answer

Put: an S in 8
    an E in 6
    an L in 1
    an N in 3 and 4
    an I in 2
    an A in 5
    a U in 7

_____

_____

_____

_____

_____

_____

_____

Library Research Questions

Answers   **Sources**

1. If your state has a state flower, what is its common name and what is its scientific name?

2. What is the genus name for the oak tree?

3. What are names of some organisms classified in the Protista kingdom?

4. When scientific names are handwritten, what rules should be followed?

5. What is the scientific name of the house cat?

Unit 3
Focus on the Senses

3.1 DISSECTION OF THE SHEEP'S EYE

You Will Need the Following Materials:

paper towels

scissors

scalpels or single-edge
safety razor blade

lab aprons

dissection trays (or newspapers)

sheep's eyes or cow's eyes (could be
obtained from a local abattoir)

Upon Completion of This Activity, Students Will

- Know the basic structures of the eye.
- Know the basic functioning of the eye.
- Be able to accurately label a cross-section diagram of the human eye.

Important note for teacher: It is recommended that you practice this dissection prior to class because the students will need help with some of the cutting procedures.

1. The Students Learn Some Introductory Material About the Eye.

Distribute copies of Handout 3.1–1. This handout provides illustrative guides throughout the dissection. Refer the students to Figure #1, which shows a basic cross section of the eye. Have the students refer to it as you give them the following information:

a. Since structures are similar, a dissection of the sheep's eye is an ideal way to learn about the human eye.

b. The eye has two main cavities, the anterior and the posterior.

c. The anterior cavity of the eye occupies the space anterior to (in front of) the lens and posterior to (behind) the cornea. It is filled with a liquid called aqueous humor.

d. The posterior cavity of the eye occupies the space posterior to (behind) the lens and anterior to (in front of) the retina. It is filled with a gel called the vitreous body.

2. The Students Gather the Materials Needed for Dissection.

Each student or group of students will need a sheep's eye, scalpel (or single-edge safety razor blade), scissors, dissection tray (or newspapers), lab aprons, and paper towels. Have the students apply hand lotion prior to dissection as it will act as a partial barrier to skin odors.

3. The Students Learn the External Anatomy of the Eye.

Refer the students to Figure #2 on their worksheets and have them locate the labeled structures on the sheep's eye. Provide the students with the following information:

a. The cornea is the transparent front of the eye. It helps to focus light rays on the retina. The blue-black appearance of the retina of the sheep's eye is due to the color of the iris, which is located on the other side of it.

b. A layer of fat on the outer surface of the eyeball acts as protection, cushioning it in its bony eye socket.

c. Extrinsic muscles (brownish in color) move the eyeball.

d. The sclera is the protective outer layer of the eyeball. It is located beneath the fat layer.

e. The optic nerve carries impulses from the retina of the eye to the brain.

It will make eye dissection easier if the students use scissors to trim away the fat and extrinsic muscles on the outside of the eyeball.

4. The Students Dissect the Sclera in Preparation for Removing the Cornea.

Have the students use the dotted line in Figure #2 as a guide to cutting through the sclera. Have them make an initial incision through the sclera using a single-edge safety razor blade. **SAFETY CAUTION: Emphasize to the students that the razor blades and scalpels must be handled very carefully. They can easily slip and cause injury to the skin.** The rest of the cut can be made with scissors. Inform the students that the liquid that drains out of the eye is the aqueous humor. One of the many important roles of this liquid is to provide shape to the front portion of the eyeball.

After they complete the cut all the way around the dotted line, they can lift the central piece of sclera, containing the cornea, from the eyeball. You might wish to help the students individually with this task, because it must be done very carefully so as not to lift the lens out. The lens tends to adhere to the posterior surface of the iris located on the back of the cornea. As the central piece is slowly lifted, have them use a finger to carefully hold the lens in its place.

After they remove the central piece, have them keep the rest of the eye in an upright position to prevent the lens and other structures from "spilling" out.

5. The Students Examine the Posterior Side of the Cornea.

They should push the central piece "inside out" using a finger, thus enabling them to examine the posterior side more easily. Using Figure #3 as a guide, have the students locate the labeled structures. Give the following information to the students:

    a. The iris is the colored part of the eye. It is a muscle that regulates the size of the pupil.

    b. The pupil is the opening through the center of the iris that lets light into the eye.

    c. The ciliary muscle controls the focusing ability of the lens by regulating tension on structures called suspensory ligaments, which run from the ciliary muscle to the lens. (The ciliary muscle, with its noticeable vertical ridges, surrounds the outer edge of the iris. The suspensory ligaments are quite difficult to observe—usually they are destroyed when the central piece is removed from the eyeball.)

6. The Students Examine the Posterior Portion of the Eye.

Refer the students to Figure #4, and have them locate the labeled structures on the section of the eye that they have been keeping in an upright position. Give the students the following information:

    a. The lens helps focus light rays on the retina.

    b. The vitreous body is a gellike material that fills the posterior cavity of the eye. Among its many important functions is to provide shape to the eyeball.

By carefully tilting the eye, the lens and the vitreous body will "spill out," allowing the students to examine them more closely.

Have them examine the structures remaining in the posterior portion of the eye. A fragile milky-colored layer, the retina, can be removed carefully using a finger. (It is to be noted that the retina sometimes adheres to the vitreous body and is therefore removed at the same time as the vitreous body.)

Once the students remove the retina, they will be able to observe a purple-black layer, the choroid coat. They can remove this coat easily using a finger. Once it is removed, the only remaining structure will be the empty sclera.

Give the students the following notes:

    a. The retina is the light-sensitive layer of the eye. It is composed of special nerve cells called rods and cones.

    b. The choroid coat is a purplish-black pigmented layer located under the retina. It absorbs excess light that has entered the eye, preventing it from being reflected off surfaces in the interior of the eye.

c. There is a small area on the retina called the fovea. The fovea is the only area on the retina of true focus of light rays.

7. The Students Work on an Activity About Eye Structure and Function.

Distribute copies of Worksheet 3.1–2 and let the students work on the Crossword Activity. Across: 1. ciliary body; 2. retina; 3. anterior; 7. cones; 8. rods; 9. darkness; Down: 1. cornea; 6. arteries; 7. choroid; Diagonal: 4. sclera; 5. fovea.

8. The Students Test Their Knowledge of Eye Structure and Function.

Distribute copies of Worksheet 3.1–3. **The answers to the evaluation exercise are** 1. retina; 2. sclera; 3. cornea and the lens; 4. choroid coat; 5. vitreous body; 6. iris; 7. ciliary muscle; 8. cornea; 9. extrinsic; 10. fat; 11. pupil; 12. optic nerve.

Structures labeled on the cross-section diagram of the eye are 1. lens; 2. anterior cavity; 3. cornea; 4. iris; 5. suspensory ligaments; 6. posterior cavity; 7. choroid; 8. retina; 9. sclera; 10. optic nerve.

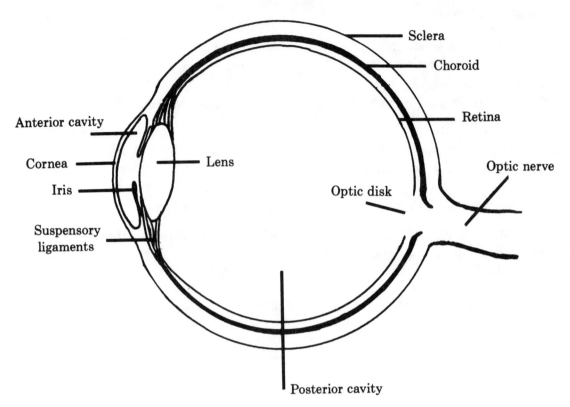

Figure 1
Basic Cross Section of the Human Eye

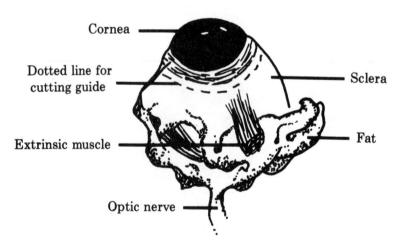

Figure 2
External View of Sheep's Eye

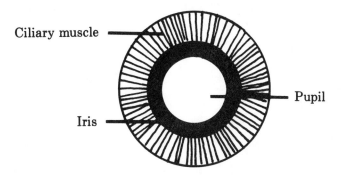

Figure 3
Posterior Side of Cornea

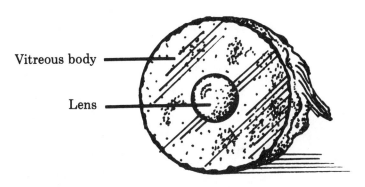

Figure 4
Lens Resting on Vitreous Body
(Eye shown is tilted on its side, which will
allow lens and vitreous body to "spill out.")

WORKSHEET 3.1–2
CROSSWORD ACTIVITY ON EYE STRUCTURE AND FUNCTION

Instructions: Using the clues given at the bottom of this sheet, fill in the crossword pattern.

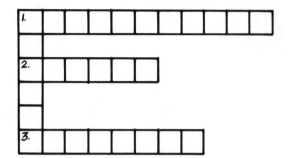

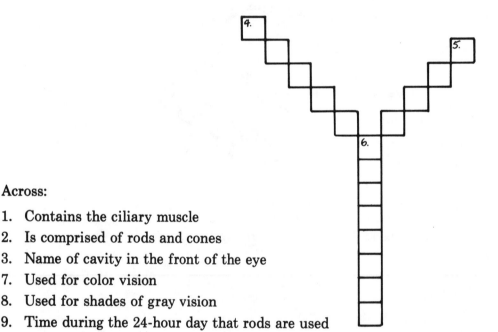

Across:

1. Contains the ciliary muscle
2. Is comprised of rods and cones
3. Name of cavity in the front of the eye
7. Used for color vision
8. Used for shades of gray vision
9. Time during the 24-hour day that rods are used

Down:

1. Transparent covering on front of the eye
6. Blood vessels on the retina that carry blood pumped from the heart
7. Coat of eye that contains a black pigment

Diagonal:

4. Outer protective coat of the eye
5. Only area on retina of true focus of light rays

Name _____   Date _____

WORKSHEET 3.1–3   EVALUATION EXERCISE

Instructions: Fill in the blanks with the correct answers.

1. The _____ is the light-sensitive layer of the eye.

2. The outer, protective coat of the eye is the _____.

3. The _____ and the _____ are both involved in focusing light rays.

4. The layer of the eye that absorbs excess light, preventing it from being reflected off structures inside the eye, is called the _____.

5. The gel that fills the posterior cavity is referred to as the _____.

6. The _____ is the muscle that regulates the size of the pupil.

7. The _____ controls the focusing ability of the lens.

8. The transparent front of the eye is the _____.

9. Muscles that move the eyeball are called _____ muscles.

10. The eyeball is cushioned in its bony socket by a layer of _____.

11. The opening through the center of the iris is called the _____.

12. Nerve impulses are carried from the retina to the brain by the _____.

Instructions: Label the following structures on the cross section of the human eye:

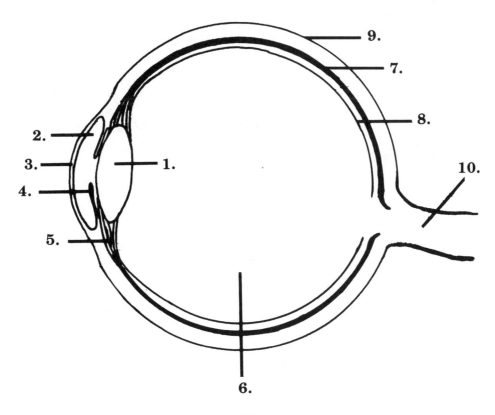

127

3.2 THE DISTRIBUTION PATTERN OF CONE TYPES ON THE RETINA

You Will Need the Following Materials:

colored pencils (red, blue, green, black)   scissors
large sheets of plain white paper (24" × 24")   microscope lamp
rulers   toothpicks (flat)

Upon Completion of This Activity, Students Will

- Have determined experimentally the distribution pattern of the three types of cones on the retina.
- Have learned the basic composition and function of the retina.

1. The Students Learn the Function of the Rods and Cones.

Give the students the following information:

a. Rods and cones are the basic structures comprising the retina.

b. Rods are specialized nerve cells that are extremely sensitive to light. They are not, however, able to detect colors. If you had only rods on your retina, your environment would look much like a black-and-white television picture. Rods function primarily for night vision.

c. Cones are specialized nerve cells that distinguish colors of light. They function primarily for daylight vision. There are three types of cones: those sensitive to red light, those sensitive to blue light, and those sensitive to green light.

2. The Students Learn the General Distribution Pattern of Rods and Cones on the Retina.

Draw the following diagram on the chalkboard:

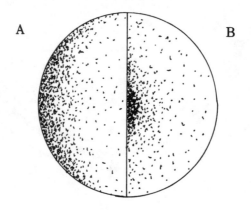

A   B

Explain to the students that the diagram represents the retina of the eye. The side labeled A shows the distribution of rods on the retina. The side labeled B shows the distribution of cones. (The students should note that rods and cones are each distributed over the entire surface of the retina and are not confined to just half of the retina.)

Ask the students to describe the distribution of rods and cones as shown on the diagram. **(Answer: The rods are most dense at the edges, or periphery, of the retina and least dense at the center. Conversely, the cones are most dense at the center and least dense at the edges of the retina.)**

3. The Students Gather Materials and Are Given Some Preliminary Information Prior to the Investigation.

Explain to the students that they are going to gather data to answer the question: Are the three types of cones equally distributed on the retina? Upon completion of the investigation, they will have prepared a diagram showing distribution patterns of the cone types.

Draw the following "retina sheet" diagram on the chalkboard:

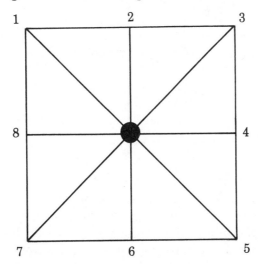

Have each student copy this diagram on a 24 inch by 24 inch piece of plain white paper. The numbers (placed at the very edges of the paper), lines, and circle (in the center of the paper) should be done in black.

Each pair of students should obtain three flat toothpicks. They should color the larger flat end of one toothpick red, another toothpick blue, and the third toothpick green.

4. The Students, Working in Pairs, Carry out the Investigation and Collect the Resulting Data.

Distribute copies of Handout 3.2–1 to the experimenters only.

Review Handout 3.2–1 with the students prior to the investigation. During the investigation, monitor the students closely for such procedures as:

a. keeping the right eye about 10 inches directly above the black circle on the retina sheet.
b. keeping the left eye completely covered with the 3-inch by 5-inch card.
c. moving the toothpick slowly along the black lines.

5. The Students Analyze Their Data Results.

The "retina sheets," upon completion, should approximate the following diagram, which should be drawn on the chalkboard using colored chalk:

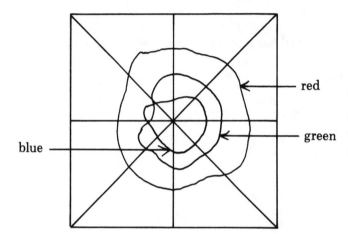

The inner circle should be colored blue, the middle circle green, and the outer circle red.

Guide the students to realize that the three types of cones are not equally distributed on the retina. For example, the color blue is perceived only when light rays strike the retina near its center because cones receptive to blue are clustered near the center. On the other hand, the color green can be perceived farther out from the center than blue because the cones are scattered farther out from the center. The cones for red are scattered even farther out.

6. The Students Are Evaluated on Their Learning.

Write the following questions on the chalkboard for the students to answer:

a. Where are the cones most densely located on the retina? (**Answer:** Toward the center.)
b. List three things learned about rods. (**Answer:** Extremely sensitive to light; unable to detect colors; used primarily for night vision.)
c. List two things you learned about the cones. (**Answer:** Used primarily for daylight vision; are sensitive to light; there are three types.)

d. Name two things that the subject had to remember about the placement of his or her head during the investigation. (**Answer:** Keep the head still; keep the head about 10 inches directly above the black circle on the retina sheet.)

e. What information did the data results provide about the three types of cones? (**Answer:** They are not evenly distributed on the retina.)

HANDOUT 3.2-1
INVESTIGATING DISTRIBUTION OF RODS AND CONES

Read through all instructions before beginning:

1. One student should be the subject and the other, the experimenter.

2. Position a microscope lamp beside the "retina sheet" and direct its light directly at it.

3. Position the subject's face directly over the retina sheet. The right eye should be about 10 inches directly above the black circle.

4. "Blindfold" the subject's left eye by covering it with a 3-inch by 5-inch card (or a cupped hand).

5. The subject stares with the right eye directly at the black circle. The subject's head should not move during the investigation.

6. Referring to the Number and Color Guide at right, the experimenter takes the appropriately colored toothpick and, beginning at the proper number on the retina sheet, moves the colored tip of the toothpick slowly along the black line toward the black circle.

7. At the instant the subject correctly identifies the color, write a small letter (r for red, g for green, b for blue) at that location on the black line.

8. Repeat procedures 6 and 7 above until you have completed the sequence on the Number and Color Guide.

9. Upon completing the sequence, connect the r's with a red line, the g's with a green line, and the b's with a blue line.

10. Repeat this investigation, reversing roles with your lab partner. Use the same Number and Color Guide.

Number and Color Guide	
Number to Start at on Sheet	Color to Use
1	red
7	blue
2	red
7	green
3	green
1	blue
5	red
6	green
4	blue
8	green
5	blue
4	red
2	green
7	red
3	red
5	green
6	red
8	red
6	blue
2	blue
4	green
3	blue
8	blue
1	green

3.3 HEARING AND THE EAR

You Will Need the Following Materials:

scissors

blindfold (or cheesecloth)

8 clickers (or clothespins that snap)

felt-tip marker

opaque projector

colored pencils

soft cloth for blocking ear

40 sheets of paper

masking tape

Upon Completion of This Activity, Students Will

- Know the basic organizational structure of the human ear.
- Know the three divisions of the ear.
- Be able to name and give the function of the ossicles.
- Know the three ways the ear can adapt itself for protection against dangerously loud noises.
- Know the function and clinical significance of the Eustachian tube.
- Have become familiar with some types of hearing impairments.
- Have become familiar with types of ear specialists.
- Have assembled a flat-plane model of the ear and learned the functions of the component parts.
- Have participated in an investigation that illustrates the need for both ears in detecting the location of a sound.

1. The Students Learn Structures and Functions of the Ear and Assemble a Model of the Human Ear.

Distribute copies of Worksheet 3.3–1 along with scissors and colored pencils. Following completion of the worksheet, project on the screen a sheet showing the unassembled parts and quiz students on their functions.

Explain to the students, as they take notes, that the ear can be divided into three sections: the outer, the middle, and the inner ear. The tympanic membrane separates the outer from the middle ear. The middle ear extends on to and includes the stapes. The inner ear is composed of the cochlea and semicircular canals (as well as certain other structures not studied here).

The malleus, incus, and stapes are known collectively as the **ossicles**. The ossicles are actually the ear's own built-in amplification system. As sound wave vibrations are transferred from one ossicle to another, the vibrations are considerably amplified. This fact helps explain how we can hear even a faint whisper.

If the noise in our environment becomes dangerously loud (such as can occur at a rock concert, or if one has the volume turned way up on a radio with a head set), the ear attempts to adapt and protect itself in three ways: (1) the stapes pulls away from the cochlea, (2) the tympanic membrane tightens up, and (3) the ossicles move slightly out of alignment with each other. These three modifications of the ear serve the purpose of making it much less efficient in conducting sound vibrations. Indeed, this explains why we may say that things sound muffled after exposure to extremely loud noise. Things will continue to sound muffled until the ear structures return to their normal state.

The Eustachian tube runs from the middle ear down to an area called the nasopharynx, which is a part of the throat located behind the nose. The Eustachian tube has the important function of maintaining and adjusting the air pressure in the middle ear so that it remains the same as the air pressure in one's environment. This assures that the air pressure on each side of the tympanic membrane remains equal. When flying, for example, as you take off and land, the air pressure in the airplane cabin changes (even though the cabin is essentially pressurized). As you ascend, the cabin pressure decreases; and as you descend, it increases. Sometimes the Eustachian tube is less than effective in keeping the proper middle ear air pressure. This can lead to some ear discomfort, which is often remedied by swallowing. Swallowing aids in opening the Eustachian tube wider, thus allowing air to move more easily either in or out of the middle ear. Of clinical significance is the fact that throat infections have the potential of spreading up through the Eustachian tube into the middle ear, a situation that can have serious consequences.

2. The Students Become Familiar with Some Types of Ear Specialists and Some Types of Hearing Impairments.

Distribute copies of Worksheet 3.3–2 to the students. As you give the students the following information, they can record the information on their worksheets.

Ear Specialists:

1. Otologist: specializes in treating diseases of the ear
2. Otolaryngologist: specializes in not only the ear, but also the nose and throat; often referred to as an ENT (ear, nose, and throat) specialist
3. Audiologist: specializes in treating the hearing impaired

Hearing Impairments:

1. Conductive hearing losses: loss of hearing due to the ear's inability to properly conduct sound vibrations

    Causes: a. buildup of ear wax, interfering with vibrations reaching the tympanic membrane

    b. a middle ear infection that interferes with the operation of the ossicles

    c. excess bony growth in the middle ear that interferes with the operation of the stapes

    d. tympanic membrane damage

    e. blockage of the Eustachian tube

2. Sensori-neural hearing loss: inability of the ear to convert the sound vibrations to nerve impulses

    Cause: a. damage to the cochlea due to physical injury, loud noises, or infections

3. Congenital nerve hearing losses: damage to the acoustic nerve occurring at or soon after birth

    Causes: a. disease

              b. lack of oxygen reaching the developing baby in the womb

4. Central hearing loss: hearing loss resulting from nervous system damage

    Causes: a. damage to the acoustic nerve

              b. damage to the brain itself

5. Psychogenic hearing loss: hearing loss that is not traceable to physical causes

    Cause: a. thought to be a mental problem because under hypnosis the afflicted person can hear

3. The Students Participate in Investigating the Detection of Sound Location.

This investigation will demonstrate that both ears are necessary for the accurate detection of sound location. When either the left or the right ear is plugged, preventing sound from entering it, the subject will have difficulty in accurately detecting sound location.

Distribute copies of Worksheet 3.3–3 to the students. They will need one copy per subject tested. Test two or three students, first using one ear and then both ears. Inform the students that they should follow the instructions on this worksheet in keeping data.

You will need 40 sheets of paper. Five sheets should have a large #1 written on them, five sheets a large #2, continuing in like manner through #8.

Place a chair for the student subject at the center of the classroom. Around the periphery of the classroom, mark eight "stations" on the floor using masking tape. (The eight stations are shown on Worksheet 3.3–3.)

Seat the subject in the chair, blindfolded. (If only one ear will be used, a soft cloth should be pressed against the other ear to block out all sound from entering. Several layers of cloth may be necessary, as it is essential that the subject not be able to perceive any sound through the blocked ear.)

Position eight students with clickers at the stations around the room.

Have a ninth student stand at the front of the room with the 40 marked sheets of paper that have been thoroughly shuffled. One at a time, this student holds up a sheet for the eight students with clickers to see. If the sheet has the number 7 on it, the student at station #7 clicks his or her clicker. The subject points an arm in the direction from which he or she thinks the sound came. Repeat this for the 40 sheets.

After the subjects have been tested, give the students a few minutes to organize the data recorded on their worksheets. Discuss the data results with the students. Were subject errors equally distributed over the eight stations, or did they make more errors at certain stations? Ask if anyone has any idea why two ears are more accurate than one in accurately detecting sound location. **(It is thought that the time difference between the sound entering the right and the left ears is used by the brain in determining the location of the sound.)**

Name _____   Date _____

WORKSHEET 3.3–1
THE ANATOMY AND FUNCTIONING OF THE EAR

Procedure:

A. Learn the names of the structures of the ear as you color each part according to the following color-coding instructions:

    1. Auricle = red

    2. Auditory canal = yellow

3, 4, 5. Malleus, incus, and stapes = blue

    6. Tympanic membrane = black

    7. Acoustic nerve = orange

    8. Three semicircular canals = purple

    9. Eustachian tube = brown

    10. Cochlea and remaining portion = leave white

B. Cut out the individual pieces and assemble. Pieces marked with like letters of the alphabet fit together. For example "a" fits with "a," "b" with "b," and so on.

C. The functions of the structures of the ear that you have assembled follow. As you learn them, refer to the appropriate structure on your model.

    1. **Auricle:** aids in directing sound waves into the auditory canal

    2. **Auditory canal:** directs the sound waves to the tympanic canal

    3. **Malleus:** transfers the vibrations to the incus

    4. **Incus:** transfers the vibrations to the stapes

    5. **Stapes:** transfers the vibrations into the cochlea

    6. **Tympanic membrane:** vibrates as the sound waves hit it and transfers the vibrations to the malleus

    7. **Acoustic nerve:** carries nerve impulses to the brain through two divisions, one from the cochlea and one from the semicircular canal area of the ear

    8. **Semicircular canals:** deal with the sensation of head movements and body equilibrium

    9. **Eustachian tube:** keeps the air pressure on the inside surface of the tympanic membrane equal to that on its outside surface

    10. **Cochlea:** contains structures that convert the vibrations into nerve impulses

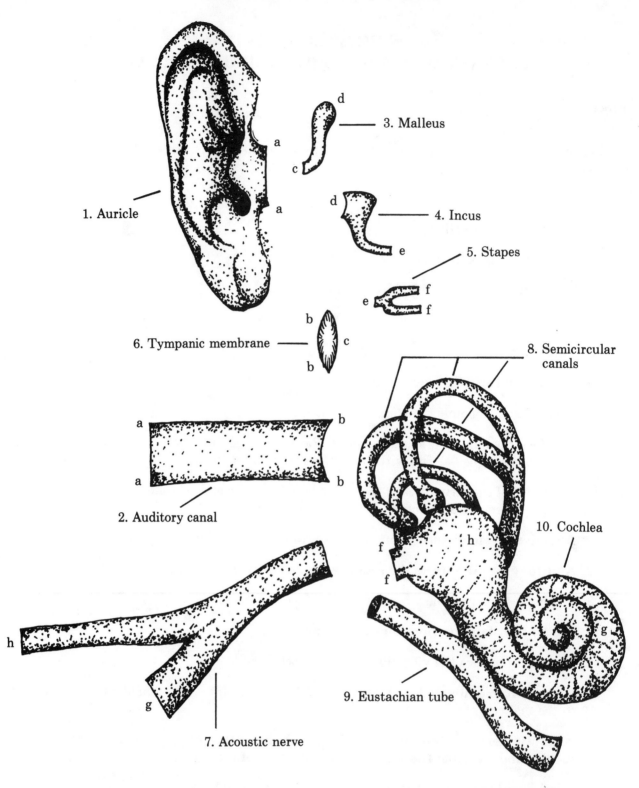

1. Auricle

d — 3. Malleus

c

d — 4. Incus

e

5. Stapes

e f
f

6. Tympanic membrane — b c b

2. Auditory canal

8. Semicircular canals

10. Cochlea

f

h

f

g

9. Eustachian tube

h

g

7. Acoustic nerve

WORKSHEET 3.3–2 SOME TYPES OF EAR SPECIALISTS AND HEARING IMPAIRMENTS

Ear Specialists:

1. _____

2. _____

3. _____

Hearing Impairments:

1. _____

    Causes: a. _____

            b. _____

            c. _____

            d. _____

            e. _____

2. _____

    Cause: a. _____

3. _____

    Causes: a. _____

            b. _____

4. _____

    Causes: a. _____

            b. _____

5. _____

    Cause: a. _____

WORKSHEET 3.3–3
DATA SHEET FOR INVESTIGATING SOUND LOCATION

Instructions:

1. As the subject responds to each clicker sound, put a plus (+) or minus (–) symbol by that clicker's station number. Use the plus symbol if the subject was correct in placing the location of the sound and a minus symbol if the subject was in error. For example, if the sound comes from the clicker at station #7 and the subject correctly points to that station, place a plus at #7. If the subject was in error, place a minus at #7.
2. At the conclusion of the investigation, tabulate the number of errors for each of the eight stations and complete the Error Data Table below.

Subject Number: _____

Number of Ears Used: _____

7	6	5
8	Subject	4
1	2	3

ERROR DATA TABLE								
	Station Number							
	1	**2**	**3**	**4**	**5**	**6**	**7**	**8**
Number of Errors								

3.4 TASTE PERCEPTION AND VISIBLE CUES

You Will Need the Following Materials:

clear lemon soda such as 7 UP™, or Sprite™   4 transparent glasses

cola   paper cups

red food coloring   yellow food coloring

one can each of an orange soda that is orange in color, a lemon soda
that is yellow in color, cola, and clear lemon soda in addition to
that listed above

Upon Completion of This Activity, Students Will

- Have experienced first hand that visual cues can influence taste sensation.

1. Teacher Preparation Prior to the Activity:

This laboratory activity is designed to provide some dramatic evidence for
the students that the sense perception of taste can be influenced by visual cues in
the environment.

Select an area in the classroom where the student subject's responses will not
be overheard by the rest of the class. Behind a screen or shield, so that they cannot
be seen by the rest of the class, arrange the following items:

a. Glass #1: filled with clear lemon soda

b. Glass #2: filled with cola

c. Glass #3: filled with clear lemon soda that has been colored with food
coloring to appear orange (This is designed as a visual cue to suggest to
the subject an orange drink.)

d. Glass #4: filled with clear lemon soda that has been colored with food
coloring to appear yellow (This is designed as a visual cue to suggest to
the subject a lemon drink.)

e. Also set in the proximity of the glasses an opened can of clear lemon
soda, cola, orange soda, and lemon soda. Position the labels on the cans to
ensure their being seen by the subjects. (The cans present a second set of
visual cues in addition to glasses #3 and #4 above.)

2. The Students Participate in a Taste Test.

Pass out copies of Worksheet 3.4–1 to the students, explaining to them that
they are about to take part in a taste test. Have them immediately fill in the name
and date information.

As each subject (student) comes behind the screen and takes the taste test, you should fill out the Part 1: Individual Data on the subject's worksheet. (You should keep each subject's worksheet, returning them at the conclusion of the investigation.) Inform the subject that he/she is going to sample four soft drinks and, based on taste, is going to try to identify the name of the drink.

In front of the subject, pour a small amount of clear lemon soda from glass #1 into a paper cup. Have the subject drink it. Ask the subject to try to identify the name of the drink. Record the subject's response. The subject's cup is rinsed out and the same procedure is repeated for the remaining three glasses. (Remember, as the subject is taking the taste test, he/she is being exposed to two sets of visual cues. One is the color of the soft drink in the glasses, and the other, the exposed cans of soft drink.)

3. The Students Analyze the Class Data Results.

Hand back to the students their Taste Test Data Table worksheets. Help the students to pool the class responses and fill in Part 2: Pooled Class Data.

Distribute copies of Worksheet 3.4–2. Work with the students in filling in the data, using the following information as a guide:

1. For glass #1 7 UP™ or Sprite™ is right. However, if subjects responded with another soft drink that tastes the same, it is to be considered a correct response.
2. Any cola soft drinks should be considered a correct response.
3. Although the correct response may be 7 UP™ or Sprite™, many students will have used the visual cues and identified the soft drink as Orange Crush™, an orange soft drink, or other orange-type beverage. (The key is any response that infers orange.)
4. Although the correct response may be 7 UP™ or Sprite™, many students will have used the visual cues and identified the soft drink as lemon soda, Mountain Dew™, and so on. (The key is any response that infers lemon.)
5. Yellow- and orange-colored 7 UP™ or Sprite™; the four different soft drink cans.
6. That visual cues can influence our taste perceptions.

4. The Students Conduct a Further Taste Test.

If you can arrange to use students from a different class, a similar taste test can be conducted, but without the four soft-drink cans as visual cues. It will be seen that color alone is sufficient to alter taste sensation.

WORKSHEET 3.4–1 TASTE TEST DATA TABLE

Part 1: Individual Data: (to be filled out by your teacher as you take the taste test)

Glass Number	Student Response
1	
2	
3	
4	

Part 2: Pooled Class Data:

	STUDENT RESPONSES			
Subject Number	Glass #1	Glass #2	Glass #3	Glass #4

WORKSHEET 3.4–2   ANALYSIS OF DATA

1. Glass #1 contained: _____

   Percentage of students correct: _____

2. Glass #2 contained: _____

   Percentage of students correct: _____

3. Glass #3 contained: _____

   Percentage of students correct: _____

   Percentage of students who said it was an orange-type soft drink: _____

4. Glass #4 contained: _____

   Percentage of students correct: _____

   Percentage of students who said it was a lemon-type soft drink: _____

5. The visual cues that were deliberately introduced into the experimental setting were:

   a. _____

   b. _____

6. What do you think that this lab activity demonstrated? _____

   _____

   _____

7. Outline an idea for another investigation using visual cues in an attempt to influence subject responses:

   _____

   _____

   _____

   _____

8. List some foods that you dislike based on appearance: _____

   _____

   _____

   _____

   _____

9. List some foods that you dislike based on the texture or "feel" of them in your mouth:

   _____

   _____

   _____

   _____

3.5 AN ANALYSIS OF ODOR IDENTIFICATION

You Will Need the Following Materials:

blindfolds (or paper towels or cheesecloth)   graph paper

colored pencils (red and blue)   opaque projector

rulers

20 items for odor identification (the following is a suggested list: instant coffee powder, orange, lemon, vinegar, nail polish remover, peanut butter, Johnson's™ baby powder, chocolate, Crayola™ crayons, Vicks VapoRub™, caramel, banana, vanilla extract, rubbing alcohol, mothballs, Bazooka™ bubble gum, Ivory™ soap, coconut, potato chip, cheese) *Note:* Five brand-name items have been included because they have been used in odor research and were referred to by their brand names. Instead of saying bubble gum, for example, a subject would say Bazooka™ bubble gum.

Upon Completion of This Activity, Students Will

- Have learned that females probably have a keener sense of odor identification than males.
- Realize that when not able to see what one is smelling, odor identification can be difficult.
- Have learned that some odors are so closely associated with their brand names that they are identified by brand name.
- Have investigated whether some odors are more accurately identified by one sex than the other.

1. Teacher Preparation Prior to the Activity:

Select an area in the classroom where the student subject's responses will not be overheard by the rest of the class.

Behind a screen or shield so that they cannot be seen by the rest of the class, arrange the 20 items to be used in the odor identification activity.

2. The Students Participate in an Odor Identification Investigation.

Distribute copies of Worksheet 3.5-1 to the students, explaining to them that they are about to participate in an odor identification investigation. Have them immediately fill in the name and date information.

As each subject (student) comes behind the screen and participates in the activity, you should record his/her responses on the Part 1: Individual Data of the subject's worksheet. (You should keep each subject's worksheet, returning them at the conclusion of the investigation.)

As each subject participates, he/she should be blindfolded, perhaps by holding a piece of clean paper towel or cheesecloth over the eyes. Decide upon the order of item presentation, and hold each item, one at a time, close to the subject's nose.

Record the subject's response as follows: A + indicates an accurate response, a B indicates an accurate response using the brand name, and an o indicates an inaccurate response.

3. The Students Pool the Class Data and Analyze the Results.

Hand back to the students their Odor Identification Data Sheets. Help the students as they pool class data and calculate percentages.

Distribute copies of Worksheet 3.5–2 and let the students complete them.

Project a completed bar graph on the screen as you discuss with the students their responses to the worksheet questions. (The answers will vary, depending upon the data collected during the investigation.)

Finally, give the students the following information:

a. Skill at odor identification seems to peak somewhere between 20 and 40 years of age.

b. Women seem to be better than men in the overall identification of odors. (Does your data indicate this?)

c. According to the article "Educating Your Nose," written by William S. Cain, which appeared in the July 1981 issue of *Psychology Today*, female participants in an odor identification test invariably identified the following odors by brand name: Johnson's™ baby powder, Crayola™ crayons, Ivory™ soap, Vicks VapoRub™, and Bazooka™ bubble gum. (Does your data support this?)

WORKSHEET 3.5–1   ODOR IDENTIFICATION DATA SHEET

Part 1:   Individual Data

Odor Identification
(+ = accurate response, B = accurate response by brand name, o = inaccurate response)

1. _____	5. _____	9. _____	13. _____	17. _____
2. _____	6. _____	10. _____	14. _____	18. _____
3. _____	7. _____	11. _____	15. _____	19. _____
4. _____	8. _____	12. _____	16. _____	20. _____

Part 2:   Pooled Class Data:

Name of Odor	Percentage of Males Correct	Percentage of Females Correct	Percentage of Total Students Correct
1.			
2.			
3.			
4.			
5.			
6.			
7.			
8.			
9.			
10.			
11.			
12.			
13.			
14.			
15.			
16.			
17.			
18.			
19.			
20.			

WORKSHEET 3.5–2
ANALYSIS OF ODOR IDENTIFICATION DATA

1. Prepare a bar graph based on the **Percentage of Total Students Correct** column. Let each square up the vertical axis equal 5 percent. List the names of the odors along the horizontal axis in order from lowest to highest percentage correct. Accurately title each axis as well as the graph.

    Questions based on the above bar graph (write your answers on a separate piece of paper):

    a. What odor was least identified?

    b. What are the next three least-identified odors?

    c. What odor was most identified?

    d. What are the next three most-identified odors?

2. Prepare a bar graph comparing the percentage of males correct with the percentage of females correct. Set up the axes exactly the same way you did for #1 above. For each odor, plot the female and male bars side by side, separated by a space. Color the female bars red and the male bars blue. Add a legend to your graph.

    Questions based on the above bar graph (answer on a separate sheet):

    a. Which odor(s) did males and females come closest to in percentage of correct identification?

    b. Which odor(s) did males and females differ most from each other in percentage of correct identification?

    c. In general, were males and females quite close, fairly close, or quite varied in terms of percentages for all of the odors considered together?

    d. List the odors correctly identified by a higher percentage of males than females.

    e. List the odors correctly identified by a higher percentage of females than males.

    f. Can you offer any explanations for the difference in answers to d and e above?

    g. List the names of any odors identified by brand name and note whether they were identified by a male or a female.

    h. List any odors that were not identified by anyone. (Do you have any explanation for why this odor(s) was not identified?)

    i. List any odors exclusively identified by females, and/or exclusively identified by males. (Do you have any explanation for this data?)

Unit 4
Focus on Microbiology

4.1 STUDY OF BACTERIA

You Will Need the Following Materials:

prepared slides of the three basic
    types of bacteria

prepared slides of bacterial spores

prepared slides of bacterial flagella

methylene staining solution

drawing paper

Lysol™ solution

Bacillus subtilis (24-hour culture
    and 4-day-old culture)

oil immersion microscope (optional)

toothpicks (flat)

inoculating loop

microscope

microscope lamp

microscope slides

autoclave

lab apron

hand soap

paper towels

Bunsen burner

Upon Completion of This Activity, Students Will

- Know the names and shapes of the three basic types of bacteria.
- Be able to identify the three basic types of bacteria.
- Know the meaning of various prefixes used in describing bacteria.
- Know the function of bacterial spores and flagella.
- Be able to identify bacterial spores and flagella.
- Know the definition and techniques of aseptic technique.
- Have experienced and learned the proper techniques for using the inoculating loop.
- Have experienced and learned the proper techniques for preparing bacterial smears.
- Know the procedure and importance of fixing bacterial smears.

1. The Students Learn the Appearance of, and the Names for, the Three Basic Types of Bacteria and Prepare Drawings of Them.

Distribute copies of Worksheet 4.1–1 to the students for note taking. (As you give notes during this activity, the students can record them in their worksheets, which are designed in a note-taking format.)

Put on the chalkboard the names of the three basic types and shapes of bacteria along with drawings:

Name:	bacillus	coccus	spirillum
Shape:	rod	round	spiral
Drawing:			

Pass out prepared microscope slides of the three types of bacteria. Have the students locate and draw the bacillus type first. (*Note:* Tell the students that the best area of the prepared slide to focus on is at the **edge of the visible smear**.) It is important for you to check a student's microscope image and focus to be certain he/she is observing the proper specimen as clearly as possible.

The students now locate and draw the coccus type of bacteria. (Be certain they are focused on single coccus bacteria, because most prepared slides also have cocci bunched together, which is confusing to the students.)

Finally, the students can locate and draw the spirillum type of bacteria. Their spiral shapes are easily observed.

2. The Students Learn Prefixes Used in Describing Bacteria, Along with Examples.

Some commonly used prefixes along with their definitions, examples, and drawings are

Prefix:	strepto-	staphylo-	diplo-	tetra-
Definition:	in chains	in bunches	in groups of two	in groups of four
Examples:	streptococcus streptobacillus	staphylococcus	diplococcus	tetracoccus
Drawings:				

3. The Students Observe Bacterial Spores and Learn Their Significance.

Pass out prepared microscope slides of bacterial spores and let the students observe them and make a drawing on their worksheets.

The spores will look like coccus-type bacteria. Explain that there are special spore-staining solutions that can be used to differentiate spores from coccus bacteria.

Spores are produced only by certain groups of bacteria and serve the function of protecting the bacteria from hostile environmental conditions that might otherwise destroy the bacteria.

4. The Students Observe Bacterial Flagella and Learn Their Significance.

Pass out prepared microscope slides of bacterial flagella and let the students observe them and make a drawing on their worksheets. Have them label both the bacteria and the flagella as shown in the following drawing:

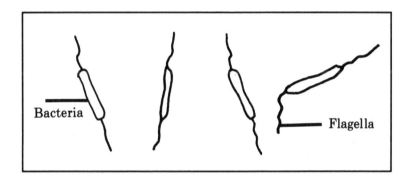

Flagella provide locomotion for the bacteria. Not all kinds of bacteria have flagella. (*Note:* Explain to students that bacteria capable of locomotion can move through liquid mediums but not across solid surfaces.)

5. The Students Learn a Definition for Aseptic Technique and the Extreme Importance for Using It at All Times in the Laboratory.

A good definition for aseptic technique is a laboratory procedure that does not allow for contamination of you or your environment. Aseptic technique is extremely important when working with microorganisms such as bacteria.

Most bacteria are safe and many are beneficial, but a few are potentially hazardous in that they are capable of causing infection and disease. Because of these few, all bacteria are handled using aseptic technique in the laboratory. Therefore, it bears repeating: Aseptic technique is of critical importance at all times when working with microorganisms such as bacteria.

6. The Students Learn the Steps for Preparing and Staining a Bacterial Smear of Mouth Bacteria.

Have the students carry out the following procedure step by step as you give them the following notes. **(SAFETY CAUTION: Students should always begin every lab activity by putting on lab aprons.)**

a. Clean microscope slides by rinsing with water and rubbing dry with a paper towel.

b. Hold the tip of a clean toothpick under a water faucet and transfer a small amount of water to the center of the microscope slide.

c. Using the tip of another clean toothpick, gently scrape along the margin between the teeth and the gums, picking up some material on the end of the toothpick.

d. Smear the material around in the drop of water on the slide to about the size of a nickel.

e. Allow the smear to air dry. (This will usually happen in a minute or two.)

f. The smear must now be **fixed**. (You will have to demonstrate this to the students prior to their doing it. The smear is fixed by passing the slide, smear side up, through a Bunsen burner flame three times at the speed of about a second per pass. If the slide becomes hot to the touch, it is being moved too slowly through the flame.) The purpose for fixing is to thoroughly dry the smear on the slide to prevent it from washing off during the staining procedure.

g. The smear is liberally flooded (covered) with methylene blue staining solution and allowed to set for about a minute.

h. The excess methylene blue staining solution is gently rinsed off the slide over a sink.

i. Allow the smear to thoroughly air dry. (*Note:* Caution the students against drying the smear by blotting it with a paper towel because the bacteria in a smear are still living and would get on the towel, contaminating it.)

j. The students should clean their work areas with a Lysol™ solution and then wash their hands thoroughly with soap and water.

(SAFETY CAUTION: Emphasize to the students that following all laboratory activities dealing with living bacteria, the work area should be cleaned with a Lysol™ solution or similar disinfectant and their hands should be thoroughly washed with soap and water.)

The students can now observe their smears through the microscope. Have them observe specifically for any of the three basic types of bacteria studied previously and make a drawing on their worksheets. (They should observe bacillus bacteria with little difficulty. Streptococcus might be observed, but spirillum probably will not.)

(If you are fortunate enough to have an oil immersion microscope, set up a demonstration smear for the students to observe.)

7. The Students Learn How to Properly Use the Inoculating Loop.

You should demonstrate the following technique as you explain it to the students for note taking on their worksheets:

a. The inoculating loop is used to aseptically transfer bacteria from one location to another.

b. **Immediately before and immediately after every use, the inoculating loop must be sterilized (made completely free of any living material).** The process of sterilizing the inoculating loop is referred to as **flaming the inoculating loop**.

c. The inoculating loop is **flamed** by holding the wire portion of the loop in a Bunsen burner flame. Allow the tip of the loop to get bright red and then slowly move the loop through the flame, allowing a band of red to move along the wire until it reaches the handle.

Have the students put on lab aprons. Then distribute inoculating loops to them. Have them practice the flaming technique as you observe. **SAFETY CAUTION: Be certain that the students are aware that the match should be lit and held over the top of the barrel of the Bunsen burner prior to turning on the gas. This helps prevent a buildup of gas that could cause a dangerous burst of flame.**

8. The Students Prepare Bacterial Smears of Living Bacillus Subtilis *Bacteria.*

Be certain that the students have lab aprons on.

In preparing this bacterial smear, the students can eventually follow e through j of their worksheet notes under #6. First, however, guide them through the following initial steps:

a. The inoculating loop should be flamed and then used to transfer two or three loops full of water to the center of a clean microscope slide.

b. The inoculating loop should immediately be flamed again.

c. You, the teacher, should transfer the *Bacillus subtilis* (24-hour culture) to the drop of water on the student slides.

d. Instruct the students to use their inoculating loops to mix the bacteria with the water while spreading (smearing) the material out to about the size of a nickel. Upon completion of the smearing, the inoculating loop should immediately be flamed.

The students can now proceed to step e on their worksheets. Upon completing their smear preparations, make certain that the students clean their work areas with Lysol™ disinfectant solution and then wash their hands with soap and water.

Finally, the students can observe their smear using the microscope. They should fill in #8 on their worksheets.

You should collect all student slides and autoclave them.

9. The Students Prepare Smears of Bacillus Subtilis *Spores.*

The same general procedure as in #8 above is used in preparing this smear, with two modifications. One, use the four-day-old culture of the bacteria. It will contain spores. And two, substitute malachite-green staining solution for methylene blue and allow it to remain on the smear for about five minutes. Malachite green will stain the spores bluish green.

Make certain that the students wear lab aprons, and at the completion of smear preparation, have them clean their work areas with Lysol™ disinfectant solution and wash their hands with soap and water.

The students can fill in #9 on their worksheets.

You should collect all student slides and autoclave them.

10. The Students Are Evaluated on Their Learning.

Distribute copies of Worksheet 4.1–2 for the students to work on as a quiz or self-evaluation exercise.

WORKSHEET 4.1–1   A STUDY OF BACTERIA

1. The three basic types of bacteria:

   Name: a. _____   b. _____   c. _____

   Shape: _____   _____   _____

   Drawing:

2. Prefixes used in describing bacteria:

Prefix:	a.	b.	c.	d.
Definition:				
Examples:				
Drawing:				

3. Bacterial spores:

   a. Significance of: b. Drawing of:

   _____

   _____

4. Bacterial flagella:

   a. Significance of: b. Drawing of:

   _____

   _____

5. Aseptic technique:

   Definition of: _____

   Extreme importance of: _____

   _____

6. The steps for preparing and staining a bacterial smear:

   a. _____

   _____

   b. _____

   _____

   c. _____

   _____

   d. _____

   _____

e. _____

_____

f. _____

_____

g. _____

_____

h. _____

_____

i. _____

_____

j. _____

_____

Technique of fixing the smear: _____

_____

Purpose for fixing the smear: _____

_____

7. Purpose for which the inoculating loop is used: _____

_____

When the inoculating loop must always be flamed: _____

_____

Reason for flaming the inoculating loop: _____

Technique for flaming the inoculating loop: _____

_____

_____

8. *Bacillus subtilis*:
   Which of the three basic types of bacteria is it?

   _____

   Drawing:

9. *Bacillus subtilis* spores:
   Name the special stain used to color the spores.

   _____

   Drawing:

WORKSHEET 4.1–2   EVALUATION EXERCISE

Instructions: Provide the answers for the following:

1. a. Describe the shape of a **bacillus** bacterium: _____

    b. Describe the shape of a **spirillum** bacterium: _____

2. a. Sketch **streptococcus** bacteria:

    b. Sketch **staphylococcus** bacteria:

3. What is the function of **flagella**? _____

_____

4. What is the function of **bacterial spores**? _____

_____

5. Define **aseptic technique**: _____

_____

6. a. Explain how one **fixes** a bacterial smear: _____

_____

_____

    b. What is the reason for fixing a bacterial smear? _____

_____

7. a. What is the function of the **inoculating loop**? _____

_____

    b. Explain how one **flames** the inoculating loop: _____

_____

_____

    c. What is the reason for flaming the inoculating loop? _____

_____

8. What two tasks should you always carry out following laboratory activities dealing with living bacteria?

    a. _____

    b. _____

4.2 THE MICROBIOLOGY OF YOGURT

You Will Need the Following Materials:

nonfat powdered milk

yogurt starter (plain yogurt, purchased
   from the grocery store, that
   contains active or live cultures

candy thermometer

saucepan

milk (whole, lowfat, or nonfat)

spoon

toothpicks

safety goggles

paper towels

vanilla extract

containers with lids

incubator (optional)

measuring cup

Bunsen burner

microscope slides

microscope

microscope lamp

methylene blue staining
   solution

lab apron

Lysol™ disinfectant

newspapers

Upon Completion of This Activity, Students Will

- Know how to make homemade yogurt at home.
- Know the names and roles of the two bacteria responsible for yogurt.
- Have observed microscopically the two types of bacteria responsible for yogurt.
- Gain experience in preparing a bacterial smear.

1. The Students Learn Some Information About Yogurt.

Yogurt is a popular food item these days. More and more consumers are realizing that nonfat yogurts with fruit flavors are an excellent low-cholesterol snack with all the vitamins and minerals found in whole milk. Few people realize that yogurt is the result of milk that has been inoculated with two specific kinds of bacteria. Fewer still have actually observed these bacteria through a microscope.

2. The Students Prepare Yogurt.

You can have the students bring in from home most of the materials needed for making yogurt. It can facilitate matters if you provide the nonfat powdered milk, yogurt starter, measuring cup, and vanilla extract.

The students should wear lab aprons and they should wash their hands prior to beginning yogurt preparation. They should also thoroughly clean their laboratory work surfaces with a disinfectant such as Lysol™. The surfaces should then be covered with newspaper. **(SAFETY NOTE: During preparation of the yogurt, let no materials come into direct contact with an uncovered laboratory work surface.)**

One quart of milk (lowfat or nonfat is recommended) is poured into a saucepan. One-third cup of nonfat dry milk powder is stirred into the milk to provide for a creamier consistency in the finished product. (You should dispense the milk powder to the students.)

(SAFETY NOTE: The students should wear safety goggles during the heating and cooling of the milk.) The milk is heated until the temperature reaches 180°F. It should be stirred frequently while it is heating. If it is not, the milk will quickly begin to burn on the bottom of the saucepan.

When the temperature of the milk reaches 180°F, the Bunsen burner should be turned off and the milk allowed to cool to about 115°F. The cooling process can be greatly speeded up by using a spoon to stir and aerate the liquid. (If there is a refrigerator in the classroom, placing the saucepan of milk in the freezer for a short period of time will speed up cooling.)

When the temperature of the milk has lowered to about 115°F, 2 tablespoons of yogurt starter should be added and mixed thoroughly using a spoon. (You can dispense the yogurt starter as students are ready. Explain to them that the yogurt starter is regular yogurt that contains live cultures of the two kinds of bacteria needed.)

The milk mixture should now be poured into four to six small containers, and lids should be added. (Dividing the milk mixture up into several small containers assures a better consistency of yogurt.) The containers should be labeled with the students' names.

The containers of yogurt should now be incubated. If you have a classroom incubator, incubate the yogurt for about 4 or 5 hours at 100°F. Then place the yogurt in a refrigerator (or cool place) for about an hour to further thicken it. If an incubator is not available, the yogurt can be left in a warm location overnight prior to refrigeration.

Finally, the students should clean up their work areas.

3. The Students Prepare a Bacterial Smear and Observe the Two Types of Bacteria That Are Responsible for Yogurt.

Have the students put on lab aprons and obtain clean microscope slides.

Using a clean toothpick, a very small amount of yogurt should be placed on the center of a clean microscope slide and spread into a smear about the size of a nickel.

Let the smear completely air dry and then cover it with methylene blue staining solution. Wait about 2 minutes and then gently rinse off the excess stain with tap water.

Let the stained smear completely air dry and then observe through the microscope using high power.

The students should observe and prepare sketches of the following types of bacteria: *Lactobacillus bulgaricus*   *Streptococcus thermophillus*

    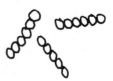

Tell the students the names of the bacteria and explain that they produce lactic acid, which is responsible for both yogurt's flavor and consistency.

The students can now eat and enjoy their yogurt. Allow them to bring in from home whatever they would like to mix with their yogurt prior to consuming. If the students mix a few drops of vanilla extract with their yogurt, this will tone down the tartness caused by the lactic acid. **SAFETY CAUTION: You should check each student's yogurt prior to their consuming it to make certain that the color and odor is that of fresh yogurt.**

4. The Students Work on an Activity to Learn About Food Poisoning.

Pass out copies of Worksheet 4.2–1. **The answers to the Library Research Questions are** 1. *Closteridium botulinum;* 2. Staphylococcal food poisoning; 3. *Staphylococcus aureus;* 4. Mayonnaise, salad dressings, cream pies and desserts, meats.

© 1992 by The Center for Applied Research in Education

Name _____ Date _____

WORKSHEET 4.2-1
MESSAGE SQUARE ACTIVITY ON FOOD POISONING

Hint: The most severe type of food poisoning

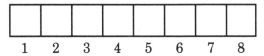

1	2	3	4	5	6	7	8

Anticipated Answer

Put: an L in 5 _____
     an I in 6 _____
     a T in 3 _____
     an M in 8 _____
     a U in 4 _____
     a B in 1 _____
     an O in 2 _____
     an S in 7 _____

Hint: The chemical substance, released by certain types of bacteria, that makes food poisonous

1	2	3	4	5

Anticipated Answer

Put: an I in 4 _____
     an O in 2 _____
     an N in 5 _____
     an X in 3 _____
     a T in 1 _____

Library Research Questions   **Answers**   **Sources**

1. What is the scientific name for
   the bacteria that causes the type
   of food poisoning named above?

2. What is the most common type
   of food poisoning?

3. What is the scientific name for the
   bacteria that causes the type of
   food poisoning named in #2 above?

4. What types of foods are often
   implicated in causes of the type of
   food poisoning named in #2 above?

4.3 TESTING THE EFFICIENCY OF FLOOR CLEANERS

You Will Need the Following Materials:

blank sterile (antibiotic) disks, 6mm in diameter

4 different liquid floor cleaners

sterile cotton swabs

nutrient broth powder

nutrient agar powder

forceps

incubator

stirring rod

safety goggles

flask

paper towels

rulers calibrated in millimeters

hand soap

masking tape

container for disposal of contaminated swabs and forceps

test tubes

cotton

beakers

sterile Petri dishes

glass-marking pencils

autoclave

Bunsen burner

laboratory balance

lab aprons

small paper cups

overhead projector

colored pencils

graph paper

Lysol™ disinfectant

Upon Completion of This Activity, Students Will

- Have experienced a consumer-oriented type of microbiological investigation.
- Have collected and interpreted data and prepared bar graphs.
- Be aware of the value of and uses of the disk-plate technique.
- Know what zones of inhibition are, as well as their importance.
- Know the definition and importance of aseptic technique.

1. The Teacher Prepares the Materials Necessary for Testing the Efficiency of the Various Floor Cleaners.

Select four liquid floor cleaners to be tested. You might wish to include a couple that are labeled as containing disinfectants. You will need to assign numbers 1, 2, 3, and 4 to the cleaners and eventually distribute beaker (or paper cup) samples to the students.

Prepare and sterilize enough nutrient agar for pouring three Petri dishes for each student (or group of students). Follow the instructions on the container, which usually indicates that 23 grams of nutrient agar powder is needed for each

1000ml of water. **SAFETY CAUTION: Put on lab apron and safety goggles. The agar should be slowly added to hot water as you are stirring the liquid. Continue stirring the liquid constantly until it comes to a boil. Failure to stir can result in the agar settling to the bottom of the beaker, causing the beaker to shatter. Once the liquid reaches a boil, the stirring can be stopped and the Bunsen burner turned off.**

If you wish, blank antibiotic disks can be prepared by punching disks out of filter paper using a paper punch. The disks can then be autoclaved.

Prepare 250ml of nutrient broth by dissolving 2 grams of nutrient broth powder in 250ml of water. Pour the nutrient broth into a flask, then plug with cotton and autoclave. The nutrient broth should be cooled. Then, using a sterile cotton swab moistened with some of the sterile nutrient broth, swab a section of the classroom floor and place the entire swab in the flask of nutrient broth. Incubate the nutrient broth in a warm place for a day or two or until the broth becomes cloudy. **SAFETY CAUTION: The broth culture now contains bacteria from the floor and is potentially dangerous if it contaminates anyone or anything.** Beakers containing samples of this broth will eventually be distributed to the students for spreading on the surface of agar.

2. The Students Prepare Their Petri Dishes for Testing Floor Cleaners.

Have the students put on laboratory aprons. Demonstrate for them how they are to inoculate the surface of the agar in each Petri dish with the broth culture. This is accomplished by dipping the tip of a cotton swab into the broth and then carefully spreading it over the entire surface of the agar, like "icing a cake." While doing this, the lid of the Petri dish should not be fully removed (this can lead to contamination of the agar by dust in the air), but one side of the lid should be lifted just enough to enable the swab to contact the surface of the agar.

(SAFETY CAUTION: Discuss with the students the concept of aseptic technique to be followed when working with the broth culture. Aseptic technique has been accomplished if the student has not contaminated anyone or anything in the environment with the broth culture. Explain to the students the nature of the broth and why it is extremely important to follow aseptic technique. Impress on them the importance of immediately telling you if broth contaminates any part of their person or environment.)

Distribute copies of Worksheet 4.3–1 and closely monitor the students for aseptic technique as they carry out Procedure, Part 1. (Be sure to read through the worksheet ahead of time.) Upon completion, collect the Petri dishes for incubation. Incubate until a surface growth of bacteria appears on the agar (usually one to three days).

Collect the beakers of broth culture. Make certain that the students have cleaned their lab areas with Lysol™ disinfectant solution and have washed their hands with soap and water.

Autoclave the contaminated cotton swabs and forceps as well as the flask and beakers of broth culture.

3. The Students Observe the Petri Dishes and Gather the Appropriate Data to Compare Floor Cleaner Effectiveness.

Prior to carrying out Part 2 of their worksheet, demonstrate to the students the proper way to gather the data results. Demonstrate by placing an inverted Petri dish (do not take the lid off) on an overhead projector and projecting the image on the screen. The following illustration shows a typical result:

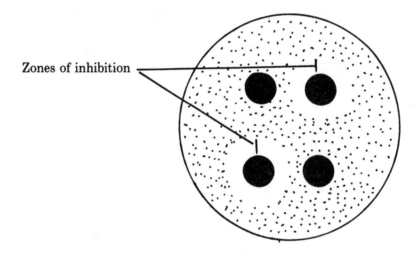

Zones of inhibition

Explain to the students that they are going to measure in millimeters the size of any **zones of inhibition** that might appear around the disks. The measurement is made from the edge of the disk to the outer edge of the zone of inhibition. Going up to the screen with a ruler, you can show the measuring of a zone quite effectively. When the students do their measuring, the lids of the Petri dishes are not to be removed, as the measurements can easily be made on the inverted surface of the dish.

The zone of inhibition is a clear area around a disk that is bacteria free. In the case of floor cleaners, a zone would indicate that the floor cleaner contains ingredients that retard the growth of bacteria. The larger the zone, the more effective the floor cleaner. This technique of investigating the effectiveness of various materials in retarding bacterial growth is called the **disk plate method (or paper disk method)**.

Explain to the students that one could study the effectiveness of mouthwash on mouth bacteria or soaps on skin bacteria by using the disk plate technique. Indeed, if one has ever had a throat culture taken because of an infection, it was then sent to a lab and the disk plate technique was used in determining the most effective antibiotic to use in treating the infection.

Have the students now carry out Part 2 of their worksheets. Upon completion of Part 2, collect and autoclave the contaminated Petri dishes.

Make certain that the students have cleaned their work areas with a Lysol™ disinfectant solution and have washed their hands with soap and water.

Work with the students in determining the class averages for the zones of inhibition for each floor cleaner sample. Finally, engage the class in a discussion of the results.

WORKSHEET 4.3–1   TESTING FLOOR CLEANERS

Procedure (Part 1):

1. Your teacher has assigned each floor cleaner a number from 1 to 4. Record this information in the following space:

   Floor Cleaner Number   Name of Floor Cleaner

   1   _____

   2   _____

   3   _____

   4   _____

2. Put on lab aprons. **SAFETY CAUTION: The broth culture you are about to work with contains millions of bacteria collected from a floor sample. These bacteria can be potentially dangerous if they come in contact with anyone or anything. Thus, it is extremely important that you follow aseptic technique and notify your teacher immediately if the broth gets on anyone or anything. The only materials that the broth should come in contact with are the cotton swab and the surface of the agar in the Petri dishes.**

3. Cover your work surface with layers of paper towels.

4. Using a glass-marking pencil, write your name and the date on the lid of each of your three Petri dishes. On the bottom of each Petri dish, draw four small circles equally spaced from each other and the edge of the dish. Number the circles 1, 2, 3, and 4. Note this illustration:

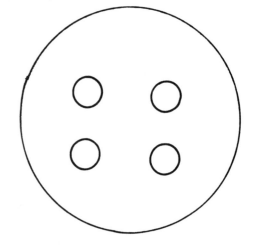

5. Obtain a beaker sample of the broth culture from your teacher. Using a sterile cotton swab, carefully coat the surface of the agar in each of your three Petri dishes, as previously demonstrated by your teacher. Carefully dip the swab into the broth culture prior to coating each agar surface.

6. Immediately dispose of the swab in the special container provided by your teacher.

7. In clean beakers (or paper cups), obtain samples of the four floor cleaners being tested. Number each beaker according to the floor cleaner it contains.

8. Place three sterile disks into each floor cleaner sample. After two minutes soaking time, transfer the disks, using forceps, to the surface of the agar in the Petri dishes. As a guide to placing the disks on the agar, refer to the numbered circles on the bottom of the Petri dish. For example, number 1 circles refer to the number 1 floor cleaner being tested. Rinse the forceps between floor cleaners.

9. Immediately place the forceps in the special container provided by your teacher.

10. Using masking tape, secure the lids on the Petri dishes.

11. Invert your three Petri dishes and your teacher will collect them and put them in an incubator for one to three days.

12. Clean your work area with Lysol™ disinfectant solution and dispose of the paper towels in the proper waste container. Wash your hands with soap and water.

Procedure (Part 2):

1. Put on lab aprons.

2. Cover your work surface with layers of paper towels.

3. Do not take the lids off the Petri dishes. Instead, invert the Petri dishes and then measure the zones of inhibition using a millimeter rule. Record your data results in the following table:

Name of Floor Cleaner	Zone of Inhibition (mm)				
	Petri Dish 1	Petri Dish 2	Petri Dish 3	Average Zone of Inhibition	Class Average Zone of Inhibition
1.					
2.					
3.					
4.					

4. Clean your work area with Lysol™ disinfectant solution and dispose of the paper towels in the proper waste container. Wash your hands with soap and water.

5. Prepare a bar graph comparing the class average zones of inhibition for each floor cleaner. Label the vertical axis, letting each square equal 1 millimeter. Along the horizontal axis, write the names of the floor cleaners, leaving a space between each. Prepare a red bar for floor cleaner 1, a blue bar for 2, a green bar for 3, and a yellow bar for 4.

6. Based on your bar graph, write a brief summary comparing the efficiency of the four floor cleaners.

4.4 CULTURING AND STUDYING FUNGI

You Will Need the Following Materials:

student microscope

stereomicroscope

microscope lamp

microscope slides

cover slips

prepared microscope slides of
  Rhizopus, Aspergillus, Penicillium,
  and *Pilobolus*

autoclave

incubator (optional)

lemon or orange

lab aprons

molasses

single-edge safety razor blade
  (such as Treet™)

selected freshly collected mushrooms

atomizer or empty spray bottle

cellophane tape

transparent food wrap

flask

bread (without preservatives)

prune juice

Petri dishes

culture dishes

aluminum foil

agar powder

colored pencils

horse, cow, or rabbit dung
  (rabbit recommended)

unlined paper

paper towels

dry yeast

peptone

sheets of white and black paper

white shellac dissolved in
  alcohol (or substitute
  fixative)

wide-mouth jar (or substitute)

scissors

forceps

Upon Completion of This Activity, Students Will

- Know structures and functions of common fungi.
- Be able to identify common fungi.
- Have prepared and labeled drawings of common fungi.
- Have learned how to manipulate materials while viewing through the stereomicroscope.
- Know some classification groups of fungi as well as characteristics and examples of each group.
- Have cultured common types of fungi.
- Have made and compared spore prints of different kinds of mushrooms.
- Have prepared wet mounts of spores from various kinds of mushrooms.

SAFETY CAUTION: Make certain that the room is well ventilated when growing molds, as some students, particularly those with asthma or severe allergies, may develop an allergic response to the spores.

1. The Students Prepare Materials on Which to Culture Fungi.

The students should prepare four culture dishes by lining the bottom of each with a layer of moist paper towel. Place a slice of bread slightly moistened with water into one dish. Place a piece of bread slightly moistened with prune juice into the second dish. Place the halves of a lemon or orange in the third dish. Place a scoop of fresh horse, cow, or rabbit dung (rabbit dung is recommended) into the fourth dish. Label all dishes with contents and student name, and, with the exception of the dishes containing dung, cover the tops with aluminum foil and place them in a warm location (either room or incubator) at approximately 25°C. Cover the dishes containing dung with a transparent food wrap and place them in a location that receives sunlight. Fungi should grow within a few days (check the dishes occasionally and add water if dry), at which time you will be ready for #8 below.

You should prepare the Petri dishes of dung agar for the students. Prepare them as follows: Autoclave fresh dung (rabbit recommended) for 30 minutes at 15 psi; place a layer of the sterile manure (approximately 12 pellets if you are using rabbit dung) in a Petri dish and cover with a thick layer of autoclaved 2 percent agar mixture. (Set aside the prepared Petri dishes of the dung agar for future use.)

2. The Students Learn Some Classification Groups of Fungi as Well as Characteristics and Examples of Each Group.

Give the students the following information regarding the classification of fungi:

Group	Characteristic(s)	Example(s)
Zygomycetes	Spores are produced in a structure called a sporangium, which ruptures, releasing the spores.	*Rhizopus* *Pilobolus*
Ascomycetes	Spores, called conidia, develop on structures called conidiophores.	yeasts *Penicillium*
Basidiomycetes	Spores, called basidiospores, develop on structures called basidia.	mushrooms puffballs bracket fungi
Deuteromycetes	No sexual type of reproduction has been observed. Conidiophores produce conidia.	*Aspergillus*

3. *The Students Study the Fungi* **Rhizopus** *and* **Pilobolus.**

Distribute prepared slides of *Rhizopus.* The following diagram is a guide to drawing and labeling the fungi:

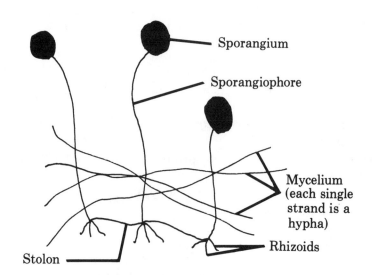

Give the following notes to the students:

a. | **Structure** | **Function** |
|---|---|
| Mycelium | The white, cottony growth associated with the fungi; allows for the spreading growth of the fungi |
| Hypha | One single filament of the mycelium; many are specialized for specific functions |
| Sporangiophore | A specialized hypha that supports the sporangium |
| Sporangium | A balloonlike structure containing the spores |
| Spores | Asexual means of reproduction; the spore lands on a suitable surface and gives rise to a new fungus |
| Rhizoids | Specialized hypha that (a) attach the fungi to the substrate (material on which the fungi is growing), (b) secrete enzymes that break down the substrate into usable nutrients for the fungi, and (c) absorb nutrients |
| Stolon | A specialized hypha that grows along the substrate, giving rise to new masses of mycelium |

b. *Rhizopus* is often referred to as common bread mold.

c. The immature sporangia are white and the mature sporangia are black.

d. Mature sporangia burst open, scattering spores for new mold growth.

e. The mold is responsible for spoilage of fruits, breads, and vegetables.

Pass out prepared slides of *Pilobolus*. The following diagram can be used as a guide in drawing and labeling:

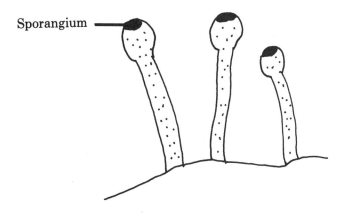

Give the following notes to the students:

a. *Pilobolus* is nicknamed the "shotgun fungus" because of its ability to discharge its sporangia over a distance of several feet.

b. It grows on animal dung and discharges its sporangia into the surrounding grass. Grazing animals ingest the sporangia, which pass through the animals' digestive system and are eliminated along with the fecal (dung) material, where it again grows on the animal dung, completing its life cycle.

4. The Students Study the Fungi Yeast and Penicillium.

You can prepare the yeast in advance by placing about ½ teaspoon of dry yeast in 100ml of water. Add 5ml of molasses and a "pinch" of peptone to the mixture. Within 24 hours, budding yeast will be available.

Have the students prepare wet mounts of the yeast mixture and observe on high power. They should prepare and label drawings as follows:

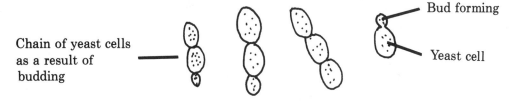

Give the following notes to the students:

a. Budding is the asexual form of yeast reproduction.

b. When you purchase a package of dry yeast at the grocery store, you are actually purchasing a package of living fungus.

c. Yeasts are very important commercially in the production of beers and wines and breads.

d. Wild yeasts are abundant in nature, growing on grapes, plums, and other fruits, as well as in the soil.

Distribute prepared slides of *Penicillium*. Students should prepare and label drawings as follows:

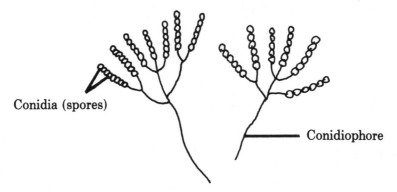

Conidia (spores)

Conidiophore

Give the students the following notes:

a. *Penicillium* fungus is also known as a mold.

b. Some species of *Penicillium* molds produce the antibiotic penicillin.

c. Some species of *Penicillium* are used in the making of cheeses such as Roquefort (blue) and Camembert.

d. Some species cause spoilage of preserves, vegetables, grains, and fruits.

e. *Penicillium* mold produces conidia (spores) on specialized structures called conidiophores, which resemble, through the microscope, a whisk broom.

f. The spores are very powdery and are a blue-green color.

5. The Students Study the Fungus Aspergillus.

Distribute prepared slides of *Aspergillus*. Students should prepare and label drawings as follows:

Spores (since this mold does not have a sporangium enclosing the spores, they can be observed around the outer edge)

Sporangiophore

Give the students the following notes:

a. *Aspergillus* is often referred to as a mold.
b. Depending upon the species, spores can be black, brown, or green.
c. It has an affinity for substrates with sugar, such as jams and jellies.
d. One species is used commercially to produce citric acid for products ranging from soft drinks and fruit-flavor jelly candies to jams and jellies.
e. One species produces a very powerful carcinogen (cancer-causing agent) called aflatoxin. It grows on plants such as rice and peanuts, and it can contaminate them with aflatoxin. For this reason, the government continuously monitors the aflatoxin levels of peanut butter.

Certain species can produce respiratory diseases in birds and humans.

6. The Students Study the Fungi Puffballs, Mushrooms, and Bracket Fungi.

Cut open a puffball and have the students prepare wet mounts and observe and prepare drawings of the spores.

Notes to be given to the students:

a. The mycelium growth of the puffball is under the ground.
b. What we know as the puffball is a large structure called a **fruiting body**, which is filled with spores.
c. When a mature puffball is kicked, perhaps while you are walking through the woods, a black cloud (of spores) is produced.

Distribute mushrooms to the students. Have them prepare and label a drawing similar to the following:

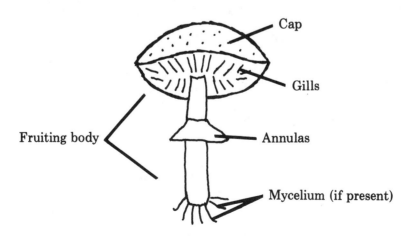

Give the students the following notes:

a. | **Structure** | **Function** |
| --- | --- |
| Fruiting body | The above-ground portion of a mushroom |
| Cap | Contains the gills on which spores are produced |
| Gills | Spores are produced in specialized structures on their surfaces |
| Annulus | A ring of tissue where the cap was originally attached to the stalk |
| Stalk | Supports the cap |

b. The mycelium is located in the soil.

c. Mushrooms are sometimes referred to as toadstools.

d. Some mushrooms are edible, whereas others are extremely poisonous. Unless one is an expert **mycologist** (one who studies fungi), **never** attempt to collect mushrooms for purposes of eating.

Have the students observe the gills using the stereomicroscope. If the mushroom is at maturity, the gills will be covered with spores. This will allow the students to prepare wet mounts and spore drawings.

Distribute bracket fungi to the students and have them observe the underside of the fungus through the stereomicroscope. Students can prepare and label a simple drawing, as shown in the following section of the undersurface:

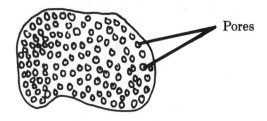

Give the students the following notes:

a. Spores are produced on the linings of tubes and drop out through the pores.

b. Bracket fungi grow on the trunks of trees and are often referred to as shelf fungi.

c. Bracket fungi are also called artist's fungi because on their flat bottom surfaces one can paint pictures.

7. *The Students Prepare Prints and Wet Mounts of Spores from Several Different Kinds of Mushrooms.*

Distribute copies of Worksheet 4.4–1 for the students to work on.

Use fresh, mature mushrooms with an abundance of spores. (**SAFETY NOTE: Have a well-ventilated area available for the students to work in when they are spraying spore prints with the fixative. Further, make certain they are wearing lab aprons and protective safety goggles.**)

The fixative can be purchased or prepared as follows: Dissolve white shellac in some alcohol and pour into a clean bottle with a spray nozzle.

8. The Students Study Living Fungi from Cultures That They Previously Set Up.

The cultures that have been previously set up should have produced the following molds:

a. Bread moistened with water—*Rhizopus* (black bread mold) should be the predominant mold. (Brown *Aspergillus* mold might also be present.)

b. Bread moistened with prune juice—*Aspergillus* (brown-colored mold) should be present, as this mold favors a substrate containing sugars.

c. Orange and/or lemon—*Penicillium* (green-gray colored mold) should be present.

d. Dung—*Pilobolus* mold should be present in at least a few of the dishes. Using the stereomicroscope, look for growths of *Pilobolus,* and, when located, let the students remove some with forceps and place them on the previously prepared Petri dishes of dung agar. These dishes should be placed in a sunny location for a day or two to establish the culture.

Distribute copies of Worksheet 4.4–2. Do not tell the students which molds are expected to be found, but let them try to identify the molds using information that they previously have learned through notes and the study of prepared slides.

9. The Students Learn About Truffles and the Amanita Group of Mushrooms.

Distribute copies of Worksheet 4.4–3 for the students to work on. **The answers to the Library Research Questions are** 1. They are actually the same thing. Sometimes the term *toadstool* is used for poisonous mushrooms. 2. Diarrhea, severe abdominal pains, blurred vision, vomiting; 3. Trained pigs; 4. Ascomycetes.

WORKSHEET 4.4–1 MUSHROOM SPORE STUDY

Your teacher has provided several different kinds of fresh, mature (spore-bearing) mushrooms for this study. You might wish to include some that you have collected yourself.

You are to do the following activities for each mushroom and record your results in the data table.

1. Prepare a true-life color sketch of the mushroom in the appropriate section of the data table. You can use colored pencils for this.

2. Prepare a **spore print** as follows:

   a. Select a draft-free location.

   b. A piece of white paper and black paper should be laid side by side and taped to each other. (Tape on the undersurface of the paper.)

   c. Carefully remove the cap from the stem of the mushroom.

   d. Place the mushroom cap, gill side down, on the paper, positioning it so that one half of the cap is on white paper and the other half on black paper.

   e. A wide-mouth jar (or substitute) should be placed as a cover over the cap.

   f. After about two hours, the jar and cap can be carefully removed from the paper.

   g. **(SAFETY CAUTION: Put on lab aprons and safety goggles for this step in preparing a spore print. Further, work in a well-ventilated area designated by the teacher.)** Gently spray the spore print with a fixative.

   h. After the fixative has dried, number the spore print to correspond with the number of the **True-Life Color Sketch of Mushroom** in your worksheet.

   i. Record spore color in the data table.

3. Prepare a wet mount by placing a drop of water on a clean microscope slide and adding some mushroom spores by tapping the mushroom cap while holding it over the drop of water. Add a cover slip and observe them using high power. Make a sketch of the spores in the data table.

Using information gathered for your data table, answer the following questions.

1. Are spores different shapes for different kinds of mushrooms? _____

   _____

2. How many different spore colors did you observe? _____

3. How do the spore prints compare for the different mushrooms studied? _____

   _____

   _____

   _____

Optional study: You might wish to obtain a mushroom guide from the library and locate pictures of and further information about the mushrooms that you studied. The information obtained can be recorded in the column **Additional Information**.

DATA TABLE

True-Life Color Sketch of Mushroom #: _____.	Sketch of Spores
	Color of Spores:
	Additional Information:

True-Life Color Sketch of Mushroom #: _____.	Sketch of Spores
	Color of Spores:
	Additional Information:

WORKSHEET 4.4–2   MOLD IDENTIFICATION

As you do the following activities, refer to your notes and drawings from your previous study of prepared slides of fungi.

1. a. Using a stereomicroscope, observe the mold growing on the water-moistened bread and prepare a labeled drawing:

   b. Using the stereomicroscope and forceps, carefully remove a very small amount of the mold and prepare a wet mount. Using the student microscope, observe and prepare a drawing:

   c. Of the molds previously studied, which one is this? _____

   To what classification group does this mold belong? _____

   What are the characteristics of this classification group? _____

   _____

2. a. Using the stereomicroscope, observe the mold growing on the prune juice-moistened bread and prepare a labeled drawing:

   b. Repeat 1.b. above for this mold:

   c. Of the molds previously studied, which one is this? _____

   To what classification group does this mold belong? _____

   What are the characteristics of this classification group? _____

   _____

3. a. Using the stereomicroscope, observe the mold growing on the orange or lemon and prepare a labeled drawing:

    b. Repeat 1.b. for this mold:

    c. Of the molds previously studied, which one is this? _____

        To what classification group does this mold belong? _____

        What are the characteristics of this classification group? _____

        _____

4. a. Using the stereomicroscope, observe the mold growing on the dung agar and prepare a labeled drawing:

        Of the molds previously studied, which one is this? _____

        To what classification group does this mold belong? _____

        What are the characteristics of this classification group? _____

        _____

5. In the space below, record the type of information collected above for any other molds found growing on the substrates. (It is not uncommon to observe white or gray *Mucor*, or pink *Neurospora* molds.)

WORKSHEET 4.4–3   MESSAGE SQUARE ACTIVITY FUNGI

A. *Hint:* The genus name of mushrooms noted for its deadly species

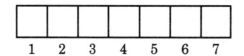

1	2	3	4	5	6	7

Anticipated Answer

Put: an I in 5
    an A in 1, 3, and 7
    a T in 6
    an M in 2
    an N in 4

_____
_____
_____
_____
_____

B. *Hint:* These fungi are a gourmet's delight

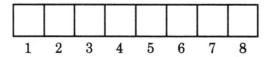

1	2	3	4	5	6	7	8

Anticipated Answer

Put: an S in 8
    an E in 7
    an F in 4 and 5
    a T in 1
    an L in 6
    a U in 3
    an R in 2

_____
_____
_____
_____
_____
_____
_____

Library Research Questions

Answers   **Sources**

1. What is the difference between a
   mushroom and a toadstool?

2. List four symptoms of mushroom
   poisoning.

3. How are humans aided in locating
   (the answer to Hint B) in nature?

4. To what classification group of fungi
   do (the answer to Hint B) belong?

4.5 CULTURING AND STUDYING PROTOZOANS

You Will Need the Following Materials:

prepared slides of protozoans, such as amoeba, paramecium, vorticella, euglena, radiolarians, blepherisma, euplotes, plasmodium

methyl cellulose (liquid)	iodine solution (dilute)
neutral red solution	paper towels
straw or hay	Petri dishes
pond water	culture dishes
rice grains	marking pencils
dry oatmeal flakes	aluminum foil
medicine droppers	nonnutrient agar powder
microscopes	lab aprons
microscope lamps	safety goggles
microscope slides and cover slips	unlined paper
lab aprons	Elodea (*anacharis*)

Upon Completion of This Activity, Students Will

- Know structures and functions of various protozoans.
- Be able to identify common protozoans.
- Have prepared and labeled drawings of protozoans.
- Have practiced techniques of using the microscope and observing specimens.
- Have practiced skills at preparing wet mount slides.
- Know the basic classification groups of protozoans as well as characteristics and examples of each group.
- Have cultured various types of protozoans using several different media combinations.

1. The Students Prepare Various Media Combinations for Culturing Several Different Kinds of Protozoans.

Distribute copies of Handout 4.5–1, which has student directions for preparing five different media combinations. (*Note:* You should prepare the Petri dishes with agar for the students. Use nonnutrient agar and follow the preparation instructions on the package, substituting pond water for distilled water.) After the students have completed the procedures on Handout 4.5–1, the dishes should be placed in a warm location for a few days.

Inform the students that the sources of the protozoans are the hay or straw and the pond water on and in which they live. Bacteria multiply and feed off the hay and straw, oatmeal flakes, and rice grains. They in turn provide food for the protozoans.

2. The Students Learn the Basic Classification Groups of Protozoans as Well as Characteristics and Examples of Each Group.

Write on the chalkboard the following material for the students to copy in their notes:

a. | Classification Groups | Characteristics | Examples |
|---|---|---|
| (1) Mastigophora | (1) Locomotion by flagella | (1) Euglena |
| (2) Sarcodina | (2) Locomotion by pseudopods | (2) Amoeba |
| (3) Ciliophora | (3) Locomotion by cilia | (3) Paramecium |
| (4) Sporozoa | (4) Nonmotile as adults | (4) Plasmodium |

b. The organism euglena is classified by some biologists as more algaelike than protozoanlike because euglena contains chloroplasts and under sunlight conditions can carry out photosynthesis.

3. The Students Study the Protozoan Euglena.

Distribute the prepared slides of euglena as well as unlined paper. The following diagram is a guide to making observations and labeling drawings:

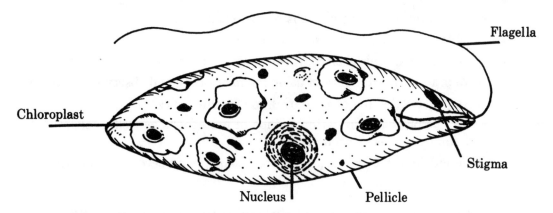

The following notes are to be given to the students:

a. | Structure | Function |
|---|---|
| Flagellum | Structure used for locomotion |
| Nucleus | Contains the genetic instructions for the cell |
| Chloroplast | Carries out photosynthesis (food manufacture) |
| Pellicle | Provides strength to cell membrane |
| Stigma | Light sensitive; directs the cell toward light |

b. Euglena is a member of the classification group Mastigophora.

c. It can be referred to as a flagellate.

d. If the water in a home aquarium turns greenish, it could be a population explosion of euglenoids.

e. Many species of euglenoids live in fresh water. They play an important role in the food chain and in oxygen production for the atmosphere.

4. The Students Study the Protozoans Paramecium, Vorticella, Euplotes, and Blepherisma.

Tell the students that the next four protozoans they are going to study are members of the classification group ciliophora and can be referred to as ciliates. It should be noted that protozoans, as a group, function ecologically as consumers and are, in turn, a source of food for larger organisms.

Distribute prepared slides of paramecia. The following diagram is a guide to making observations and labeling drawings:

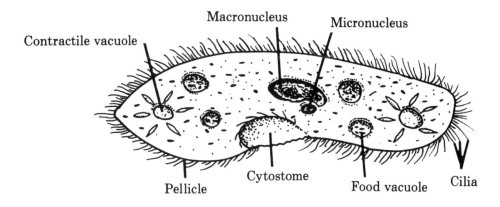

The following notes should be given to the students:

Structure	Function
Contractile vacuole	Pumps excess water out of the cell
Pellicle	Provides strength to cell membrane
Cilia	Structure used for locomotion and food getting
Cytostome (oral groove)	Entranceway for food
Micronucleus	Contains genetic instructions and functions only during reproduction
`Macronucleus	Contains genetic instructions for cell metabolism
Food vacuole	Storage site for food

Distribute prepared slides of vorticella. The diagram at right is a guide to making observations and drawings:

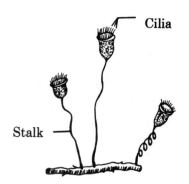

Give the students the following notes about vorticella:

a. **Structure**   **Function**

   Cilia   Structure used for locomotion and food getting

   Stalk   Used for attaching vorticella to a solid substrate; can also contract to pull the organism away from danger

b. Vorticella is a member of the classification group ciliophora.

c. It is a sessile (attached to a solid substrate) form of ciliate.

Distribute prepared slides of euplotes. The following diagram is a guide to making observations and labeling drawings:

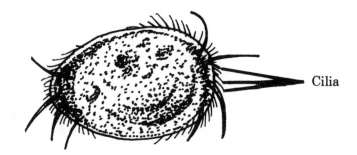

Give the students the following notes about euplotes:

Structure   **Function**

Cilia   Structure used for locomotion and food getting

Distribute prepared slides of blepherisma. The following diagram is a guide to making observations and labeling drawings:

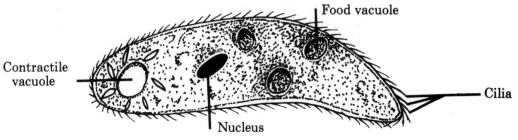

Again, the students should realize that the cilia are involved both in locomotion and in food getting.

5. The Students Study the Protozoans Amoeba and Radiolarian.

Distribute prepared slides of amoeba and use the diagram at right as a guide to making observations and labeling:

Plasmalemma

Contractile vacuole

Food vacuole

Nucleus

Pseudopod

Give the students the following notes:

a. **Structure**   **Function**

Contractile vacuole   Pumps excess water out of the organism
Food vacuole   Storage site for food
Pseudopod   Used for locomotion and food getting
Nucleus   Contains genetic instructions for the cell
Plasmalemma   Protective cell membrane

b. The amoeba is a member of the classification group Sarcodina.

Pass out prepared slides of radiolarians and use the diagram at right as a guide to making observations and labeling:

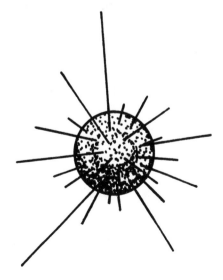

Give the students the following notes:

a. Radiolarians are marine organisms.
b. They have silica shells.

c. They are an important part of zooplankton (marine protozoans).

d. They are members of the classification group Sarcodina.

6. *The Students Study the Protozoan Plasmodium.*

Distribute prepared slides and use the following diagram as a guide to making observations and labeling:

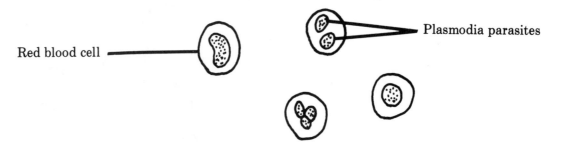

Give the following notes to the students:

a. Plasmodium organisms belong to the classification group Sporozoa.

b. Sporozoans are parasites.

c. Adult sporozoans are nonmotile.

d. Plasmodia often invade red blood cells.

e. Various types of plasmodium organisms cause human diseases, such as malaria.

7. *The Students Observe Living Protozoans Found in Their Own Cultures.*

It is difficult to say that a particular protozoan is going to be found in a particular culture medium that the students have set up. Instead, it is advisable to take one culture medium at a time and have the students prepare wet mounts. If a particular student has a wet mount abundant with vorticella, for example, have all the students prepare wet mounts from that same culture dish. Follow this procedure for exploring each of the four different media combinations. It is very important that students make wet mounts which include scrapings from the sides and bottoms of the dishes. Organisms such as paramecium and vorticella are not free swimming.

As various protozoans are found, the following are some interesting activities and observations that can be carried out by the students:

a. **Food vacuoles in paramecium:** Place a small drop of neutral red solution on a slide. Add a drop of culture containing paramecia. Add a cover slip and observe for red food vacuoles. (Paramecia take in the neutral red, which ends up in the food vacuoles.)

b. **The cilia of paramecia:** Add a drop of dilute iodine solution to a wet mount of paramecia and the organisms will come to a standstill, with the cilia easily visible. (This technique can be used with other ciliates as well.)

c. **The contractile stalk of vorticellae:** The stalk of a vorticella will rapidly coil up tightly if the organism is disturbed. When you have vorticellae visible under the microscope and the stalks are fully extended (as when the vorticellae are feeding), jar the microscope slide and watch the stalks quickly coil up and then extend again.

d. **Food getting by vorticellae:** Observe the cilia-lined, bell-shaped structure at the end of the stalk and watch the cilia beating rapidly to draw a steady stream of food particles into the organism.

e. **Food getting in paramecia:** Observe the cilia around the oral groove, drawing food into the organism.

f. **Locomotion and food getting in amoebae:** Watch for a period of time as the amoeba slowly moves by extending pseudopods in its direction of motion. If you are fortunate, you might observe the amoeba capturing food particles by surrounding them with pseudopods.

g. **Slowing down protozoans:** To slow down the movements of protozoans, place a drop of methyl cellulose on the slide prior to preparing the wet mount. The methyl cellulose adds viscosity to the wet mount, slowing down cilia movement.

h. **Observing pyrenoids in euglena:** Add a drop of dilute iodine solution to the wet mount of euglena organisms. Pyrenoids contain food stored in the form of starch, and starch turns blue-black in the presence of iodine.

8. The Students Are Evaluated on Their Knowledge of Protozoans.

Pass out copies of Worksheet 4.5–2 and use it, perhaps, as a sponge activity. **The answers are Across**—1. Protozoans; 3. Chloroplast; 4. Flagella; 5. Contractile vacuole; 8. Radiolarians; 9. Sporozoa. **Down**—1. Pyrenoid; 2. Sarcodina; 4. Food vacuole; 5. Cilia; 6. Amoeba; 7. Euglena.

HANDOUT 4.5–1 CULTURING PROTOZOANS

1. **Pond water and hay or straw:**

   a. Loosely fill a culture dish with hay or straw.

   b. Fill the dish with pond water.

   c. Cover the top of the dish with aluminum foil and label with the contents and your name.

2. **Pond water with rice grains:**

   a. Pour some pond water into a Petri dish.

   b. Add 6 or 7 grains of rice.

   c. Place a lid on the dish and label it with the contents and your name.

3. **Pond water with oatmeal flakes:**

   a. Pour some pond water into a Petri dish.

   b. Add a "pinch" of oatmeal flakes.

   c. Place a lid on the dish and label it with the contents and your name.

4. **Agar gel with pond water and rice grains:**

   a. Petri dishes with agar have already been prepared for you.

   b. Embed 3 or 4 rice grains into the surface of the agar.

   c. Add a layer of pond water.

   d. Place a lid on the dish and label it with the contents and your name.

5. **Elodea in pond water:**

   a. Place an elodea plant in some pond water in a culture dish.

   b. Cover the top of the dish with aluminum foil and label the dish with the contents and your name.

   Note: Elodea plants are an excellent source of amoebae. When preparing your wet mount, include scrapings from the plant surface as well as the dish bottom and sides. Amoebae are not free-swimming organisms.

Hints for excellent observations:

   a. Thoroughly clean a microscope slide.

   b. Place a drop of the liquid you are studying on the slide.

   c. Add any other solutions that are called for.

   d. Carefully place a cover slip on top of the liquid.

   e. Make certain that the ocular, objective lenses, and mirror are clean.

   f. Always focus on low power first, using the coarse adjustment.

   g. When using high power, use only the fine adjustment.

   h. Adjust light intensity using the diaphragm.

   i. Remember, the image through the microscope should have plenty of light and be in sharp focus.

Name _____   Date _____

WORKSHEET 4.5–2   PROTOZOANS EVALUATION EXERCISE

Instructions: Fill in the crossword puzzle below using answers to the clues provided.

Across:
1. General name for organisms studied in this activity
3. Structure that carries out photosynthesis
4. Structure used for locomotion
5. Structure that pumps excess water out of the cell (two words)
8. Organisms that are an important part of zooplankton
9. Classification group that contains parasites

Down:
1. Structure that stores starch
2. Classification group for amoebae
4. Storage site for food (two words)
5. Structure used for locomotion and food getting
6. Organism that belongs to sarcodina
7. Organism that belongs to mastigophora

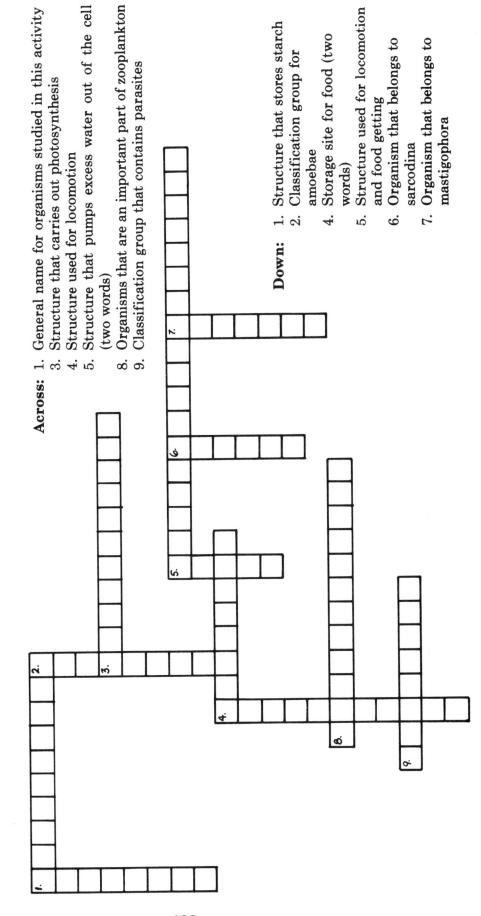

Part II
BASIC SCIENCE PROCESS LESSONS AND ACTIVITIES

Unit 5

Laboratory Techniques

5.1 USING THE STUDENT MICROSCOPE

You Will Need the Following Materials:

microscopes
prepared microscope slides
opaque projector

microscope lamps
lens paper

Upon Completion of This Activity, Students Will

- Know the parts of the microscope and how they function.
- Have experienced the proper way to focus the microscope.
- Be aware of how to keep the microscope's mirror and lenses clean.

1. The Students Label a Diagram of the Student Microscope.

Distribute copies of Worksheet 5.1–1 along with student microscopes. Instruct the students to label as many parts as they can on their worksheets. Upon completion of this task, distribute copies of Handout 5.1–2, which describes the functions of the parts of the microscope. Have the students learn this information as they use it to help them label any parts left blank on Worksheet 5.1–1.

2. The Students Check the Accuracy of Their Labeling.

Label a diagram of the microscope and, using an opaque projector, project it on the classroom screen. Let the students check the accuracy of their labeling. Follow this by projecting an unlabeled diagram of the microscope and having students volunteer to go to the screen and name the parts and/or functions of the parts.

3. The Students Learn the Proper Techniques for Focusing the Microscope.

Have the students set up the microscope lamps. Next have them adjust the diaphragm so that it is fully open to allow light to enter the microscope. (Various types of diaphragms differ somewhat in their structure, but all can be adjusted easily.) While looking through the ocular, the students should adjust the mirror so that it is reflecting light from the microscope lamp up through the diaphragm into the microscope. **(SAFETY CAUTION: The sun should never be used as a direct source of illumination for the microscope because its intensity can seriously damage the retina of the eye.)** If the illumination is too bright for the eyes, the diaphragm or condenser should be adjusted to cut down on the amount of light entering the microscope.

Provide the students with prepared microscope slides, perhaps of a cross section of a stem. Instruct them that the first thing they should always do with a microscope slide (prepared or otherwise) is to check it for cleanliness. If need be, gently clean the slide with a piece of lens paper. Further, a microscope slide should be handled by its edges so as not to touch the surface, leaving a fingerprint that will interfere with focusing.

The students should now focus the microscope using low power and the coarse adjustment knob. **Emphasize** to them that the low-power objective is always used first in focusing. Further, the coarse adjustment knob is used only with the low-power objective. Check each student's microscope for proper illumination and focus.

The students are now ready to focus on high power. They should turn the revolving nosepiece to rotate the high-power objective into place. An important thing to **emphasize** is that as the students do this, they should visually observe the objective lens to make certain that it does not physically hit the microscope slide.

The students can now look through the ocular and "fine tune" the focus by using the fine adjustment only. The coarse adjustment should never be used with the high-power objective, as this might cause the objective lens to hit the microscope slide, possibly damaging the lens and/or slide.

4. The Students Learn How to Clean the Microscope Ocular, Mirror, and Objective Lenses.

Instruct the students that they should use only lens paper in cleaning the microscope parts. Have them clean the mirror and the ocular. In cleaning the objective lens, it might be necessary to twist a corner of a piece of lens paper into a point. This is because many lenses are recessed and are difficult to reach in order to clean. Have them press the point into the recess against the lens and rotate it back and forth a few times. (If you use a lens-cleaning agent, have the students dip the point into the solution prior to cleaning.)

5. The Students Test Their Knowledge of Microscope Function, Structure, and Technique.

Distribute copies of Worksheet 5.1–3. You might wish to use this as a quiz, self-test, or home assignment. The answers to the worksheet follow:

Labeling the Six Parts of
the Microscope:

1. coarse adjustment
2. stage clips
3. base
4. ocular
5. high-power objective
6. diaphragm (or condenser)

Learning matchups:

1. i
2. g
3. f
4. b
5. c
6. k

Questions:

1. To observe the objective lens to make certain it does not hit the microscope slide
2. Multiply the power of the ocular by the power of the objective lens.
3. 430 (This may vary with different microscopes.)
4. The coarse adjustment is used only with the low-power objective.
5. When you want to adjust the amount of light entering the microscope
6. Handle by edge of slide only
7. The retina of the eye can be damaged.
8. To secure the slide to the stage
9. Keeps both eyes opened

6. The Students Learn Some Additional Information Related to the Microscope.

Pass out copies of Worksheet 5.1–4. **The answers are Message Square =** Van Leeuwenhoek; 1. microorganisms; 2. microbiology or protozoology; 3. 1723 at age 91; 4. examines tissues through the microscope, looking for evidence of disease, most notably cancer; 5. the ability to observe specimens in three dimensions.

Name _____   Date _____

WORKSHEET 5.1-1   THE STUDENT MICROSCOPE

Instructions: Label the parts of the microscope.

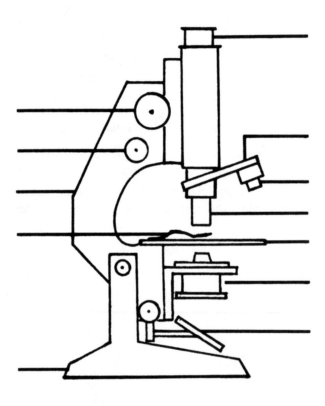

HANDOUT 5.1–2 FUNCTIONS OF MICROSCOPE PARTS

Ocular: This is the eyepiece lens that usually magnifies by a power of 10. (*Note:* To determine the power of the microscope, one multiples the power of the ocular by the power of the objective lens being used.)

High-power objective: It is located just above the stage. It is the longer of the objectives. Its lens has a magnifying power usually of 43.

Low-power objective: It is located just above the stage. It is the shorter objective. Its lens has a magnifying power usually of 10.

Stage: This is a horizontal platform just below the objectives that supports the microscope slide for observation.

Revolving nosepiece: The objective lenses are attached to this part. It can be manually rotated to select the objective lens that you wish to use.

Stage clips: They clamp over the edges of the microscope slide to secure it to the stage.

Diaphragm (or condenser): Located just below the stage, it can be hand adjusted to regulate the amount of light entering the microscope. An image viewed through the microscope should not be dark but should have plenty of light.

Mirror: This is adjusted to reflect light from the microscope lamp up into the microscope. Although the mirror is sometimes used to regulate the amount of light entering the microscope, this is not good technique.

Coarse adjustment: This is used to focus the microscope. It is always used first, and it is used *only* with the low-power objective.

Fine adjustment: This is used to focus the microscope. It is used with the high-power objective to "fine tune" the focus.

Arm: This is the back of the microscope and it is used along with the base to transport the microscope.

Base: This is the bottom of the microscope and it is used along with the arm to transport the microscope.

Note: Both eyes should be open when viewing through the microscope. This prevents eye fatigue, which occurs when the nonviewing eye is kept closed. Keeping both eyes open does take some practice, but it is highly recommended.

WORKSHEET 5.1–3 EVALUATION EXERCISE

Instructions: Label the following six parts of the microscope:

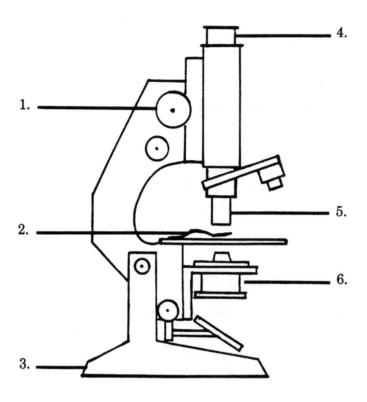

Learning Matchups: Fill in the blanks in the left-hand column with the letter of the proper answer from the right-hand column.

_____ 1. Can be hand adjusted to regulate the amount of light entering the microscope

_____ 2. Used first and with low-power objective in focusing

_____ 3. The lens that has a magnifying power usually of 43

_____ 4. The lens that magnifies the image usually by a factor of 10; also referred to as the eyepiece

_____ 5. The two parts used in carrying the microscope

_____ 6. Can be manually turned in selecting the objective lens that you want to use

a. mirror
b. ocular
c. arm and base
d. fine adjustment
e. stage
f. high-power objective
g. coarse adjustment
h. low-power objective
i. diaphragm
j. stage clips
k. revolving nosepiece
l. base and ocular

Worksheet 5.1–3   (cont'd.)

Questions:

1. Explain an important thing to remember as you turn the high-power objective into place.

   _____

   _____

2. How do you determine the power of a microscope?

   _____

   _____

3. What is the power of your classroom microscope when you are using the high-power objective?

   _____

   _____

4. What should you always remember when using the coarse adjustment?

   _____

   _____

5. Under what conditions would you use the diaphragm?

   _____

   _____

6. What should you remember when handling microscope slides (prepared or otherwise)?

   _____

   _____

7. Why should you never use direct sunlight as a source of light for the microscope?

   _____

   _____

8. What is the function of the stage clips?

   _____

   _____

9. In terms of your eyes, what should you try to learn as you use the microscope?

   _____

   _____

WORKSHEET 5.1–4   MESSAGE SQUARE ACTIVITY
THE MICROSCOPE

Hint: He is called the Father of the Microscope.

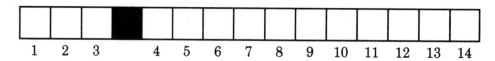

| 1 | 2 | 3 | | 4 | 5 | 6 | 7 | 8 | 9 | 10 | 11 | 12 | 13 | 14 |

Put: an A in 2
   an H in 11
   an E in 5, 6, 9, and 13
   a K in 14
   a V in 1
   an L in 4
   an N in 3 and 10
   a U in 7
   a W in 8
   an O in 12

Anticipated Answer

_____
_____
_____
_____
_____
_____
_____
_____
_____
_____

Library Research Questions

Answers   **Sources**

1. What did (the answer above) first observe and describe?

2. He is also considered to be the "father" of what science?

3. In what year did he die? How old was he?

4. The microscope is vital to the cytotechnologist. What does a cytotechnologist do?

5. What does the prefix *stereo-* mean in stereomicroscope?

5.2 USING THE STEREOMICROSCOPE

You Will Need the Following Materials:

stereomicroscopes   microscope lamps
opaque projector
an assortment of objects to observe, such as coins, paper money,
   rings, watches, salt, colored pictures from magazines, leaves

Upon Completion of This Activity, Students Will

- Know the parts of the stereomicroscope and how they function.
- Have learned proper focusing techniques.
- Have learned and practiced techniques of microscope lamp placement.
- Have learned and practiced techniques of mirror angle adjustment.
- Have become familiar with the general types of materials suitable for observation using a stereomicroscope.

1. The Students Learn the Parts of the Stereomicroscope and Their Functions.

Distribute copies of Worksheet 5.2–1. Let the students label as many parts as they think they can identify. At the completion of this task, distribute copies of Handout 5.2–2. Have the students learn the information on this handout as they use it to help them label any parts left blank on Worksheet 5.2–1.

2. The Students Check the Accuracy of Their Labeling.

You should label a copy of Worksheet 5.2–1 and then project it on the classroom screen using an opaque projector. This will allow the students to check their own accuracy. The correct labels are 1. ocular; 2. eyecap; 3. zoom lens adjustment; 4. adjustment knob; 5. arm; 6. base; 7. stage. Follow this by projecting an unlabeled diagram of the stereomicroscope and having students volunteer to go to the screen and name the parts and/or functions of the parts.

3. The Students Practice Proper Techniques of Focusing and Illuminating.

Distribute stereomicroscopes and microscope lamps.
First, have the students observe salt crystals. They are going to need some help in adjusting the two oculars for their inter-eye width. (Students have a tendency to remove the eyecaps from the stereomicroscope, not realizing that they play a role in helping to adjust the oculars to their inter-eye width.)
Let the students turn the zoom adjustment knob (or revolving nosepiece on stereomicroscopes that do not have a zoom adjustment knob) to varying

powers of magnification and observe the differences in the image sizes of the salt crystals.

Now have the students experiment with the mirror by tilting it to various angles and noting how it affects the appearance of the salt crystals by reflecting light at them from different directions and at different intensities. (This technique of mirror adjustment is very important, but it is often overlooked by the students.)

Next, the students should adjust the microscope lamp to various positions of illumination. Have them illuminate the salt crystals from above, below, and the sides, noting the effects each has on the appearance of the crystals. (This is another technique that should be remembered but is often overlooked by the students.)

4. The Students Become Familiar with the Types of Materials That Are Suitable for Observation Using the Stereomicroscope.

Explain to the students that the student microscope is used for observing microscopic specimens (specimens too small to be seen with the unaided eye). In comparison, the stereomicroscope is used for observing macroscopic specimens (specimens that, in general, can be seen with the unaided eye and are too large to be observed using the student microscope).

Let the students take some time and observe several different macroscopic objects of their choosing. Students really enjoy using the stereomicroscope and are fascinated by the appearance of objects through it. This is an excellent time to get students to volunteer for some extra-credit projects using the stereomicroscope. For example, a student might wish to observe and prepare drawings of an assortment of different kinds of crystals. Another might wish to observe and prepare drawings of the external anatomy of some insects.

5. The Students Apply Knowledge Learned.

Distribute copies of Worksheet 5.2–3. You might wish to use it as a quiz, or possibly for extra credit. **The answers are** 1. stereomicroscope; 2. ocular; 3. zoom; 4. macroscopic; 5. mirror; 6. stage; 7. mirror; 8. microscopic; 9. adjustment knob; 10. eyecap.

WORKSHEET 5.2–1   THE STEREOMICROSCOPE

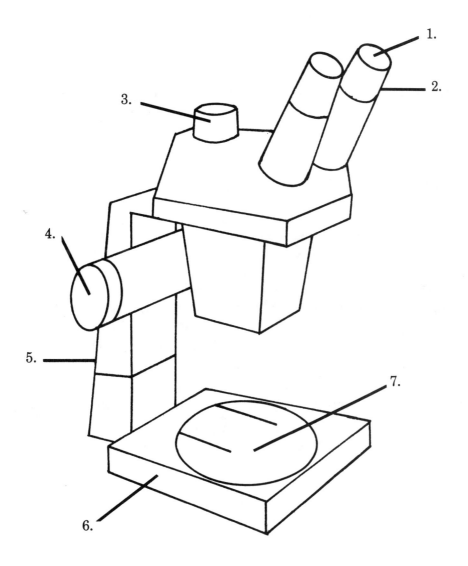

HANDOUT 5.2–2   FUNCTIONS OF THE PARTS
OF THE STEREOMICROSCOPE

Eyecap: This fits over the ocular lens. It makes adjusting the two oculars to your inter-eye width easier.

Ocular: This is the eyepiece lens. It usually magnifies by a power of 10. Note that the two oculars can be moved back and forth to adjust to your own specific inter-eye width. Due to the fact that you are viewing the specimen looking through two oculars, the specimen image will appear in three dimensions (or stereo). Unless the oculars are very accurately adjusted for inter-eye width, you will not view in three dimensions.

Adjustment knob: This allows you to focus the microscope.

Mirror and mirror adjustment knob (not shown on microscope diagram): When present, the mirror reflects light up through the microscope. **(SAFETY CAUTION: Never reflect direct sunlight up through the microscope, as its intensity can cause damage to the retina of the eye.)**

Zoom lens adjustment: Note that this adjustment has numbers on it from 0.7 to 3. By turning the knob toward the number 3, one can "zoom in" on a specimen, increasing from a magnifying power of 0.7 to 3. (Since the ocular has a magnifying power of 10, one multiplies the number turned to on the zoom lens adjustment by 10 to obtain the total magnification power of the stereomicroscope. For example, if the zoom lens adjustment is on 2, then 2 times 10 equals a total magnification power of 20.)

    Not all stereomicroscopes have a zoom lens adjustment. Instead, they have a revolving nosepiece that can be manually turned to change the magnifying power.

Stage: This is the place where specimens are placed for observation. On some stereomicroscopes the stage is glass, and on others it is metal.

Arm: This is the back of the stereomicroscope, and it is used along with the base to transport it.

Base: This is the bottom of the stereomicroscope and it is used along with the arm to transport it.

Note: For best viewing of a specimen, it is important to have proper illumination, proper mirror angle, and proper inter-eye width adjustment of the oculars.

WORKSHEET 5.2–3   AROUND THE SQUARE REVIEW ACTIVITY

Instructions: Begin at Start and fill in the squares, moving clockwise with the answers to the following clues. The same answer may be used twice. (There is no overlapping of letters; if an answer is two words, leave a space between them.)

1. Name of microscope that allows you to view in three dimensions
2. Name of one of the two eyepieces
3. Name of lens adjustment that has numbers 0.7 to 3
4. Name given to specimens too large to be viewed using the student microscope
5. Reflects light up through the microscope
6. Location where specimen is placed for viewing
7. Has a knob to tilt it at various angles for reflecting light
8. Specimens that are too small to be seen with the unaided eye
9. Allows you to focus
10. One fits over each ocular lens

Start

5.3 PREPARING WET MOUNT SLIDES
AND LABORATORY DRAWINGS

You Will Need the Following Materials:

microscopes	microscope lamps
microscope slides	cover slips
lab aprons	drawing paper
colored pencils	forceps
methylene blue staining solution	onion
dilute iodine solution	potato
elodea (*Anacharis*)	paper towels
toothpicks (flat)	medicine droppers
scalpel (or single-edged safety razor blade such as Treet™)	

Upon Completion of This Activity, Students Will

- Have experienced the technique of preparing wet mount slides.
- Know a basic format to use when preparing laboratory drawings.
- Have practiced skills of observation through the microscope.
- Have learned the value of staining solutions.
- Have had the opportunity to practice good technique in using the microscope.

1. The Students Learn How to Prepare Wet Mount Slides.

Emphasize to the students that microscope slides should be cleaned before every use. Even new slides must be cleaned prior to their first use because they have an oily surface. A simple and effective way to clean slides is to rinse them with water and scrub them dry with a paper towel.

A wet mount slide is one in which the specimen is in a drop of liquid, such as water, and covered with a cover slip. Have the students prepare a wet mount of cells from the lining of the cheeks inside the mouth. Using a medicine dropper, place a drop of water on the center of a clean microscope slide. Using the flattened end of a clean toothpick, gently scrape cells from the lining of the cheek, mixing them with the drop of water. Add a drop of methylene blue staining solution to the water and carefully place a cover slip on top.

Instruct the students to focus first on low power and find one or two cheek cells. After centering the cheek cell in the microscope's field of vision, they can focus on high power to improve detail. Check each student's final focus for clarity and illumination. If either needs modification, have the student check the mirror angle, the diaphragm setting, and the cleanliness of the objective and ocular lenses. (Many students have difficulty in maintaining adequate clarity and illumination of specimen images.)

The students should leave their wet mounts set up, coming back to them in a few minutes, after the following notes are taken.

2. The Students Learn a Basic Format for Preparing Laboratory Drawings.

Have the students take notes as you discuss the following information. Explain to the students that accurate laboratory drawings are a vital part of collecting data in the laboratory. They must also be convinced that artistic ability is not a prerequisite for accurate drawings. The most important prerequisite is good observation.

Laboratory drawings are made in pencil because this allows for clean erasures as you occasionally modify the drawing to make it more accurate. Colored pencils can be used if there is a need to record specimen colors in the drawing.

Drawings should be prepared large and should be centered on the paper. (Students frequently exhibit the opposite tendencies—preparing drawings that are quite small and relegated to a corner of the paper.) Drawing large allows for adding detail and makes labeling neater.

Structures should be neatly labeled on label lines drawn with the aid of a ruler.

Drawings should be accurately labeled either above or below the drawing itself. If a stain has been used, this should be noted. In addition, the microscope power used in observation should be noted and preceded by an X (referring to the power of magnification). For example, a drawing might be labeled as follows: "Starch grains from rice; iodine solution stained; X430."

3. The Students Prepare Several Different Wet Mount Slides and Practice Skills at Making Laboratory Drawings.

Distribute copies of Worksheet 5.3–1 to the students along with drawing paper. They begin the worksheet by returning to their cheek cell wet mounts. Have the materials needed for the remaining wet mounts set out for them. Continually help the students as they attempt to make accurate drawings of what they observe through the microscope. Look at what they have drawn and then look through the microscope to see if the two match. Constantly encourage the students to concentrate on their powers of observation and to draw exactly what they observe through the microscope.

Following are examples of labeled drawings of the wet mounts that the students will prepare:

Cheek Cells:

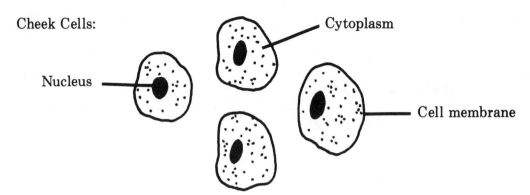

Potato Tissue:

The potato tissue contains starch grains that stain blue-black in the presence of iodine.

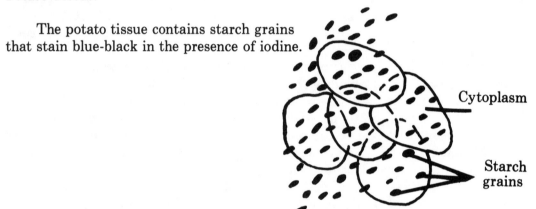

Onion Tissue:

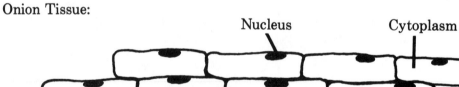

Elodea Tissue:

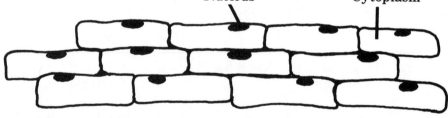

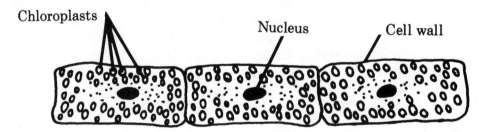

4. The Students Are Evaluated on Their Learning.

Write the following questions on the chalkboard for the students to work on:

a. Describe how you would prepare a wet mount.

b. What is the value of using staining solutions?

c. What is a good way to clean microscope slides prior to use?

d. When you title a drawing, what two other pieces of information should be included?

e. List three different reasons for preparing wet mounts.

5. The Students Learn Some General Information Pertaining to the Cell.

Pass out copies of Worksheet 5.3–2. **The answers to the Around the Square Activity are** endoplasmic reticulum, ribosomes, nucleus, vacuole, cytology, Golgi complex, ctyoplasm, lysosome, and muscle.

WORKSHEET 5.3–1   PREPARING WET MOUNTS

1. Cheek Cells:

   Return to your wet mount of cheek cells. On a sheet of drawing paper, prepare a drawing of one or two cells. Label the following structures: nucleus, cytoplasm, and cell membrane. Title the drawing with the name of the cell drawn, the stain used, and the microscope power used. (This is an example of a wet mount that is prepared in order to observe the overall structure of a cell.)

2. Potato Tissue:

   From a potato that has been cut in half, scrape a small amount of material from the exposed area, using a toothpick, and mix in a drop of water on a clean microscope slide. Stain by adding a drop of dilute iodine solution. Cover with a cover slip. Prepare a drawing and label the following structures: cytoplasm and starch grains. The starch grains will have been stained blue-black by the iodine solution. Properly title the drawing. (This is an example of a wet mount that is prepared to observe specific cell structures.)

   Note: An interesting follow-up activity that you might find enjoyable would be to prepare wet mounts of the contents of a variety of seed species—such as corn, oats, wheat, and beans—in an attempt to find out if the starch grains are similar or different for each. The seeds are soaked in water overnight, cut open, and a small amount of exposed tissue is used in a wet mount. Dilute iodine solution is used for staining.

3. Onion Tissue:

   Peel loose a small piece of a single layer of onion tissue from an onion, cut in half or quarters, that has the outer four or five layers of tissue removed. This single layer of onion tissue can best be obtained using forceps or your fingernails. Prepare a wet mount of this single layer. Stain with dilute iodine solution. Prepare a drawing and label the nucleus and the cytoplasm. Properly title the drawing. (This is an example of a wet mount that is prepared to observe the overall structure of a cell.)

4. Elodea Tissue:

   Place a small piece of the growing tip of an elodea plant in a drop of water and add a cover slip. Prepare a drawing and label the nucleus, cell wall, and chloroplasts. The small green chloroplasts can easily be seen being carried along by the cytoplasm moving (or streaming) around the border of the cell. The process of cytoplasmic moving or streaming is called cyclosis. The chloroplasts carry out the food-manufacturing process of photosynthesis. The drawing should be properly titled. (This is an example of a wet mount that is prepared to observe a specific activity going on inside a cell.)

   Attach your drawings.

WORKSHEET 5.3–2   CELL STRUCTURES:
AN AROUND-THE-SQUARE ACTIVITY

Instructions: Begin at Start and fill in the squares, moving clockwise with the answers to the following clues or questions. See the answer list below. (There is no overlapping of words.)

1. Acts as a type of transportation system for the cell
2. Structures that carry out protein synthesis
3. Controls the activities of the cell
4. Storage chamber
5. The term that means "the study of cells"
6. Packages proteins after manufacture
7. The liquidlike substance that fills the cell
8. A small sac containing digestive enzymes
9. The biceps and triceps are made of these specialized cells

Answer list: Golgi complex   nucleus
               ribosomes   endoplasmic reticulum
               lysosome   vacuole
               cytology   muscle
               cytoplasm

Start

5.4 THE METRIC SYSTEM

You Will Need the Following Materials:

meter sticks	triple-beam balance
measuring cups	graduated cylinders
1 pound weights	rulers calculated in both English and metric units

Upon Completion of This Activity, Students Will

- Have become familiar with metric units of length.
- Have become familiar with metric units of volume.
- Have become familiar with metric units of weight (mass).

1. The Students Become Familiar with Units of Measurement Used in the Metric System for Expressing Length.

Explain to the students that the system of measurement used by scientists throughout the world is the **metric system**. Although this system is initially confusing to people accustomed to the **English system** (used, for example, in the United States), it can easily be learned and is quite simple.

Pass out copies of Worksheet 5.4–1, along with the laboratory materials needed and allow the students to complete them. **The answers to the worksheet are** 1.a 12 in.; b. 30.5 cm; c. cm; d. 2.5 (30.5 ÷ 12); e. 37.5 (15 × 2.5); 2.a. 10mm; b. 120 in.; 3.a. 1,000ml; b. 39 in.; c. 3.2; d. m; 4.a. 1,600 m; 5.a. 1.6 km; b. mile. Summary: 1.a. mm; b. cm; c. m; d. km; 2.a. m; b. km; c. mm; d. cm.

2. The Students Become Familiar with Units of Measurement Used in the Metric System for Expressing Volume and Weight (Mass).

Distribute copies of Worksheet 5.4–2, along with the laboratory materials needed and allow the students to complete them. **The answers to the worksheet are** Part 1: 1.a. ml; b. 1,000; c. 1,000; 2.a. 950; b. no; c.1 L; d. 4 L; Part 2: 1.a. 454; b. 28; c. answer will vary; 2.a. 2.2; b. divide your weight by 2.2; c. 1.1.; d. 1 kg.

WORKSHEET 5.4–1 METRIC SYSTEM UNITS OF LENGTH

1. Examine a foot-long ruler that has one edge calibrated in inches and the opposite edge calibrated in metric system units of **centimeters (cm)**.

   a. How many inches long is the ruler? _____

   b. How many centimeters (numbered along the edge of the ruler) long is the ruler? _____

   c. Which is the shorter unit of length measurement, the inch or the centimeter? _____

   d. How many centimeters are there in 1 inch? _____

   e. How many centimeters are there in 15 inches? _____

2. Examine more closely the centimeter edge of the ruler. The shorter lines that are found between the longer centimeter lines are **millimeter (mm)** lines.

   a. How many millimeters are there in 1 centimeter? _____

   b. How many millimeters are there in 12 centimeters? _____

3. Examine a **meter** stick.

   a. How many millimeters long is the meter stick? _____

   b. How many inches is equivalent to a meter? _____

   c. How many feet are equal to a meter? _____

   d. Which is longer, 1 meter or 1 yard? _____

4. There are 5,280 feet in a mile. How many meters are there in a mile? _____

5. One thousand meters are equal to 1 **kilometer (kl)**.

   a. How many kilometers are there in 1 mile? _____

   b. Which is longer, 1 kilometer or 1 mile? _____

Summary: Based on information provided and gathered in numbers 1 to 5 above, complete the following:

1. List in order from smallest to largest the metric system units of length studied:

   a. _____

   b. _____

   c. _____

   d. _____

2. Which of the metric system units of length studied would be most appropriate to use when:

   a. measuring the distance from the front to the back of your classroom? _____

   b. measuring the distance between two towns several miles apart? _____

   c. measuring the diameter of the head of a common pin? _____

   d. measuring the width of a textbook? _____

WORKSHEET 5.4–2
METRIC SYSTEM UNITS OF VOLUME AND WEIGHT (MASS)

Part 1: Volume

1. In the English system of measurement, the term *quart* is used. In the metric system, the closest equivalent is the **liter (L)**. Obtain a 1-liter capacity graduated cylinder. Examine the graduated scale printed on it.

   a. The graduated cylinder is marked off (graduated) in units called **milliliters**. The initials for these units will be found toward the top of the cylinder. What are the initials? _____

   b. What is the capacity of the graduated cylinder in milliliters? _____

   c. How many milliliters are there in 1 liter? _____

2. Using a measuring cup, pour 1 quart (4 cups) of water into the graduated cylinder.

   a. The quart of liquid is how many milliliters? _____

   b. Is 1 quart equal to 1 liter? _____

   c. Which contains more liquid, 1 quart or 1 liter? _____

   d. Which contains more gasoline, 1 gallon (4 quarts) or 4 liters? _____

Part 2: Weight (Mass)

1. Weigh a 1-pound weight on the triple-beam balance.

   a. One pound equals how many **grams (g)**? _____

   b. How many grams are there in 1 ounce? _____

   c. How many grams does your pencil or pen weigh? _____

2. One unit of weight in the English system is the pound. The closest equivalent in the metric system is the **kilogram (kg): 1,000 grams equal 1 kilogram**.

   a. One kilogram equals how many pounds? _____

   b. How would you calculate your own weight in kilograms? _____

   c. If you purchased ½ kilogram of cookies, how many pounds would you have?

   _____

   d. Which is heavier, 1 pound or 1 kilogram? _____

5.5 USING SOME COMMON PIECES OF LABORATORY EQUIPMENT

You Will Need the Following Materials:

triple-beam balances   Bunsen burners
item(s) to weigh   graduated cylinders (10ml)
pipettes with rubber bulbs   colored pencils
beaker   screen or shield

Upon Completion of This Activity, Students Will

- Know the proper steps to follow when using the triple-beam balance.
- Know the proper way of igniting the Bunsen burner and obtaining a desirable flame.
- Learn how to accurately read a graduated cylinder.
- Learn how to accurately transfer specific volumes of liquids using the pipette.

1. The Students Test Their Skills at Using the Triple-Beam Balance.

Make certain that the laboratory balance is balanced at zero grams and that the sliding weight riders are in their zero positions.

Determine the weight of the item that is going to be weighed by the students.

Place the balance behind a screen or shield so each student can work unobserved by the rest of the class. Prior to each student's weighing of the item, return the sliding weight riders to their zero positions.

Give each student an opportunity to weigh the item. As each student completes the weighing, he/she is to come to you and write the answer on a sheet of paper (assuring that no one else is aware of the answer). Note which students did not get the correct answer. (This will allow for individual remedial help.)

At the conclusion of the weighing activity, write the actual weight of the item as well as the weights determined by the students on the chalkboard. Calculate the percentage of students that made an error in weight determination.

2. The Students Learn the Proper Steps in Using the Triple-Beam Balance.

Generate classroom discussion and obtain some ideas as to what types of errors might have been made by the students when using the balance. At the conclusion of the discussion, give the students the following notes regarding the steps that should be followed when using the triple-beam balance:

a. Make certain that the three sliding weight riders are in their zero positions.

b. Always make certain that the triple-beam balance is balanced to zero prior to use. This is done by turning a small knob located beneath the pan of the balance. The knob is adjusted until the pointer of the balance indicates zero. (*Note:* Often a small piece of paper is placed on the pan prior to weighing out, for example, a powdered chemical. The balance must be balanced out to zero prior to placing the powder on the paper. If this is not done, the final weight will include that of the paper. **The students should be made aware that this balancing procedure is often overlooked.**)

c. Place the material to be weighed on the center of the pan (weighing surface).

d. Determine the weight by properly positioning the sliding weight riders on the three beams of the balance. The front beam is graduated from 0 to 10 grams. The middle beam is graduated into divisions of 100 grams each up to 500 grams. The back beam is graduated into divisions of 10 grams each up to 100 grams.

e. Take an accurate reading of the weight. This is done by simply adding together the weights of the three beams.

3. The Students Have Additional Practice at Using the Triple-Beam Balance.

If several of the students have made errors in weight determination, you might wish to have them participate in this additional activity. Set out several items—such as a pencil, paper clip, small beaker filled with sand, and so on. Let each student weigh these same items. Upon completion, the items can be listed on the chalkboard along with their accurate weights and each student's weight determination.

4. The Students Learn the Proper Way to Use a Bunsen Burner.

Distribute copies of Worksheet 5.5–1 and colored pencils to the students. As they are filling them in with the following notes, also demonstrate using an actual Bunsen burner.

a. If using a match, always light the match prior to turning on the gas. **(SAFETY CAUTION: If you turn on the gas first, fumes build up while you light the match. The gas can then ignite in a potentially dangerous burst of flame.)**

b. Check the color of the flame. **(SAFETY CAUTION: On occasion, such as when the room is brightly lighted, it is difficult to determine whether or not the Bunsen burner ignited. NEVER LEAN OVER THE BUNSEN BURNER OR POSITION YOUR FACE CLOSE TO IT TO HAVE A CLOSER LOOK. If you are not certain whether or**

not the Bunsen burner is ignited, check with your teacher. Its color should be blue, not yellow. (Refer the students to their worksheet illustration of the Bunsen burner and have them color the flame blue.)

c. If the flame is yellow, adjust the **collar** of the Bunsen burner by turning it until the desired blue flame is achieved. (Have the students color the collar red.)

d. The height of the flame is controlled by turning the **wheel** located at the base of the Bunsen burner. (Have the students color the wheel green.) The height of the flame above the **barrel** is usually kept at 5 or 6 centimeters. (Have the students color the barrel brown.)

e. Never leave a lighted Bunsen burner unattended.

f. When you are finished using the Bunsen burner, make certain that you turn off the gas jet outlet completely.

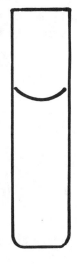

5. The Students Learn How to Properly Read a Graduated Cylinder.

Fill a 500ml graduated cylinder to a predetermined level—for example, 347ml. Have several students individually determine the volume of water in the cylinder and then write their answers on pieces of paper. You might be surprised at the range of answers.

Draw the illustration at the right on the chalkboard and explain to the students that the volume of liquid in a graduated cylinder is determined by reading the low central portion of the **meniscus (curved surface of the liquid).**

6. The Students Learn How to Accurately Transfer Specific Volumes of Liquid Using the Pipette.

Explain to the students that the pipette is used when extreme accuracy is required in measuring out and/or transferring specific volumes of liquid.

Set out a beaker of water, a 10ml graduated cylinder, and a 1/10 (graduated into 10ml) pipette fitted with a rubber bulb. (**SAFETY CAUTION: The mouth should never be used in drawing in or expelling out fluids from the pipette. Instead, use a rubber bulb.**) Have a student volunteer use the pipette in transferring 10ml of water from the beaker to the 10ml graduated cylinder. Upon reading the graduated cylinder at the completion of the task, it is highly probable that more than 10ml of water will have been transferred. You might wish to engage the students in a discussion to determine what error might have been made in making the transfer. Eventually, draw the following illustration on the chalkboard and explain the proper steps to use:

a. Using the rubber bulb and holding the pipette vertically, draw the water into the pipette until it is above the 0 gradation line.

b. Slowly expel excess water back into the beaker until its level in the pipette is exactly at the 0 gradation line.

c. Slowly expel the water into the graduated cylinder until the level of the water in the pipette reaches the gradation line immediately below 10. **Error occurs when liquid below the 10 gradation line is also expelled.**

d. Safely dispose of the remaining liquid. (In this case, it is water, but under other circumstances it might be a potentially dangerous liquid.)

Finally, give the students pipettes with rubber bulbs, beakers, and graduated cylinders, and allow them to practice measuring out and transferring specific amounts of water.

7. The Students Learn the Names and Functions of Various Pieces of Classroom Equipment. (Students will need to use the library or classroom resource material)

Distribute copies of Worksheet 5.5–2 for the students to work on. **The answers to the crossword activity are Across:** 1. Dial-O-Gram; 3. autoclave; 4. Erlenmeyer; 5. spectroscope; 7. prism; 9. magnetic; 10. spatula; 12. mortar and pestle; 13. photometer; **Down:** 2. manometer; 6. pH meter; 8. ammeter; 10. spirometer; 11. test tube.

Name _____   Date _____

WORKSHEET 5.5–1   USING THE BUNSEN BURNER

Instructions: As your teacher explains and demonstrates the steps to follow in using the Bunsen burner, record notes on this worksheet.

a. _____

_____

_____

_____

_____

SAFETY CAUTION: If you turn on the gas first, fumes will build up while you light the match. The gas might then ignite in a potentially dangerous burst of flame.

b. _____

_____

_____

_____

_____

SAFETY CAUTION: On occasion, such as when the room is brightly lighted, you may find it difficult to determine whether the Bunsen burner is ignited. NEVER LEAN OVER THE BUNSEN BURNER OR POSITION YOUR FACE CLOSE TO IT to have a closer look. If you are not certain whether the Bunsen burner is ignited, check with your teacher.

c. _____

_____

_____

d. _____

_____

e. _____

_____

f. _____

_____

Flame

Barrel

Collar

Wheel

Bunsen Burner

219

WORKSHEET 5.5–2   LABORATORY EQUIPMENT CROSSWORD

Instructions: Fill in the
crossword with the answers
to the clues provided below:

Across: 1. A type of weighing scale that has a dial
            that is turned until the scale is balanced
         3. Used to sterilize lab materials
         4. A type of flask
         5. An instrument used to examine the optical spectrum
         7. Breaks white light up into its component colors
         9. A type of automatic stirrer
        10. Used for scooping small amounts of materials
        12. Used to pulverize materials
        13. Measures light intensity

Down: 2. Measures small amounts of gas
             involved in biological reactions
         6. Used to measure acidity and alkalinity
         8. Used to measure electric current
        10. Measures volume of air inhaled and exhaled
        11. A lipped glass tube open at one end

Unit 6
Designing Methods of Research

6.1 THE HYPOTHESIS, POPULATION, AND RANDOM SAMPLE

You Will Need the Following Materials:

> lollipops of several different colors, including red, enough of each
> color for all students
> paper and pencil

Upon Completion of This Activity, Students Will

- Be able to define the term *subject.*
- Understand the importance of a random sample and how to obtain one.
- Be able to define the term *hypothesis* and prepare one using the proper format.
- Be able to explain what is meant by the population of an investigation.
- Have participated in an investigation designed to test a specific hypothesis.

1. The Students Begin by Responding to a Specific Question Posed to Them.

Inform the students that you are going to ask them to write down something and that they must respond as rapidly as possible with the first thing that comes to their mind. When ready, ask the students to write down the first color that comes to their mind.

Determine the class responses, along with the frequency of each response, and have the students record them in their notes. Red is usually the color reported with the highest frequency. (Should it be another color, then have the students substitute that color for red when they receive Worksheet 6.1–1 later on. Also, make the substitution in the hypothesis below.)

2. The Students Participate in a Classroom Investigation.

You are going to carry out a classroom investigation testing the hypothesis: If each student in a group is offered a choice of lollipops of different colors, then more students will select red than any other color. The students must be kept unaware that this particular hypothesis is being investigated. You should tell them that the investigation involves "sense of direction." Thus, you will have the students involved in collecting one set of data while you will be collecting the pertinent set of data.

Tell the students that they are going to participate in a "sense of direction" activity.

One by one, have the students come to the front of the room. The student faces the front of the room and closes his/her eyes. You turn the student around once or twice clockwise and then counterclockwise. Stop the student facing either the front, back, right, or left of the classroom.

Ask the student to indicate the direction he/she is facing and have the rest of the class keep data on response accuracy.

Prior to this activity you should arrange on a plate a selection of lollipops of several different colors, including red (or the color that was most frequently reported in #1 above). Have the different colors "casually" arranged in separate groups on the plate. Have the plate set casually out of sight, perhaps behind a set of texts. Giving the impression of sort of an afterthought, tell the students that you have some lollipops left over from a previous class and for lack of anything better to do with them, they might as well be used for rewards for participation in this activity. Thus, as each student completes participation, have the student select a lollipop.

At the conclusion of the activity, let the students in on the pertinent data that was actually being collected. Also, explain to them why they had to be unaware of this during the activity.

Count the number of remaining lollipops of each color to determine choice frequency by the students and give that information to the class.

3. The Students Learn About the Design of Hypotheses and Investigations.

Distribute copies of Worksheet 6.1–1 to the students and have them study it and respond to the questions.

Answers to worksheet questions are 4. Flavor associated with a particular color. 5. Regardless of the color of the M & M™, the chocolate flavor is the same.

4. The Students Are Evaluated on Their Learning.

Pass out copies of Worksheet 6.1–2 to the class and use it as a self-test or perhaps a quiz.

Name _____ Date _____

WORKSHEET 6.1–1
THE HYPOTHESIS, POPULATION, AND RANDOM SAMPLE

It is interesting that when a group of people are asked to quickly name the first color that comes to their mind, the color reported with the greatest frequency is red. You have already tried this in your class. Let's assume that this leads you to an idea that red might be a popular choice of candy color. You have just begun to form a **hypothesis**. A hypothesis is often referred to as **an idea that can be tested**. Further, it is often developed into an **if-then statement** that can be tested. You might continue to develop the idea as follows: If a group of people are offered a choice of lollipops of different colors, **then** more people will select red than any other color of lollipop. Now you have a developed hypothesis; that is, AN IF-THEN STATEMENT OR IDEA THAT CAN BE TESTED.

If you decide to test your hypothesis, you will have to determine who is to be tested. Individuals who are actually tested in a research situation are called **subjects**. If there are 25 students in your class and you want to test them all, then you have 25 subjects. The **population** is the total number of potential subjects that could participate in the research. If your research is limited only to your class, then the class is referred to as the population.

Now with only 25 subjects in your total population, it will be a simple matter to test the entire population. However, there are situations in which the population you want to test is so large that it would be impossible to test every one of the potential subjects. In this case, you would want to select only a portion of the population to test. This portion of the population is called a sample. However, you would want to go one step further and make certain that the sample is a **random sample**. For a sample to be random, each potential subject from the population has to have an equal chance of being selected. Let us say that instead of 25 in your class, the population is 125. To obtain a random sample of 25 you must use a technique of selection that assures each student (subject) an equal chance of being selected.

One technique of selecting the random sample is to write each student's name on a tag. The 125 tags would then be placed in a container and thoroughly mixed. A blindfolded person would then pick one of the tags from the container, and the name would be recorded. The chance of that name having been selected from the container is 1 in 125. Remember this important point: For the next name to be selected with an equal 1 in 125 chance, the previous tag must be placed back in the container and the contents again mixed. This procedure must be followed until 25 subjects have been selected from the population.

1. Define the following terms:

   a. subject _____

   _____

   _____

   b. population _____

   _____

   c. random sample _____

   _____

   _____

d. hypothesis _____

_____

2. a. What color did your class select with the greatest frequency when asked to write down the name of a color? _____

   b. List at least three ideas why you think that color is so popular.

   a. _____

   b. _____

   c. _____

3. a. What color lollipop was most frequently selected in your class? _____

   b. Was the lollipop color and the color named in 2a above the same? _____ If not, provide some ideas that might help explain why not:

   _____

   _____

   _____

   _____

4. What factor(s) other than color might be involved in choosing lollipops?

_____

_____

_____

_____

5. What might be an advantage in using M & M™ type candies in testing color preference?

_____

_____

_____

_____

6. Develop a hypothesis, using the if-then format to test an idea that people might like chunky peanut butter more than the smooth kind.

_____

_____

_____

_____

_____

_____

WORKSHEET 6.1–2   EVALUATION EXERCISE

Instructions: Read the following material and then answer the questions.

    Let's assume that you are interested in investigating an idea that you have that the majority of students who participate in the high school weight-training program are nonsmokers. You find out that there are 375 participants in the program. You end up selecting 50 of them to actually participate in your investigation.

1. What is the format often used in developing a hypothesis? _____

   _____

2. Using the above format, state the hypothesis that you would be investigating regarding the weight-training participants: _____

   _____

   _____

3. a. Define the term *population:* _____

   _____

   b. How many students are in your population? _____

4. a. Define the term *subject:* _____

   _____

   b. How many subjects did you have in the investigation? _____

5. a. Define the term *random sample:* _____

   _____

   b. Under what conditions does one use a random sample? _____

   _____

   c. Explain, step by step, how you would go about obtaining your random sample. _____

   _____

   _____

   _____

   _____

   _____

   _____

   _____

   _____

   _____

6.2 THE SURVEY

You Will Need the Following Materials:

Ditto™ masters for students to use in preparing the final copies of their surveys (or you might wish to use other means for preparing class quantities of the students' surveys)

Upon Completion of This Activity, Students Will

- Be able to describe the survey type of investigation.
- Know seven important factors in developing and carrying out survey investigations.
- Know what to be concerned about when deciding upon the population to be surveyed.
- Know the most important characteristic of a good survey question.
- Understand the concept of test validity.
- Have designed and carried out survey investigations.

1. The Students Are Provided with Some Background Information About the Survey Technique of Investigation.

Have the students take notes as you give them the following background information.

Inform the students that the survey is a widely used technique for gathering data relevant to a particular question. The best surveys are based on very specific questions. If the survey results accurately answer the questions posed, then the survey is said to be **valid**. Many surveys are really not valid because they ask the subjects **ambiguous** and/or **biased** questions. An example of an ambiguous survey question is, "Where do you watch television from the most?" The words "where" and "from" are confusing. From rooms in the home? From specific chairs or sofas? From your own home as opposed to a friend's home? An unambiguous question would be: "When watching television, in what room of your home do you do most of your viewing?"

An example of a biased survey question is, "Which one of the following choices best expresses your feeling toward our candidate? a. very positive, b. a combination of positive and negative." This survey question does not provide a choice of "very negative." It tends to influence the subject who might have a "very negative" feeling to choose "b" because that comes closest to expressing his/her feeling.

The students have probably participated in many academic surveys. For example, standardized national achievement tests are administered to survey student achievement for a variety of subjects. Tests that you give in class are, in fact, surveys used to determine how much information the students have learned.

Politicians sometimes send surveys to their constituents or do telephone surveys in an attempt to obtain a "political pulse" on a specific problem.

2. The Students Learn the Essentials of Preparing Survey Investigations.

Distribute copies of Worksheet 6.2–1. Instruct the students to study the material and answer the questions.

3. The Students Experience Designing Their Own Survey Investigations.

Inform the students that eventually they are going to carry out their surveys.

Work with the students individually when they reach that part of their worksheet that deals with the survey design. For example, they will probably need help designing their data tables and with the wording of their survey questions.

4. The Students Receive Copies of Each Other's Surveys.

Provide the students with Ditto™ masters on which to prepare the final drafts of their surveys. Make class-quantity copies and distribute them to the students. Discuss selected surveys with the class, emphasizing the proper wording of questions and also data table design.

5. The Students Conduct Their Own Surveys.

Allow the students to administer their surveys. Allow each student to share findings with the rest of the class, at which time each student can fill in the data tables on his/her copy of the survey.

Generate class discussion on survey findings.

6. The Students Are Evaluated on Their Learning.

Distribute copies of Worksheet 6.2–2 and allow the students to complete them.

WORKSHEET 6.2–1   THE SURVEY

The **survey** is a type of investigation in which a questionnaire is prepared and then administered to subjects for their responses. Surveys are widely employed and cover a broad range of topics. These topics can range from political surveys to health surveys to environmental surveys to TV viewing surveys, to name just a few.

The following factors are important in developing and carrying out survey investigations.

1. The Purpose for the Survey: Is the purpose to collect specific information from a specific group? Are you interested in investigating a particular hypothesis? An example of a purpose might be to determine weekend television viewing habits of different groups of high school students.

2. The Title of the Survey: Exactly what type of information do you wish to obtain? Be as specific as possible as you narrow down a title. An example of a title might be comparing biology students with physics students in terms of the specific weekend television programs watched on a regular basis.

3. The Description of the Population You Want to Survey: Is there a specific age group that you want to survey? Will it involve both sexes or just one? Will it deal with the general population or a more specialized segment of the population? Will you be administering the survey to each subject in the population, or will you have to obtain and administer it to a random sample?

4. The Preparation of the Data Table: Designing a data table prior to preparing the survey questions can be an advantage. It can help you in two ways: (1) Having a data table designed and ready for your future data will allow you to focus in on the type of data you wish to obtain from the survey, and (2) it makes designing the survey questions easier.

5. The Survey Questions: Be very specific in wording each question. Make each question simple and to the point. A good survey question should not be biased or open to several different interpretations. A good survey question does not have the subject asking, "I wonder what type of information is being asked for?"

6. The Administering of the Survey: Under what conditions will the survey be administered to the subjects? Will it be a telephone survey? Will it be conducted through the mail? Will it be a personal one-on-one survey or perhaps be administered to a group in a room?

7. The Presentation of Findings: Your findings are then summarized and supported by the data recorded in your data table.

1. What is a survey? _____

_____

2. What must you keep in mind when deciding upon the title for a survey? _____

_____

_____

3. List at least three concerns when deciding upon the population to be surveyed.

    a. _____

    b. _____

    c. _____

4. What is an important characteristic of a good survey question? _____

_____

5. In what two ways does designing the data table prior to preparing the survey questions help you?

    a. _____

    b. _____

      You are now going to design a survey investigation of your own. Keep in mind the important factors to consider as you do so. Use the following format:

Purpose for the Survey: _____

_____

Title of the Survey: _____

_____

The Population Description (list as many descriptive factors as you can): _____

_____

_____

The Data Table Design (design the data table to allow you to organize your findings in a meaningful format). Draw your data table design on a separate piece of paper.

      The Survey Questions (prepare at least ten questions that are clearly worded and ask for specific information):

  1. _____

  2. _____

  3. _____

  4. _____

  5. _____

  6. _____

  7. _____

  8. _____

  9. _____

10. _____

Administering the Survey (explain how you plan to conduct the survey): _____

_____

_____

Presentation of Results (present your findings, supporting them with data from your data table):

_____

_____

_____

WORKSHEET 6.2–2   EVALUATION EXERCISE

Instructions: Answer each question after reading it carefully.

1. What is a **survey?** _____

_____

2. Under what conditions is a survey **valid?** _____

_____

3. What two types of questions make a survey invalid?

    a. _____

    b. _____

4. What is an important characteristic of a good survey question? _____

_____

5. What must you keep in mind when deciding upon the title for a survey? ___

_____

6. How is the title of a survey best expressed? _____

_____

7. Give at least three specific examples as you explain what is meant by **the population**

    description. _____

_____

_____

_____

_____

_____

8. Designing the data table prior to preparing the survey questions may be an advantage in what two ways?

    a. _____

    b. _____

9. Give one example of a type of survey one might receive through the mail. ____

_____

© 1992 by The Center for Applied Research in Education

6.3 THE FIELD RESEARCH

You Will Need the Following Materials:

Ditto™ masters for students to use in preparing final copies of their field research investigations (or you might wish to use other means for preparing class quantities of their investigations)

Upon Completion of This Activity, Students Will

- Be able to describe the field research type of investigation.
- Know six important factors to keep in mind in developing and carrying out the field research.
- Know two roles of the investigator in carrying out field research.
- Know what is meant by "manipulating the environment."
- Know what is meant by "a real-life setting."

1. The Students Are Provided with Some Background Information About the Field Research Type of Investigation.

Have the students take notes as you give them the following background information:

It is often necessary for the researcher to go out into the real-life environment or, in research terms, **out into the field** in order to collect data. Not to be confused with naturalistic observations, which also are conducted in the field, field research differs in the following way: In field research, the investigator alters a part of the environment. This will be further explored by the students when they develop their own field research investigations.

2. The Students Learn the Essentials of Preparing Field Research.

Distribute copies of Worksheet 6.3–1. Instruct the students to study the material and answer the questions.

3. The Students Experience Designing Their Own Field Research Investigations.

Work with the students individually, especially when they reach the point of developing data tables, determining the real-life settings, and explaining how the environment is going to be manipulated.

4. *The Students Receive Copies of Each Other's Field Researches.*

Provide the students with Ditto™ masters on which to put the final drafts of their field researches. Make class-quantity copies and distribute them. Discuss selected papers with the students in terms of overall design.

5. *The Students Carry Out Their Own Field Research Investigations.*

Whenever practical, allow the students to carry out their field researches and share the findings with the rest of the class, at which time each student can fill in the data tables on his/her copy of the field research investigation.

Engage the class in a discussion of research findings.

WORKSHEET 6.3–1   FIELD RESEARCH

Field Research is an investigation carried out by observing people in real-life situations (as opposed to a laboratory setting). In field research, the investigator manipulates or changes something in the real-life environment. The subject(s), of course, is not aware that his/her behavior is being observed.

Assume that bars of a particular brand of soap are, for some reason, not selling as well as might be expected. Someone suggests that a bright-gold wrapper to replace the current dark-green one might increase sales. Field research is therefore designed whereby the consumer will have a choice of two wrapper colors to choose between: the original dark green and the new bright gold. The soaps will be placed in separate bins, side by side. Data is eventually obtained comparing the relative sales of each soap. This is field research because the consumer's environment has been manipulated by deliberately presenting the same soap in two different wrapper colors. The consumer, of course, is unaware that his/her purchasing choice constitutes data for a research project.

The television program *Candid Camera* is an excellent example of the use of the field research technique. The environment is always manipulated—from talking mailboxes to faulty salt shakers—and unknown to the subjects, their behavior is observed by hidden cameras.

When designing field research, keep in mind the following important factors (a few of which have been previously explained):

1. The Purpose (See Activity 6.2.)
2. The Title (See Activity 6.2.)
3. The Preparation of the Data Table (See Activity 6.2.)
4. The Real-Life Setting: This is a complete description of the real-life setting in which the field research is going to take place.
5. The Manipulation of the Environment: This is a specific explanation of how you are going to manipulate or change a part of the real-life setting in which you are conducting field research.
6. The Presentation of Findings.

1. What are two roles of the investigator in carrying out *field research*?

   a. _____

   b. _____

2. What is meant by "manipulating the environment"? _____

   _____

3. What is meant by "a real-life setting"? _____

   _____

You are now going to design your own field research. Use the following format:

The Purpose: _____

_____

The Title: _____

The Data Table (Use a separate sheet of paper.): _____

The Real-Life Setting: _____

_____

_____

The Manipulation of the Environment: _____

_____

_____

The Presentation of Results: _____

_____

_____

_____

_____

_____

_____

_____

_____

_____

_____

_____

_____

_____

_____

_____

6.4 THE NATURALISTIC OBSERVATION

You Will Need the Following Materials:

Ditto™ masters for students to use in preparing final copies of their naturalistic observation investigations (or you might wish to use other means for preparing class quantities of the investigations)

Upon Completion of This Activity, Students Will

- Be able to describe the naturalistic observation type of investigation.
- Know the basic difference between a naturalistic observation and field research.
- Have designed and carried out a naturalistic observation.

1. The Students Are Provided With Some Background Information About the Naturalistic Observation Type of Investigation.

Have the students take notes as you give them the following background information:

The naturalistic observation is a direct way in which to obtain data because you are observing first hand the behavior of humans and animals as they interact with their environment. A type of research scientist that specializes in observing animal behavior is an **ethologist**.

A naturalistic observation might be as complex as studying social interactions among groups of specific animals or as simple as observing the number of food items in shopping carts going through the ten-item-or-less line at your local supermarket.

2. The Students Learn the Essentials of Preparing Naturalistic Observation Investigations.

Pass out copies of Worksheet 6.4–1 to the students. Have the students study the material and answer the questions.

3. The Students Experience Designing Their Own Naturalistic Observation Investigations.

Inform the students that eventually they are going to carry out their own naturalistic observations.

Work individually with the students as they design naturalistic observation investigations. They will probably need help with hypothesis development and data table design.

4. *The Students Receive Copies of Each Other's Naturalistic Observation Investigations.*

Provide the students with Ditto™ masters on which to put the final draft of their investigations. Make class-quantity copies and distribute them. Discuss selected investigations with the students.

5. *The Students Carry Out Their Own Naturalistic Observation Investigations.*

Allow the students to carry out their investigations. Finally, let them share their findings with the rest of the class, at which time the students can fill in the data tables on their copies of the investigation.

WORKSHEET 6.4-1   THE NATURALISTIC OBSERVATION

The naturalistic observation is similar to field research in that it involves observing people in real-life situations. But it differs from field research in one important way: The investigator **does not manipulate the environment in any way.**

The following description is an example of a naturalistic observation: In a food market, the laundry detergent section has various brands of detergents from the top shelf to the bottom shelf. The bottom shelf often requires that a customer bend way down to pick up the package of detergent. Suppose you have an idea that detergents on the bottom shelf have the least chance of being selected over those on any other shelf. You then decide to spend a few afternoons observing customers selecting detergents. This is a naturalistic observation because your subjects are being observed in a real-life situation and you did nothing to manipulate or change the environment in any way. As with field research, your subjects should not be aware that they are being observed.

1. In what important way does a naturalistic observation differ from field research?

   _____

   _____

2. Think of at least three examples of a naturalistic observation:

   a. _____

   b. _____

   c. _____

3. Develop an if-then hypothesis (see Activity 6.1) for the naturalistic observation described in your reading.

   _____

   _____

   _____

   _____

You are now going to design your own naturalistic observation. (Use the format descriptions that are presented in the worksheets that accompany Activities 6.1, 6.2, and 6.3.)

The Purpose: _____

   _____

The Title: _____

The Hypothesis to Be Investigated: _____

   _____

   _____

   _____

   _____

The Data Table:

The Real-Life Setting: _____
_____
_____
_____

Presentation of Findings: _____
_____
_____
_____
_____
_____
_____
_____
_____
_____
_____
_____

6.5 THE CORRELATION INVESTIGATION

You Will Need the Following Materials:

paper and pencils

Upon Completion of This Activity, Students Will

- Be able to describe the correlation-type investigation.
- Understand why it is difficult to conclude with certainty that a particular correlation does or does not exist between two sets of data.
- Have had experience in designing and carrying out a simple correlation investigation.

1. The Students Learn Some Essential Information Relating to the Correlation Investigation.

Distribute copies of Worksheet 6.5–1. Have the students study the material and answer the questions. After they have finished, give them the following supplemental notes regarding correlation investigations:

When many people think of correlation, they think of a direct cause-and-effect relationship; for example, that there is a correlation between eating salty foods and becoming thirsty. It so happens that it is also a cause-and-effect situation. Eating salty foods does cause the effect of being thirsty. However, a correlation can exist without a direct cause-and-effect relationship. For example, more people die in bed than in any other place. There is a correlation between the bed and dying, but is it a direct cause-and-effect relationship? Obviously not, since a bed does not cause death. The cause is disease and illness, during the final stages of which the patient is often bedridden.

2. The Students Discuss Some Examples of Correlation Investigations.

Prepare a list on the chalkboard of the various student responses to question 2 on the worksheet. The following are several examples. Is there a correlation between: numbers of days absent from school and marking period grades; numbers of hours of studying per week for a particular subject and the marking period grade for that subject; participation in weight training and smoking cigarettes; sitting in the back seat of the school bus and sitting in the back seat of classes; watching television and academic grades; behavior and seating position in the classroom?

3. *The Students Design and Carry Out a Correlation Activity.*

Pass out copies of Worksheet 6.5–2. Work together with the class as a unit in designing a correlation activity. The task will be to design a questionnaire to provide data that might suggest whether there is a correlation between student's seat choices on a school bus and seat choices in classrooms.

The following information, which correlates with Worksheet 6.5–2, should be used as a guideline in working with the students: (***Note:*** Upon completion of #7 on the worksheet, have some students volunteer to prepare the questionnaire in a final format for presentation to the subjects. A title for the top of the questionnaire sheet might be, Some Questions Regarding School. A few simple instructions should be added, asking the subjects to answer the questions as accurately as they can. After all questionnaires have been administered to subjects, proceed with #8 on the worksheet.) Worksheet answers:

1. **Correlation investigation question:** Is there a correlation between student's seat choices on a school bus and seat choices in classrooms?

2. **Number of student subjects participating:** Answer will vary.

3. **A major concern of this investigation:** That the students remain unaware of the real question being investigated. Therefore, the questionnaire will be designed to suggest that student health might be the major concern of the investigation.

4. **Drawing of the seating chart of a school bus:** Work with the students as they draw up a simple floor plan of the arrangement of seats.

5. **The 15 questions of the questionnaire:** Some of the key questions have already been included in the worksheet. The task is to design the remaining questions appropriately so that the subjects will think that health is the general concern of the questionnaire.

6. **An ideal way to administer the questionnaire:** A one-on-one format is excellent. Students who might not otherwise take the investigation seriously will be more apt to do so when they are filling out the questionnaire alone.

7. **The key questions that will be used in data analysis:** Questions b and h.

8. **Data analysis:** Help the students organize the data for analysis.

9. **Does a correlation seem to exist?** Answer to be determined.

WORKSHEET 6.5-1   THE CORRELATION INVESTIGATION

The **correlation investigation** is carried out to determine the relationship between two different sets of data.

   Today, a great deal of research is being conducted to determine correlations, or relationships, between diets and blood serum cholesterol levels, or between blood serum cholesterol levels and heart attacks. To be more specific, correlation investigations are being done to determine the relationship between a diet low in cholesterol and saturated fats and blood serum cholesterol level. Other correlation investigations are dealing with a possible relationship between Omega-3 fish oils in the diet and blood serum cholesterol level.

   It is important to realize that once a relationship is suggested by a correlation investigation, it cannot be considered conclusive that the relationship exists solely between the two sets of data compared. There exist other possibilities due to other variables or influences. For example, when comparing diet and blood serum cholesterol levels, one might find a positive correlation. However, it is possible that people who watch their diets are more apt to have exercise programs. Perhaps it is the exercise that is lowering the cholesterol levels. Or is it possible that both diet and exercise are involved in lower cholesterol levels?

1. What is the purpose of a correlation investigation? _____

   _____

2. List four possible correlation investigations other than those mentioned in your reading.

   a. _____

   b. _____

   c. _____

   d. _____

3. Discuss why it is difficult to conclude with certainty that a particular type of correlation does indeed exist between two sets of data.

   _____

   _____

   _____

   _____

   _____

   _____

   _____

   _____

   _____

   _____

WORKSHEET 6.5–2
DESIGNING A CORRELATION INVESTIGATION

1. Correlation investigation question: _____

   _____

2. Number of student subjects participating: _____

3. A major concern of this investigation: _____

   _____

4. Drawing of the seating chart of a school bus:

5. The 15 questions of the questionnaire:

   a. Are you aware of any hearing problems that you might have?

   b. On the attached diagram, please put an X in the seat you most prefer to sit in when riding to and from school on the school bus.

   c. _____

   d. _____

   e. _____

   f. _____

   g. Do you have any vision problems that you are aware of? _____

   _____

h. In the following space, please list the classes that you attend during the school day, during which you can sit wherever you want. Also note your seating location by putting a #1 if you sit toward the front of the classroom, a #2 if you sit toward the middle, and a #3 if you sit toward the back.

Name of Class	Seating Location	Name of Class	Seating Location
_____	_____	_____	_____
_____	_____	_____	_____
_____	_____	_____	_____
_____	_____	_____	_____
_____	_____	_____	_____
_____	_____	_____	_____
_____	_____	_____	_____

i. Do you follow a weekly exercise program? _____

j. _____

k. _____

l. _____

m. _____

n. _____

o. _____

6. An ideal way to administer the questionnaire: _____

_____

_____

7. The key questions that will be used in data analysis: _____

_____

_____

8. Data analysis: _____

_____

_____

_____

9. Does a correlation seem to exist? _____

_____

6.6 THE EXPERIMENTAL METHOD OF RESEARCH

You Will Need the Following Materials:

> screen or shield
> 3″ × 5″ cards
> paper and pencil
> hand calculators (optional)

Upon Completion of This Activity, Students Will

- Know what an experimental group is and will be able to identify it in a description of an investigation.
- Know what a control group is and will be able to identify it in a description of an investigation.
- Be able to differentiate between the independent and the dependent variables of an investigation.
- Realize the importance of controlling experimental variables in an investigation.

1. The Students Learn Some Background Information About ESP.

Explain to the students that ESP stands for extrasensory perception. There are several categories of ESP that are being researched. One type that will be investigated here is **clairvoyance.** Clairvoyance can be defined as an ability to perceive an object without using any of the known senses.

2. The Students Help Prepare Materials Needed for an Investigation of Clairvoyance.

You are going to need 11 decks of 3 inch by 5 inch ESP cards. You can prepare one deck and have ten students each prepare an additional deck. Each deck is prepared as follows: write the number 1 on five cards and repeat in like manner for numbers 2 through 5.

At the front of the room, set up a screen or shield. It will be used to prevent your deck of cards from being seen by the students during the investigation.

3. The Students Learn About Experimental and Control Groups, Which Are Used When Developing an Experimental Method of Research.

Inform the students that the procedure that is going to be used in investigating clairvoyance will be designed as an **experimental method of research.** One characteristic of the experimental method is that it involves two distinct groups of subjects. They are an **experimental group** of subjects and a **control group** of subjects. Ten students (number will vary according to your class size) will participate in each group.

The experimental group is the group that is going to be subjected to the experimental treatment; that is, they will be tested for evidence of clairvoyance.

The control group is a group that will not be subjected to the experimental treatment.

4. The Students Participate in an Investigation of Clairvoyance.

Have ten students volunteer for each of the experimental and control groups. They should each number a piece of paper from 1 to 25.

Each student in the control group should be given a deck of ESP cards. The cards should then be thoroughly shuffled and the deck placed, number side down, on the desk.

You, the teacher, should hold your deck of thoroughly shuffled ESP cards, number side down, behind a screen or shield. Beginning with the top card and proceeding through the entire deck, you are going to discard the cards, one by one, into a stack, while saying to the students, "Card one, card two," all the way to card 25. (You are not to look at the numbered side of the cards.)

As you call out each card, the students in the experimental group will write down the number they think is on the card. **(These students are being subjected to the experimental treatment; that is, they are being tested for evidence of clairvoyance.)** The students in the control group will turn over the corresponding card in their ESP decks and write down the number on the card as the response. **(These students are not being subjected to the experimental treatment; that is, they are not being tested for evidence of clairvoyance.)**

After completing the deck, give the students the correct answers so that they can determine their number of correct responses.

Repeat the investigation for four more trials.

5. The Students Learn the Difference Between the Independent Variable and the Dependent Variable When Using the Scientific Method of Research.

Inform the students that another characteristic of the experimental method of research is that of independent and dependent variables.

The independent variable is the feature that differentiates the experimental group from the control group. In this investigation the independent variable is the human brain. The responses of the experimental subjects are provided by their brains, and the responses of the control group are provided by numbers on cards.

The dependent variable is the data being collected in the investigation. The dependent variable **depends** upon the independent variable. For example, in the experimental group the data depends upon the responses provided by human brains. In the control group the data depends upon the responses from numbers on cards.

6. The Students Learn the Importance of Controlling Experimental Conditions.

Explain to the students that another characteristic of the scientific method of research is that of controlling the conditions under which an investigation is conducted. For example, in designing a clairvoyance investigation, it is important to control the card-visibility factor to make certain that they cannot be seen by the subjects. It is important to control the shuffling of cards to ensure a random sequence of numbers in the deck. It is important to control the independent variable, making certain that it is the only feature that differentiates the experimental group from the control group.

7. The Students Analyze the Clairvoyance Data Collected.

One way to analyze the data is to simply compare the number of correct responses for the five trials between the ten subjects in the experimental group and the ten subjects in the control group. (One could expect, by chance alone, that each subject would get 5 right out of 25 per trial. For five trials, therefore, chance alone accounts for 25 correct responses by each subject. Since there were ten subjects in each group, one would expect by chance alone that each group would get 250 correct responses.)

Another more precise method of analyzing the data is to calculate the Chi-square (procedure explained in Activity 7.7). If you choose this method, put the following table on the chalkboard for the students to copy and use. (The Expected column of the table has been filled in, assuming that five trials have been run with ten subjects in each group.)

	Observed (O)	Expected (E)	O – E	$\dfrac{(O-E)^2}{E}$
Experimental group		250		
Control group		250		

Total = chi-square = _____

8. The Students Evaluate Their Knowledge of the Characteristics of the Experimental Method of Research.

Distribute copies of Worksheet 6.6–1 for the students to work on. **The answers are** Problem A: 1. The plants not exposed to any music vibration. 2.a. The plants exposed to music vibration. b. It is the group of plants being subjected to the experimental treatment (exposure to music vibrations). 3. Music vibration. 4. Height and weight. 5. Temperature and humidity and the daily cycle of light and darkness. Problem B: 1. The brand of gasoline. 2. Automobile mileage. 3. The automobiles should be tested over the same roads. The automobiles should be tested at the same speed. The automobiles should be tested on the same day to assure identical weather conditions. The same make and model of automobile should be used in all the tests. The automobiles should make the same number and duration of stops and starts.

9. The Students Learn More About the Experimental Method of Research.

Distribute copies of Worksheet 6.6–2. **The answers to the Library Research Questions are** 1.a. An inert substance used as a control against the substance being tested in an experimental group in a research test. b. Answers will vary. Example: A vaccine is being tested for its effectiveness. The experimental group receives the vaccine while the control group receives inert saline solution. 2.a. A subject in the control group responds positively to the placebo. b. Answers will vary. Example: Subjects in an experimental group receive injections of a new vaccine that is being tested for preventing colds. Subjects in the control group receive injections of saline solution (the placebo). Some subjects in the control group get fewer colds, results that cannot be attributed to saline solution.

WORKSHEET 6.6–1
THE EXPERIMENTAL METHOD OF RESEARCH

A. The following describes an investigation carried out to determine whether music vibrations have any effect upon plant development in terms of height and weight. Read carefully and answer the questions.

Twenty-five bean plants were placed in a growth chamber and were exposed to the same 30-minute passage of recorded violin music three times a day, at 7 A.M., at 1 P.M., and again at 6 P.M. Twenty-five other bean plants were placed in another growth chamber but were not exposed to any music vibrations.

Each growth chamber was kept at the same temperature and humidity. Also, the daily cycle of light and darkness was the same.

At the conclusion of the investigation, after 21 days, the heights and weights of all the bean plants were determined. The data results were compared between the two groups of 25 plants.

1. Which plants were in the control group? _____

2. a. Which plants were in the experimental group? _____

   b. Why is this group of plants the experimental group? _____

3. Name the independent variable. _____

4. Name the two dependent variables. _____

5. List the experimental conditions that were controlled by the investigators.

   _____

   _____

   _____

   _____

B. Assume that you wish to design an investigation to determine whether brand A gasoline provides better mileage than brand B.

1. Name the independent variable. _____

2. Name the dependent variable. _____

3. List a few conditions in the investigation that will have to be controlled.

   _____

   _____

   _____

   _____

   _____

WORKSHEET 6.6–2   MESSAGE SQUARE ACTIVITY
THE EXPERIMENTAL METHOD OF RESEARCH

A.   *Hint:* A type of investigation in which neither the investigator nor the subject know which is the experimental group and which is the control group

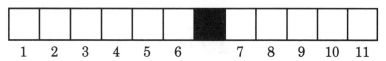

Anticipated Answer

Put: an L in 5 and 8.   _____
    a D in 1 and 11.   _____
    a B in 4 and 7.   _____
    an O in 2.   _____
    an N in 10.   _____
    an I in 9.   _____
    a U in 3.   _____
    an E in 6.   _____

B.   *Hint:* These must always be kept under control when comparing experimental with control groups.

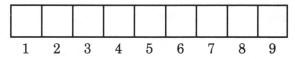

Anticipated Answer

Put: an S in 9.   _____
    an A in 2 and 5.   _____
    a B in 6.   _____
    a V in 1.   _____
    an E in 8.   _____
    an R in 3.   _____
    an I in 4.   _____
    an L in 7.   _____

Library Research Questions   **Answers**   **Sources**

1. a. What is a placebo?

    b. Give an example of a placebo being used in an investigation.

2. a. What is the placebo effect?

    b. Give an example of a placebo effect in an investigation.

Unit 7
Graphing and Simple Statistics

7.1 GRAPHING

You Will Need the Following Materials:

graph paper   colored pencils (red and blue)
rulers   opaque projector

Upon Completion of This Activity, Students Will

- Know the format to use in preparing graphs.
- Know the difference between the line graph and the bar graph.
- Be aware of the importance of titling the three major components of a graph.

1. Help the Students to Learn the Proper Format for Constructing Line and Bar Graphs.

Distribute copies of Worksheet 7.1–1 (Graphing Format). Have the students refer to the graph illustrations at the top of the worksheet as you provide the following information to them to write in their notebooks under the heading "Important Points Regarding Graphs":

a. The graph is an excellent way to make data visual.

b. There are two main types of graphs: the line graph and the bar graph.

c. Graphs have two axes. They are the horizontal axis (also referred to as the abscissa or the x axis) and the vertical axis (also referred to as the ordinate or the y axis).

d. The bottom left of the graph where the horizontal and vertical axes meet is the zero point. From this zero point, numbers increase across the horizontal axis and up the vertical axis.

e. The width of a graph is usually greater than its height, so graph paper is usually turned sideways before preparing a graph.

f. It is important that the graph be properly titled to indicate the type of information it is designed to show.

g. It is important that the horizontal and vertical axes be individually titled to indicate what the numbers or symbols along them mean.

h. When constructing graphs, rulers should be used in drawing the axes and, eventually, in connecting any plotted dots unless a trend line is asked for.

2. The Students Practice What They Have Learned Above by Doing the Two Problems on Their Worksheet.

When evaluating the students' work, keep the following factors in mind:

a. The zero point is often disregarded. Numbering is often begun where the zero belongs.

b. Students sometimes do not keep the values constant when labeling the values along the horizontal and vertical axes.

c. Make certain that the horizontal and vertical axes along with the graph are accurately titled.

d. Students may err in determining the scale to use along the horizontal and vertical axes. In general, the graph height is two thirds to three fourths its width. Scales should be determined accordingly.

3. The Students Reinforce Learning with Additional Graph Problems.

Distribute copies of Worksheet 7.1–2. You might wish to use it as a homework assignment.

The answers to the problems are: Additional Graphing Problems 1.1. 3 and 7; 2. 5 and 7

Additional Graphing Problems 2.1. A; 2. 1, 2, 5, 6; 3. Day 9. Additional tasks: When the students bring in their graph examples, use an opaque projector and project several examples on the screen. Discuss each one in terms of ease of interpretation.

WORKSHEET 7.1–1 GRAPHING FORMAT

The two main types of graphs are illustrated as follows:

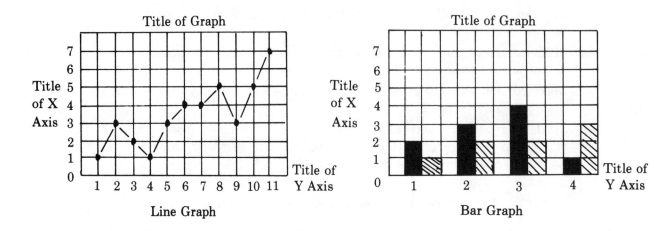

Line Graph   Bar Graph

Problem 1:

1. A line graph will be prepared based on the following data:

Trial Number	Time in Minutes for a Mouse Running a Maze	Trial Number	Time in Minutes for a Mouse Running a Maze
1	10	6	7
2	8	7	5
3	9	8	3
4	8	9	4
5	7	10	2

2. Along the horizontal axis, number the trials from 1 to 10, separating each by two spaces. Title the horizontal axis Trial Numbers.

3. Along the vertical axis, number from 1 to 10, letting each space equal one. Title the vertical axis Time in Minutes.

4. Title the graph Time Trials in Minutes for a Mouse Running a Maze. Note that the title explains what the graph has been designed to show. This is always important.

5. Plot (in other words, place) the data from the data table onto the graph in the form of dots.

6. Connect the dots with a line to complete the line graph.

7. Examine your completed line graph. Note that it provides a "picture" of time improvement for the mouse over ten trials.

Problem 2:

1. Prepare a bar graph based on the following data of memorized word definitions recalled immediately after learning and two days after learning.

Subject Number	Immediately After Learning	Two Days After Learning	Subject Number	Immediately After Learning	Two Days After Learning
1	10	6	6	9	8
2	10	8	7	10	5
3	9	4	8	9	5
4	5	5	9	7	6
5	10	10	10	9	4

2. Along the horizontal axis, number the subjects from 1 to 10, separating each by three or four spaces. Title the axis Subjects.

3. Along the vertical axis, number from 1 to 10, letting each space equal one. Title the axis Number of Word Definitions Recalled.

4. Title the graph, Number of Word Definitions Recalled Immediately After Learning vs. Two Days After Learning.

5. Below the graph title, a legend is needed. A legend indicates how certain graph symbols are to be interpreted. In this case, the legend should be

(colored red) = immediately after learning

(colored blue) = two days after learning

6. Plot the information from the data table on the graph paper in the form of bars. For subject #1, plot a red bar one space wide up to the number 10 of the vertical axis. Skip a space or two to the right and plot a blue bar up to the number 6 of the ordinate. You now have two bars for subject #1. Proceed in like manner to plot the data for the remaining subjects.

7. Examine your completed bar graph. Note that it provides a clearer "picture" of definition recall than the data table alone.

WORKSHEET 7.1–2   ADDITIONAL GRAPHING PROBLEMS

Problem 1:

A mouse was allowed to run a maze for ten trials. For each trial, the number of wrong turns made by the mouse was recorded. The data collected follows:

Trial	Number of Wrong Turns
1	13
2	11
3	12
4	10
5	8
6	5
7	2
8	2
9	1
10	1

Prepare a line graph based on the data. Remember to title all parts of the graph accurately.

Use your finished graph to answer the following questions:

1. Between what trials does the graph show a continuing improvement by the mouse? _____

2. Between what two trials did the mouse improve by six fewer errors? _____

Problem 2:

Two groups of similar plants were compared in terms of daily average height as measured in inches. Each group received a different fertilizer. The following data was collected:

Plants With Brand A Fertilizer		Plants With Brand B Fertilizer	
Day	Average Height (inches)	Day	Average Height (inches)
1	1	1	1
2	1	2	1
3	2	3	1
4	3	4	2
5	3	5	3
6	4	6	4
7	5	7	4
8	8	8	5
9	12	9	6
10	15	10	7

Prepare a line graph based on the above data. Plot both sets of data on the same piece of graph paper, using a red pencil for the group of plants fertilized with brand A and a blue pencil for the other group. Do not forget to add a legend to your graph to indicate what the red and blue lines represent.

Use your finished graph to answer the following questions:

1. Which fertilizer brand was the most effective in promoting the growth of the plants? _____

2. On what day(s) were the plants of both groups equal in height? _____

_____

3. What is the first day that the plants are more than three inches average height in difference?

_____

Problem 3:

Ten students were given a spelling test consisting of ten words. The results follow:

Student	Number of Words Correctly Spelled
1	10
2	10
3	9
4	4
5	5
6	9
7	6
8	8
9	9
10	7

Prepare a bar graph based on the data. Arrange the student numbers along the horizontal axis from lowest to highest scores.

Do not forget to add the proper titles to your completed bar graph.

Additional tasks:

a. Bar and line graphs appear frequently in news magazines and newspapers. Bring to the classroom three examples of graphs, noting for each graph whether or not it has been labeled clearly and is easy to interpret.
b. Another type of graph, which we have not explored, is called the circle graph or pie chart. It is a circle that has been divided into segments representing frequencies. This type of graph is also found in news magazines and newspapers. Bring in one example of this type of graph.

7.2 THE RANGE AND FREQUENCY DISTRIBUTION

You Will Need the Following Materials:

paper and pencils

Upon Completion of This Activity, Students Will

- Be able to provide definitions for the terms *range* and *frequency distribution.*
- Be able to calculate the range and frequency distribution for a set of data.
- Know a definition of the term *statistics.*

1. The Students Become Acquainted with the Terms Range *and* Frequency Distribution.

Explain to the students that the **range** is defined as the difference between the lowest and the highest scores in a set of data. The **frequency distribution** shows the frequency with which each score of a set of data occurs. Both terms are statistical terms. **Statistics is a branch of mathematics dealing with the collection and analysis of data.**

2. The Students Calculate the Range and Frequency Distribution.

Write the following golf scores on the chalkboard: 35, 30, 42, 42, 32, 51, 50, 42, 51, 36, 41, 40, 44, 55, and 50.

Write the two column headings, side by side, on the chalkboard: **Scores (Xi)** (Xi is a symbol for individual scores) and **Frequency (f)**. Explain that they are the headings for a **frequency distribution table**. Have a volunteer go to the chalkboard and write the golf scores, from highest to lowest, in the **Scores (Xi) column**, then write the frequency of each of the scores in the **Frequency (f) column**.

Have the students determine the range for the scores. **(Answer: = 25.)** Which golf score occurred with the highest frequency? **(Answer: = 42.)** What is the frequency for golf score 51? **(Answer: = 2.)**

Tell the students that a good example of the necessity of using a frequency distribution table in business is when an inventory is taken. Taking an inventory is actually preparing a frequency distribution table. In a shirt store, for example, when an inventory of shirts is taken, the number (frequency) of each brand of shirt, in each color and size, is taken.

3. The Students Calculate the Range and Frequency Distribution on Their Own.

Distribute copies of Worksheet 7.2–1 for the students to work on either in class or as homework.

The answers are 1.a. 9; b. 12, 10, 9; c. 2; d. 16; 2.a. 125, 120, 115, 110, 100, 98, 95; b. 105; c. 44; 3. The difference between the highest and the lowest scores. 4. The frequency with which each score in a set of data occurs. 5. It would allow you to determine the sales frequency for each food product so that you would know how many units of each food product to order.

4. The Students Are Evaluated on Their Learning.

Pass out copies of Worksheet 7.2–2 and use as either a self-evaluation or a quiz.

The answers are 1.b. Examples: If you were going to purchase a car, you would want to determine the range of prices between the different dealers. If you were playing golf in a foursome, you might want to know the handicap range among the other three. When you get a test grade back, you might want to know the range of test scores for the entire class. 2.c. It would tell you how many units of each particular type of paint have been sold so you will know how many units of each to order. 4.a. 10,000. b. 4. c. 7,000; 11,000; 14,000.

WORKSHEET 7.2–1
THE RANGE AND FREQUENCY DISTRIBUTION

1. Twenty students have a summertime job mowing lawns. When asked how many lawns they mowed per week, the replies were 10, 12, 15, 9, 12, 18, 14, 12, 14, 9, 14, 9, 10, 14, 16, 14, 16, 14, 10, and 14. Prepare a frequency distribution table of the above data, then answer the following questions:

   a. What is the range for the distribution?

   _____

   b. Which three lawns-mowed-per-week numbers

   have the same frequency? _____

   c. What is the frequency for 16 lawns mowed per

   week? _____

   d. How many students mowed 14 or fewer lawns

   per week? _____

Scores (Xi)	Frequency (f)

2. Prepare a frequency distribution table for the following weight data, expressed in pounds, for 25 individuals and then answer the questions. Weight in pounds: 110, 105, 139, 105, 95, 98, 125, 100, 120, 115, 114, 123, 105, 110, 123, 125, 120, 105, 95, 105, 115, 99, 100, 123, and 98.

   a. Which weights have a frequency of 2?

   _____

   b. Which weight has the highest frequency?

   _____

   c. What is the range for the weight data?

   _____

3. The range is defined as: _____

4. What does the frequency distribution table show?

   _____

Scores (Xi)	Frequency (f)

5. If you were the manager of your own grocery store and had to do all the purchasing of the store's food supplies, how would a frequency distribution table help you?

_____

_____

_____

_____

WORKSHEET 7.2–2   EVALUATION EXERCISE

1. a. What is determined by calculating the **range**? ⎯⎯⎯⎯⎯⎯⎯⎯⎯⎯⎯⎯⎯⎯⎯⎯

⎯⎯⎯⎯⎯⎯⎯⎯⎯⎯⎯⎯⎯⎯⎯⎯⎯⎯⎯⎯⎯⎯⎯⎯⎯⎯⎯⎯⎯⎯⎯⎯⎯⎯⎯⎯⎯

   b. Give an everyday example of when you might want to calculate a range: ⎯⎯⎯⎯⎯⎯

⎯⎯⎯⎯⎯⎯⎯⎯⎯⎯⎯⎯⎯⎯⎯⎯⎯⎯⎯⎯⎯⎯⎯⎯⎯⎯⎯⎯⎯⎯⎯⎯⎯⎯⎯⎯⎯

2. a. What does a **frequency distribution table** show? ⎯⎯⎯⎯⎯⎯⎯⎯⎯⎯⎯⎯⎯⎯

⎯⎯⎯⎯⎯⎯⎯⎯⎯⎯⎯⎯⎯⎯⎯⎯⎯⎯⎯⎯⎯⎯⎯⎯⎯⎯⎯⎯⎯⎯⎯⎯⎯⎯⎯⎯⎯

   b. How is the frequency distribution table usually organized? ⎯⎯⎯⎯⎯⎯⎯⎯⎯⎯

⎯⎯⎯⎯⎯⎯⎯⎯⎯⎯⎯⎯⎯⎯⎯⎯⎯⎯⎯⎯⎯⎯⎯⎯⎯⎯⎯⎯⎯⎯⎯⎯⎯⎯⎯⎯⎯

   c. If you were employed in a paint store and were responsible for ordering each new supply of

   paint, how would a frequency distribution table help you? ⎯⎯⎯⎯⎯⎯⎯⎯⎯⎯⎯

⎯⎯⎯⎯⎯⎯⎯⎯⎯⎯⎯⎯⎯⎯⎯⎯⎯⎯⎯⎯⎯⎯⎯⎯⎯⎯⎯⎯⎯⎯⎯⎯⎯⎯⎯⎯⎯

⎯⎯⎯⎯⎯⎯⎯⎯⎯⎯⎯⎯⎯⎯⎯⎯⎯⎯⎯⎯⎯⎯⎯⎯⎯⎯⎯⎯⎯⎯⎯⎯⎯⎯⎯⎯⎯

⎯⎯⎯⎯⎯⎯⎯⎯⎯⎯⎯⎯⎯⎯⎯⎯⎯⎯⎯⎯⎯⎯⎯⎯⎯⎯⎯⎯⎯⎯⎯⎯⎯⎯⎯⎯⎯

⎯⎯⎯⎯⎯⎯⎯⎯⎯⎯⎯⎯⎯⎯⎯⎯⎯⎯⎯⎯⎯⎯⎯⎯⎯⎯⎯⎯⎯⎯⎯⎯⎯⎯⎯⎯⎯

3. What is the role of **statistics** in science? ⎯⎯⎯⎯⎯⎯⎯⎯⎯⎯⎯⎯⎯⎯⎯⎯⎯⎯

⎯⎯⎯⎯⎯⎯⎯⎯⎯⎯⎯⎯⎯⎯⎯⎯⎯⎯⎯⎯⎯⎯⎯⎯⎯⎯⎯⎯⎯⎯⎯⎯⎯⎯⎯⎯⎯

⎯⎯⎯⎯⎯⎯⎯⎯⎯⎯⎯⎯⎯⎯⎯⎯⎯⎯⎯⎯⎯⎯⎯⎯⎯⎯⎯⎯⎯⎯⎯⎯⎯⎯⎯⎯⎯

⎯⎯⎯⎯⎯⎯⎯⎯⎯⎯⎯⎯⎯⎯⎯⎯⎯⎯⎯⎯⎯⎯⎯⎯⎯⎯⎯⎯⎯⎯⎯⎯⎯⎯⎯⎯⎯

⎯⎯⎯⎯⎯⎯⎯⎯⎯⎯⎯⎯⎯⎯⎯⎯⎯⎯⎯⎯⎯⎯⎯⎯⎯⎯⎯⎯⎯⎯⎯⎯⎯⎯⎯⎯⎯

4. Twenty drivers were surveyed regarding the average number of miles that they drove their cars per year. Their answers were 10,000; 23,000; 8,000; 10,000; 13,000; 14,000; 10,000; 8,000; 8,000; 10,000; 7,000; 11,000; 9,000; 20,000; 10,000; 8,000; 11,000; 10,000; 7,000; 14,000. Prepare a **frequency distribution table**, then answer the following questions:

Scores (Xi)	Frequency (f)

   a. Which mileage has the greatest

   frequency? ⎯⎯⎯⎯⎯⎯⎯⎯

   b. What is the frequency for 8,000 miles?

   ⎯⎯⎯⎯⎯⎯⎯⎯

   c. What mileage figure(s) has a frequency

   of 2? ⎯⎯⎯⎯⎯⎯⎯⎯

7.3 THE MEAN AND THE MEDIAN

You Will Need the Following Materials:

paper and pencil   hand calculator (optional)

Upon Completion of This Activity, Students Will

- Be able to provide definitions for the terms *mean* and *median*.
- Have become acquainted with some statistical symbols used in representing a mathematical formula.
- Know three measures of central tendency.
- Be able to calculate the mean and the median from a set of data.

1. The Students Learn the Definition for the Mean.

First, explain to the students that, when analyzing data, three **measures of central tendency** are often used. They are referred to as the **mean**, the **median**, and the **mode**. (*Note:* The mode is discussed in Activity 7.4.) All three tend to indicate the middle, or central, number of a list of figures or scores. They will be more clearly understood as they are used in analyzing data.

The **mean** can be defined as **the sum of individual figures or scores divided by the total number of figures or scores**. The mean is also known as the arithmetic average. If a student has ever been instructed to "add up the numbers and determine the average," the student has actually been instructed to determine the arithmetic average, or mean.

2. The Students Learn the Symbols That Scientists Use For Expressing the Formula for the Mean.

Explain that scientists use the following four symbols for expressing the formula used in calculating the mean:

a.   The first is $\bar{X}$, and it is the symbol for the *mean*.
b.   The second is Xi, and it is the symbol for *individual figures or scores*.
c.   The third is Σ, and it is the symbol for *the sum of*.
d.   The fourth is N, and it is the symbol for *total number of figures or scores*.

Using all of the above symbols, the formula for calculating the mean is written as follows:

$$\bar{X} = \frac{\Sigma Xi}{N}.$$

Interpreted in words, the formula sates, "the *mean* equals *the sum of the individual figures or scores divided by the total number of figures or scores.*"

3. The Students Practice Calculating the Mean.

Distribute copies of Worksheet 7.3–1. **The answers are as follows:**
1a. $\bar{X} = \frac{\Sigma Xi}{N}$; b. $\bar{X} = \frac{21}{7}$; c. 3; 2.a. 3, 4, 3, 4, 5; b. #5; (*Note:* The data for students three and five contains zeros. A common error is for students not to count the zero(s) when calculating the mean. For example, when dividing the sum for student #3, some students might divide by 12 instead of by 14.) 3.a. 14.5; b. 73; c. 213.8; d. 1,478.6.

4. The Students Learn the Definition for the Median and How to Calculate it from a Set of Data.

Tell the students that the **median** is defined as **that figure or score which falls in the exact middle of a frequency distribution of figures or scores that have been arranged from highest to lowest.** The median figure or score has as many figures or scores higher than it as lower than it.

Write the following test scores on the chalkboard: 10, 8, 3, 11, 14, 2, 5, 9, 8, 8, 3, 6, 9, 12, 12, 3, and 2.

Next, write the following two headings, side by side, on the chalkboard and explain to the students that they are headings for a frequency distribution table: **Individual Scores (Xi)** and **Frequency (f)**. Have a volunteer go to the chalkboard and write the test scores from highest to lowest in the Individual Scores (Xi) column and the frequency of each of the scores in the Frequency (f) column. Upon completion of this task, ask the students which test score is the median. In other words, which test score has as many scores higher than it as lower than it? **(Answer: 8.)**

5. The Students Practice Calculating the Median.

Distribute copies of Worksheet 7.3–2.
The answers are 1.a. 80; b. 7; c. 7; 2.a. 84; b. 8; 3.a. 67.

6. The Students Are Evaluated on Their Learning.

Distribute copies of Worksheet 7.3–3 and use it as homework or as an in-class evaluation. **The answers are:** 4. There are an equal number of scores above and below 86. 6.a. $76.09; b. $74; c. yes; 7.a. $25; b. 5; c. $30.

WORKSHEET 7.3–1   THE MEAN

1. In a pie-eating contest, the winner devoured 6 cherry pies. The seven other contestants each devoured the following numbers of pies: 5, 3, 4, 3, 2, 3, 1. Calculate the mean number of pies devoured by the seven other contestants.

   a. Write the formula for the mean: _____

   b. Write the formula, substituting numbers for the symbols: _____

   c. The mean = _____

2. Five students each kept a diary of miles they jogged every day over a period of two weeks. The following data chart contains the results:

NUMBER OF MILES JOGGED DAILY

Student	Days													
	1	2	3	4	5	6	7	8	9	10	11	12	13	14
1	3	2	2	4	3	3	4	2	3	2	3	4	3	4
2	5	3	4	4	4	4	5	3	4	4	4	2	5	5
3	3	3	4	4	3	4	3	4	3	4	3	0	0	4
4	6	2	6	5	3	3	2	6	2	4	6	3	4	4
5	6	6	6	5	5	6	2	0	6	6	6	6	5	5

   a. Calculate the mean for each student:

      1 = _____

      2 = _____

      3 = _____

      4 = _____

      5 = _____

   b. Which student averaged the most miles for the 14 days? _____

3. Calculate the means for the following sets of data, rounding answers off to the nearest tenth:

   a. 10, 18, 12, 13, 15, 19. X = _____

   b. 85, 63, 65, 73, 82, 80, 63. X = _____

   c. 210, 215, 190, 212, 216, 219, 211, 221, 230. X = _____

   d. 1,350; 1,690; 1,420; 1,380; 1,620; 1,500; 1,390. X = _____

Name _____   Date _____

WORKSHEET 7.3-2   THE MEDIAN

1. The following are class scores from a science test: 30, 80, 70, 90, 90, 85, 75, 70, 100, 100, 80, 85, 90, 60, 70, and 70. Set up a frequency distribution table and determine the median.

Scores (Xi)	Frequency (f)

a. The median = _____

b. How many scores are higher than the median

score? _____

c. How many scores are lower than the median

score? _____

2. The following are class scores from a science quiz: 100, 40, 30, 85, 95, 60, 85, 83, 74, 98, 100, 85, 94, 60, 83, and 83. Set up a frequency distribution table and determine the median. (*Note:* The median in this problem will not be an actual score obtained by a student but will fall midway between two actual scores.)

Scores (Xi)	Frequency (f)

a. The median = _____

b. How many scores are above the median and how many scores are below the median?

_____

3. Set up a frequency distribution table and determine the median for the following set of data: 66, 75, 80, 52, 73, 63, 66, 63, 80, 68, 66, 80, 68, 55, 73, 65, 80, 52, 68, 68, 75, 63, 73, 66, 66, and 66.

Scores (Xi)	Frequency (f)

a. The median = _____

WORKSHEET 7.3–3 EVALUATION EXERCISE

1. Provide a definition for the **mean**. _____

   _____

2. a. What does the symbol **N** mean in the formula for the mean? _____

   b. What does the symbol **Σ** mean in the formula for the mean? _____

3. Provide a definition for the **median**. _____

   _____

4. Assume that you have taken a nationally standardized test in science. You receive your test score, which is 86. You are told that a test score of 86 represents the median score. How did you do on the test relative to all of the others who took it?

   _____

   _____

5. The mean and the median are two of three "measures of central tendency." What is the third one?

   _____

6. The following is a list of prices for a variety of sneakers on the market: $55, $49, $95, $48, $105, $50, $86, $74, $65, $100, $110.

   a. What is the **mean** price for the variety of sneakers? _____

   b. What is the **median** price for the variety of sneakers? _____

   c. Are the mean and the median sneaker data close in dollar value? _____

7. Fifteen people who own portable stereocassette players were asked how much they paid for them. Their responses follow: $19, $20, $19, $35, $50, $25, $25, $15, $65, $25, $60, $19, $25, $25, and $30. Set up a frequency distribution table, then answer the following questions:

Scores (Xi)	Frequency (f)

   a. What is the median price? _____

   b. How many people purchased the cassette players at the median price? _____

   c. What price paid was closest to the mean? _____

7.4 THE MODE AND FREQUENCY POLYGON GRAPH

You Will Need the Following Materials:

pencil   graph paper

Upon Completion of This Activity, Students Will

- Be able to define the term *mode.*
- Be able to determine the mode from a set of data.
- Be able to explain what a frequency polygon graph is.
- Have prepared a frequency polygon from a set of data.

1. The Students Learn the Definition of the Term Mode *and How to Determine it from a Set of Data.*

Explain to the students that the mode is one of three **measures of central tendency** used in analyzing data. (The other two measures of central tendency, the mean and the median, are discussed in Activity 7.3.) Any measure of central tendency indicates the middle, or central, score of a set of numerical data.

Write the following numbers on the chalkboard: 5, 3, 2, 5, 1, 9, 11, 2, 3, 6, 12, 2, 2, 12, and 2. Ask the students what number appears with the greatest frequency. (**Answer: 2.**) Inform them that this is the mode, because **the mode is defined as that figure or score that appears with the greatest frequency in a set of data.**

Assume that out of a group of 50 students who have summer jobs, 30 of them receive an hourly salary of $6.50. Therefore, $6.50 is the mode because it is the salary that appears with the greatest frequency. As another example, assume that the mode of test scores for a class of students was 76. This means that more students received a score of 76 than any other single score.

2. The Students Learn How to Prepare a Frequency Polygon Graph.

Distribute copies of Worksheet 7.4–1. In organizing the data for plotting on a frequency polygon graph, the students are, in essence, preparing a frequency distribution table, which is further discussed in Activity 7.2.

The frequency polygon graph that results from Worksheet 7.4–1 is

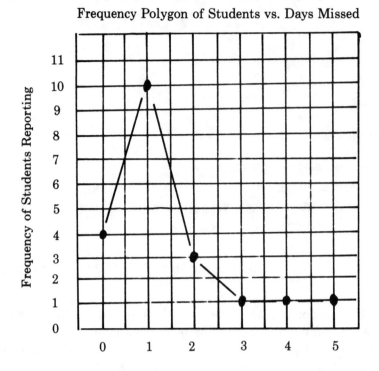

Frequency Polygon of Students vs. Days Missed

Reported Number of Days Missed

3. The Students Prepare a Frequency Polygon Graph from a Set of Data.

Hand out copies of Worksheet 7.4–2 and use it as homework or as an in-class evaluation.

The answers, and the frequency polygon graph, follow:

Test Scores	Frequency of Each Test Score
16	1
15	1
14	5
13	1
12	3
11	2
10	1
9	1
8	4
7	2
6	1

a. The figure or score that appears with the greatest frequency

b. 14

c. 8

d. Because the vertical axis represents frequency, and the mode represents the most frequent figure or score

The frequency polygon graph:

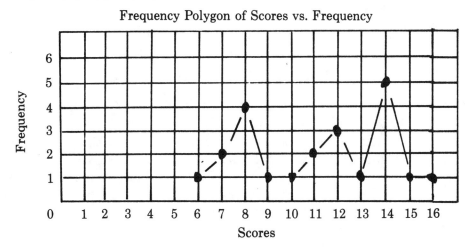

Frequency Polygon of Scores vs. Frequency

WORKSHEET 7.4–1
THE MODE AND THE FREQUENCY POLYGON GRAPH

The frequency polygon graph is a type of graph that is prepared to make visual the mode and its relationship to the rest of the data. The following is the procedure used for the organization of data and the preparation of the graph:

1. The data: Twenty students were asked how many days of school they missed during the last nine weeks. Their responses were 1, 0, 1, 1, 0, 3, 4, 1, 2, 0, 5, 0, 2, 1, 1, 1, 2, 1, 1, and 1.

2. The organization of the data: The data must be organized into what is referred to as a frequency distribution table. This is simply a table that lists each individual figure or score, usually in order from highest to lowest, in the left-hand column and the frequency (how many times it occurs in the set of data) of each score in the right-hand column. The following is a frequency distribution table set up for the data:

Each student's individual figure or score for the reported numbers of days missed:	The frequency of each figure or score:
5	1
4	1
3	1
2	3
1	10
0	4

   The figure or score that appears with the greatest frequency is one day missed. This figure or score is, therefore, the mode. More students reported one day missed than any other number of days missed.

3. The preparation of the frequency polygon graph: On a piece of graph paper, let each space along the vertical axis equal one. Title this axis, **Frequency**. Along the horizontal axis, list the number of days missed. Label this axis, **Reported Number of Days Missed**. Title the entire graph, **Frequency vs. Days Absent**. Plot the data on the graph and then connect the dots with a line.

   Look at your completed graph. Note the mode, 1, along the horizontal axis. Because the mode is the figure or score with the greatest frequency, it should be the **highest point on your graph**. And it is, because more students (10) reported this number than any other.

WORKSHEET 7.4-2   PREPARING A FREQUENCY POLYGON GRAPH

Instructions: Based on the following data, prepare a frequency distribution table, a frequency polygon graph, and answer the questions:

The data: The following are test scores received by 22 students: 8, 7, 12, 11, 16, 8, 11, 13, 8, 14, 14, 15, 9, 14, 12, 12, 10, 14, 14, 8, 7, and 6.

In the following space, organize the data in a frequency distribution table:

Test Scores	Frequency of Each Score

On a piece of graph paper, prepare a frequency polygon graph. Let each space along the vertical axis equal one. Title this axis, **Frequency**. List the scores along the horizontal axis. Title this axis, **Test Scores**. Title the graph **Test Scores vs. Frequency**.

a. Give a definition for mode. _____

_____

b. What test score represents the mode? _____

c. What score is one less in frequency than the mode? _____

d. Explain why the mode is always the highest point on a frequency polygon graph. _____

_____

_____

_____

7.5 THE SCATTERPLOT AND CORRELATION

You Will Need the Following Materials:

pencil   graph paper

Upon Completion of This Activity, Students Will

- Know the definition of the *correlation*.
- Know the three basic types of correlation.
- Have prepared scatterplots.
- Be able to interpret scatterplots.

1. The Students Learn the Definition and Three Basic Types of Correlation.

Explain to the students that the term *correlation* is defined as **the type of relationship that exists between two sets of data.** One might ask, for example, if there is a correlation between the time of the full moon and criminal behavior. If it was determined that criminal behavior neither increases nor decreases during the full moon, it can be said that a **zero correlation** exists. If criminal behavior was found to increase during the full moon, it can be said that a **positive correlation exists**. If criminal behavior was found to decrease during the full moon, a **negative correlation** then exists.

2. The Students Learn the Value of the Scatterplot.

Tell the students that a scatterplot is a special type of graph that is prepared to show in a visual manner the type of relationship between two sets of data.

3. The Students Prepare and Interpret Three Scatterplots.

Pass out copies of Worksheet 7.5–1 along with graph paper. (The students are going to prepare scatterplots that show each of the three basic types of correlations.)

The students' scatterplots should look like the following:

Scatterplot 1. Number of Study Hours per Week vs. Grade Point Average:

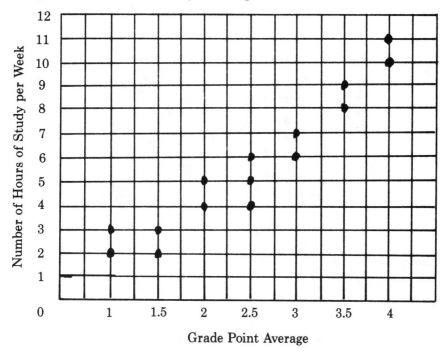

Scatterplot 2. Number of Minutes of Daily Brushing vs. Number of New Cavities:

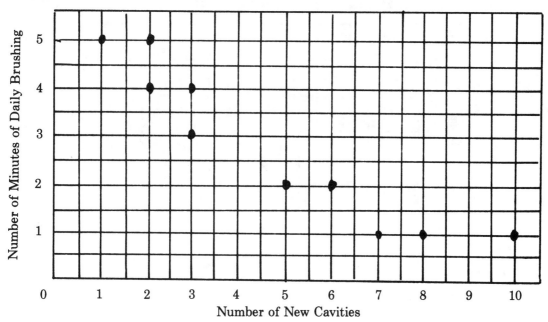

Scatterplot 3. Grades in History vs. Grades in Math:

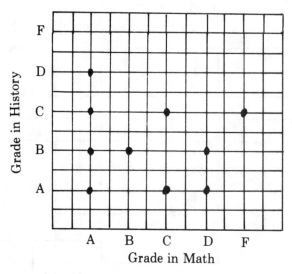

4. The Students Are Evaluated on Their Learning.

Pass out copies of Worksheet 7.5–2 along with graph paper. **The scatterplot and the answers follow:**

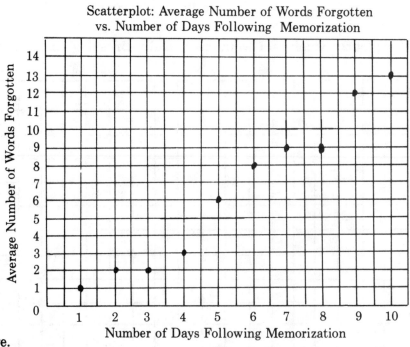

Scatterplot: Average Number of Words Forgotten vs. Number of Days Following Memorization

a. Positive.
b. As the number of days increases, the number of words forgotten increases.
c. A relationship that exists between two sets of data.
d. Decreases.

Name _____   Date _____

WORKSHEET 7.5–1   THE SCATTERPLOT AND CORRELATION

1. Assume that you want to determine the type of correlation that exists between grade point average and the number of hours spent studying per week. The following is data collected from 15 students:

Student	Number of Study Hours per Week	Grade Point Average
1	2	1
2	11	4
3	10	4
4	5	2.5
5	4	2
6	2	1.5
7	4	2.5
8	6	3
9	7	3
10	3	1.5
11	8	3.5
12	9	3.5
13	3	1
14	5	2
15	6	2.5

Set up a piece of graph paper with each space along the vertical axis equaling 1 hour of study. Along the horizontal axis, let every two spaces equal 0.5 grade point. Begin with 1, which is equivalent to a D, and end with 4, which is equivalent to an A.

Title the vertical axis **Number of Study Hours per Week**. Label the horizontal axis **Grade Point Average**. The graph can be titled **A Scatterplot of Study Hours per Week vs. Grade Point Average**.

Plot the data on the graph. For example, student #1 studied 2 hours per week and has a grade point average of 1. Go up the vertical axis to 2 and then horizontally to 1, placing a dot on the graph paper at that position. For student #2, go up the vertical axis to 11 and then across horizontally to 4 and place a dot at that position. Continue plotting all of the data.

Look at your completed scatterplot. It should show a positive correlation between the number of hours studied and the grade point average. In other words, generally, the higher the number of hours studied, the higher the grade point average. The trend pattern of the dots should be from lower left to upper right.

2. Prepare a scatterplot to determine the type of correlation that exists between the number of minutes spent daily brushing the teeth and the number of new cavities. Use the following data:

Subject	Number of Minutes of Daily Brushing	Number of New Cavities
1	5	1
2	3	3
3	4	3
4	1	8
5	1	7
6	5	2
7	4	2
8	2	6
9	1	10
10	2	5

Allow every two spaces up the vertical axis to equal 1 minute of brushing time. Allow every two spaces across the horizontal axis to equal 1 cavity.

Properly title the axes as well as the graph.

Look at your completed scatterplot. It should show a negative correlation. (*Note:* Do not make the mistake of thinking that a negative correlation is no correlation.) It is a negative correlation because, in general, as the number of minutes of daily brushing **increases** the number of new cavities **decreases**. The trend pattern of the dots should be from upper left to lower right.

3. Prepare a scatterplot to determine the type of correlation that exists between grades received in history and grades received in math. The data follows:

Student	Grade in History	Grade in Math
1	A	C
2	B	B
3	D	A
4	A	A
5	C	F
6	C	C
7	C	A
8	B	A
9	B	D
10	A	D

Place the grades A through F for one course up the vertical axis, beginning with A and leaving two spaces between grades.

Place the grades A through F for the other course along the horizontal axis, beginning with A and leaving two spaces between grades.

Accurately title each axis and the graph.

Looking at your completed scatterplot, it should show **zero correlation**. There does not seem to be a relationship between grades received in history and grades received in math. The dots are scattered over the graph and do not show a pattern, as they did in your previous two scatterplots.

WORKSHEET 7.5–2   EVALUATION EXERCISE

1. Prepare a scatterplot based on the following two sets of data which have been collected to determine what type of correlation exists between the number of days that have gone by since a list of words had been memorized and the average number of words forgotten:

Number of Days Following Memorization	Average Number of Words Forgotten
6	8
2	2
9	12
1	1
3	2
10	13
8	9
4	3
7	9
5	6

a. What type of correlation exists between the two sets of data? _____

_____

_____

b. Why is this correlation the type that you answered in a above? _____

_____

_____

c. Define the term correlation: _____

_____

_____

_____

d. Suppose that a scatterplot was prepared and it showed a negative correlation between the number of hours of exercise per week and blood serum cholesterol level. As the number of hours of exercise increases, how does the level of cholesterol change?

_____

_____

_____

_____

7.6 THE t-TEST

You Will Need the Following Materials:

paper and pencil   bull's eye target
hand calculator (optional)   ruler
safety darts

Upon Completion of This Activity, Students Will

- Understand the importance of the t-test in analyzing data.
- Know under what conditions the t-test can be used.
- Know how to calculate and interpret the results of the t-test.

1. The Students Learn How to Calculate the t-Test.

Inform the students that the t-test is an important statistic that can best be explained by using an example. Lead them step by step through the calculation of a t-test. (It is suggested that you do not require the students to memorize the steps but have them sequence the steps in their notes for future reference for tests and so on.)

Write the following data on the chalkboard for the students to copy as notes:

BRAND A TOOTHPASTE		BRAND B TOOTHPASTE	
Subject Number	Number of New Cavities Over Test Period	Subject Number	Number of New Cavities Over Test Period
1	1	1	2
2	3	2	2
3	2	3	6
4	2	4	4
5	0	5	1
6	2	6	5
7	4	7	3
8	3	8	3
9	2	9	2
10	1	10	2

Have the students assume that the data is from a study carried out to determine if one of the toothpaste brands is more effective than the other in preventing cavities. In other words, is there a **significant difference** (meaning one brand is really better than the other) as opposed to a **chance difference** (meaning that one brand is not really better than the other) between the two brands of toothpaste in preventing cavities? To arrive at an answer, scientists use the t-test. The step-by-step calculation follows:

Step 1: Determine the mean, or arithmetic average ($\bar{X}$), for each set of data, as shown at the right.

NUMBER OF NEW CAVITIES OVER TEST PERIOD	
Brand A	**Brand B**
1	2
3	2
2	6
2	4
0	1
2	5
4	3
3	3
2	2
1	2
Sum (Σ) = 20	Sum (Σ) = 30
$\bar{X} = \dfrac{20}{10}$	$\bar{X} = \dfrac{30}{10}$
$\bar{X} = 2$	$\bar{X} = 3$

Step 2: For each set of data, determine the difference between each individual measurement and the mean. Then square the difference.

BRAND A TOOTHPASTE			
Number of New Cavities	**Mean**	**Difference**	**Difference Squared**
1	2	1	1
3	2	1	1
2	2	0	0
2	2	0	0
0	2	2	4
2	2	0	0
4	2	2	4
3	2	1	1
2	2	0	0
1	2	1	1

Note: Students often make simple errors in their math. Constantly check their accuracy.

BRAND B TOOTHPASTE			
Number of New Cavities	**Mean**	**Difference**	**Difference Squared**
2	3	1	1
2	3	1	1
6	3	3	9
4	3	1	1
1	3	2	4
5	3	2	4
3	3	0	0
3	3	0	0
2	3	1	1
2	3	1	1

Step 3: For each set of data, add up the difference-squared columns and divide the sums by the number of individual measurements minus 1.

For example, you would *divide the 12 by 9* (the number of individual measurements minus 1).

Then you would *divide the 22 by 9* (the number of individual measurements minus 1).

Brand A Toothpaste (difference squared)	Brand B Toothpaste (difference squared)
1	1
1	1
0	9
0	1
4	4
0	4
4	0
1	0
0	1
1	1

Sum (Σ) = 12   Sum (Σ) = 22

The answers are expressed using the symbol s^2. The calculations are illustrated as follows:

$$s^2 \text{ (Brand A)} = \frac{12}{9} = 1.3 \qquad\qquad s^2 \text{ (Brand B)} = \frac{22}{9} = 2.4$$

Step 4: The t formula is now calculated, since you now have all of the numbers needed. The formula for t is

$$t = \frac{\text{The difference between the means}}{\sqrt{\dfrac{\text{The sums of the } s^2\text{'s for the two sets of data}}{\text{The number of subjects in the sample}}}}$$

$$t = \frac{3-2}{\sqrt{\dfrac{3.7}{10}}} \qquad t = \frac{1}{\sqrt{.37}} \qquad t = \frac{1}{.6} \qquad t = 1.6$$

Step 5: Now that the value of t has been determined, one must use what is called the t-probability table. Therefore, distribute Worksheet 7.6–1.

Note the **Degrees of Freedom column** at the left of the table. This column is numbered from 1 at the top to ∞ at the bottom. To determine what number you are going to use in this column, you add **the number of measurements minus 1 from one set of data** to **the number of measurements minus 1 from the other set of data**. This works out to 10 minus 1 (which equals 9) for each set of data. Adding the two 9s together equals 18. Therefore, go to #18 in the Degrees of Freedom column.

To the right of #18 are four different numbers, each in its own column. The numbers are 1.734, 2.101, 2.878, and 3.922. Now look at the top of the table and you will see that the columns have headings. The headings are: 0.1, 0.05, 0.01, and 0.001.

If the value calculated for t is equal to or greater than the number on the 0.05 column (in this case, the number in the column is 2.101), then the difference between the two sets of data is significant and your risk of being wrong in saying this is less than 5 times out of a 100. However, if the value calculated for t is less than the number in the 0.05 column, then the difference between the two sets of data is due to chance. (Under this condition, if you had said it was significant, your risk in being wrong would be greater than 5 times out of 100, which is not acceptable.)

Since the value of t that we arrived at is 1.6, it is less than the number 2.101, and therefore the difference between the two sets of data is due to chance. In other words, neither brand of toothpaste is more effective than the other in preventing new cavities.

2. The Students Participate in a Data-Collecting Activity and Calculate a t-Test.

Divide the class into two groups (perhaps those who have had previous experience in dart throwing and those who have not). Compare abilities at throwing darts at a bull's eye target. Allow each student to throw three darts and record the average distance in centimeters from the bull's eye. **(SAFETY NOTE: Use safety darts to prevent student injury. Also be certain that no one is in the vicinity or pathway of the darts being thrown.)**

Work with the class in calculating the value for t and in answering the following questions:

a. t =

b. What number did you use in the Degrees of Freedom column?

c. With what number in the t-Probability Table did you compare the value of t?

d. Is the difference between the two dart-throwing groups a significant one or is it due to chance?

3. The Students Calculate a t-Test from a Set of Data.

Hand out Worksheet 7.6–2. **The answers are** a. 3; b. 18; c. 2.101; d. significant.

HANDOUT 7.6–1   THE t-PROBABILITY TABLE

		Probability			
		0.1	**0.05**	**0.01**	**0.001**
	1	6.314	12.706	63.657	636.619
	2	2.920	4.303	9.925	31.598
	3	2.353	3.182	5.841	12.941
	4	2.132	2.776	4.604	8.610
	5	2.015	2.571	4.032	6.859
	6	1.943	2.447	3.707	5.959
	7	1.895	2.365	3.499	5.405
	8	1.860	2.306	3.355	5.041
	9	1.833	2.262	3.250	4.781
	10	1.812	2.228	3.169	4.587
D	11	1.796	2.201	3.106	4.437
e	12	1.782	2.179	3.055	4.318
g	13	1.771	2.160	3.012	4.221
r	14	1.761	2.145	2.977	4.140
e	15	1.753	2.131	2.947	4.073
s	16	1.746	2.120	2.921	4.015
	17	1.740	2.110	2.898	3.965
o	18	1.734	2.101	2.878	3.922
f	19	1.729	2.093	2.861	3.883
	20	1.725	2.086	2.845	3.850
F	21	1.721	2.080	2.831	3.819
r	22	1.717	2.074	2.819	3.792
e	23	1.714	2.069	2.807	3.767
e	24	1.711	2.064	2.797	3.745
d	25	1.708	2.060	2.787	3.725
o	26	1.706	2.056	2.779	3.707
m	27	1.703	2.052	2.771	3.690
	28	1.701	2.048	2.763	3.674
	29	1.699	2.045	2.756	3.659
	30	1.697	2.042	2.750	3.646
	40	1.684	2.025	2.704	3.551
	60	1.671	2.000	2.660	3.460
	120	1.658	1.980	2.617	3.373
	∞	1.645	1.960	2.576	3.291

Name _____   Date _____

WORKSHEET 7.6–2   CALCULATING THE t-TEST

Two groups of people were in a competition where they were shooting arrows at a target with a bull's eye. Each group wanted to win the prize money awarded for the best shooting. The following data was collected:

DISTANCE FROM THE BULL'S EYE IN CENTIMETERS	
Group A Participants	**Group B Participants**
4	1
3	1
3	3
2	2
10	2
8	2
8	3
7	1
2	4
3	1

Although it can be seen by looking at the data that Group B's arrows hit closer to the bull's eye, Group A wanted a t-test calculated to see if the difference was significant or due to chance (since the prize money was to be awarded only if the difference was significant).

Calculate the t-test and then answer the following questions:

a. t = _____

b. What number did you use in the Degrees of Freedom column? _____

c. With what number in the t-Probability Table did you compare the value of t? _____

d. Is the difference between the two groups significant or due to chance? _____

7.7 THE CHI-SQUARE

You Will Need the Following Materials:

paper and pencil   small beaker (or paper cup)
hand calculator (optional)   page of phone numbers from a
1 die   phone directory

Upon Completion of This Activity, Students Will

- Understand the value and importance of the chi-square in analyzing data.
- Become familiar with some types of data that call for chi-square analysis.
- Know how to calculate the chi-square.

1. The Students Are Guided Step by Step Through the Calculation of the Chi-Square.

Explain to the students that the chi-square is an important statistic that is used in comparing two sets of data in an effort to determine whether there is a **significant (real) difference** between them or a **difference due to chance**. The one set of data is called the **observed results** and the other set of data is called the **expected results**.

The chi-square can best be approached by leading the class, step by step, through the calculations involved. As you accomplish this task, put the relevant information on the chalkboard.

Familiarize the students with the following problem:

Let's assume that you are going to flip a quarter 200 times using your fingers. The probability (odds) of a head or a tail coming up as a result of each individual flip is 50-50. If asked how many times a head might be expected to come up by chance as a result of 200 flips, the answer would be 100 times.

The same would be true for tails. Thus, our **expected results** are 100 heads and 100 tails.

Assume now that a quarter was actually flipped 200 times and the data results were 82 heads and 118 tails. Since this is the data that we observed, it is referred to as **observed results**. The question now posed is, Is the difference between the observed results and the expected results a significant difference or a difference due to chance? To answer this question, one must calculate a chi-square.

To organize the data and calculate the chi-square, the following table is set up:

Attributes	Observed Results (O)	Expected Results (E)	O – E	$\frac{(O-E)^2}{E}$
Heads	82	100	18	3.2
Tails	118	100	18	3.2

Total = 6.4 = Chi-square (X^2)

Now that it has been determined that chi-square = 6.4, a table called Critical Values of X^2 (Worksheet 7.7–1) must be referred to. Therefore, pass out copies of Worksheet 7.7–1 and explain to the students how it is used. The students can take notes in the proper space on the worksheet. Note the Degrees of Freedom column at the left of the table. It is numbered from 1 to 10. The number to use in this column is simply the number of attributes that data was taken for minus 1. In our problem, data was taken for two attributes: the number of times heads came up and the number of times tails came up. It follows that 2 – 1 = 1. The number 1, therefore, is the number to use in the table.

To the right of #1 are six different numbers, each in its own column. The numbers are 0.0158, 0.455, 1.642, 3.841, 6.635, and 10.827. Note that each column has a p (probability) number at the top. The p numbers are 0.9, 0.5, 0.2, 0.05, 0.01, and 0.001. If the value of chi-square is equal to or greater than the number in the p = 0.05 column (which in this case is 3.841), this suggests that the difference between the observed results and the expected results can be considered significant. If the chi-square value is less than this number, the difference between the observed results and the expected results can be considered due to chance. The chi-square value arrived at in our problem is 6.4, which is greater than 3.841. Therefore, our findings suggest that the difference is significant.

Since it has been suggested that chance alone cannot account for the results of the coin flipping, a further investigation could be carried out to determine what factor(s) was responsible for the significant difference. Although the investigation will not be pursued here, one could hypothesize. The students might suggest such factors as the possibility that the quarter was not balanced (maybe the head side was heavier than the tail side, which is doubtful), or perhaps the technique of flipping the coin with the fingers varied from flip to flip, thus accounting for the results (most probable).

2. The Students Collect Data to Use in Calculating Another Chi-Square.

An interesting data-collecting activity that illustrates a practical use of the chi-square is that of testing the honesty (the ability to produce random results) of a die. Discuss with the students the fact that when you roll a die, it will "come up" either a 1, 2, 3, 4, 5, or 6. They should realize that the chance of any one of those numbers coming up per roll should be one in six. Now have a student roll the die 120 times. Shaking the die in a beaker or paper cup prior to rolling it will help assure consistent technique. The students keep data on the frequency with which each number comes up for the 120 trials. Although you will be using the actual data collected in your class, hypothetical data is used in the example that follows:

Attributes	Observed Results (0)	Expected Results (E)	0 – E	$\frac{(0-E)^2}{E}$
1	22	20	2	0.2
2	18	20	2	0.2
3	20	20	0	0.0
4	23	20	3	0.5
5	18	20	2	0.2
6	19	20	1	0.1

Total = 1.2 = Chi-square (X^2)

Now that it has been determined that chi-square = 1.2, one has to refer to the table Critical Values of X^2. Since the number of attributes that data was taken for is 6, one goes to the number 5 in the Degrees of Freedom column. Since the value for chi-square is less than the number in the $p = 0.05$ column, it can be concluded that the die is honest in that it does not favor any one number over another. In other words, the difference between the observed results and the expected results is due to chance and is not significant.

3. The Students Gain Further Experience in Calculating the Chi-Square.

Now that the students have had experience in calculating the chi-square for two problems, they can transfer what they have learned to some new situations. Distribute copies of Worksheet 7.7–2. Also distribute copies of a page of phone numbers from a telephone directory. (Refer below to teacher instructions regarding the phone numbers.)

The answers, along with an explanation, to the chi-square problems follow.

1. The table is organized as follows:

Attributes	Observed Results (0)	Expected Results (E)	0 – E	$\frac{(0 - E)^2}{E}$
Red	20	25	5	1
Blue	30	25	5	1
Green	15	25	10	4
Orange	35	25	10	4

Total = 10 = Chi-Square (X²)

Since the value of chi-square = 10 and the number in the Degrees of Freedom column of the Critical Values of X^2 Table is 3, the chi-square value is greater than the number (7.815) in the p = 0.05 column. Therefore, the difference between the observed results and the expected results is not due to random chance but is significant. Make certain that the students realize that this implies that the electric game is not programmed to flash the colors in a random sequence.

Inquire as to whether any students have such games at home that rely on random sequences. If they do, have them bring them in, and they can be chi-square tested in class. An activity such as this serves well in demonstrating the practical use of chi-square.

2. Teacher instructions regarding the phone numbers: Refer the students to their copy of the page from the phone directory. Are numbers chosen in a truly random way? Have them all use the same set of 100 phone numbers. Make certain that they use only the last four digits of each seven-digit number. This will provide a total of 400 individual numbers. Although you will be using actual data collected in class, the following hypothetical results serve as an example:

Attributes	Observed Results (0)	Expected Results (E)	0 – E	$\frac{(0 - E)^2}{E}$
0	35	40	5	0.6
1	45	40	5	0.6
2	43	40	3	0.2
3	36	40	4	0.4
4	43	40	3	0.2
5	34	40	6	0.9
6	40	40	0	0.0
7	46	40	6	0.9
8	34	40	6	0.9
9	44	40	4	0.4

Total = 5.1 = Chi-Square

Since the value of chi-square = 5.1 and the number in the Degrees of Freedom column is 9, the chi-square value is less than the number (16.919) in the $p = 0.05$ column. This means that the numbers used for these phone numbers were selected at random. In other words, a significant difference does not exist between the observed frequency of numbers and the expected frequency of numbers.

HANDOUT 7.7–1   CRITICAL VALUES OF X^2 (t) TABLE

Degrees of Freedom	$p = 0.9$	$p = 0.5$	$p = 0.2$	$p = 0.05$	$p = 0.01$	$p = 0.001$
1	0.0158	0.455	1.642	3.841	6.635	10.827
2	0.211	1.386	3.219	5.991	9.210	13.815
3	0.584	2.366	4.642	7.815	11.345	16.268
4	1.064	3.367	5.989	9.488	13.277	18.465
5	1.610	4.351	7.289	11.070	15.086	20.517
6	2.204	5.348	8.558	12.592	16.812	22.457
7	2.833	6.346	9.803	14.067	18.475	24.322
8	3.490	7.344	11.303	15.507	20.090	26.125
9	4.168	8.343	12.242	16.919	21.666	24.877
10	4.865	9.342	13.442	18.307	23.209	29.588

Notes provided by the teacher on how to use this table:

_____

_____

_____

_____

_____

_____

_____

_____

_____

_____

_____

_____

_____

_____

_____

_____

_____

_____

_____

WORKSHEET 7.7–2
SOME ADDITIONAL CHI-SQUARE PROBLEMS

1. Assume that you have an electronic game that has been programmed to flash the colors red, blue, green, or orange on a screen in a random sequence. Your task, according to the game instructions, is to guess which one of the four colors is going to be flashed next on the screen. Before playing the game, you decide to determine whether the game has really been programmed to flash colors in a truly random sequence. Since each flash will be one of four colors, the random chance of any color being flashed is obviously one in four. Suppose you keep a record of the colors that are flashed for 100 consecutive flashes. If the colors are flashed in a random sequence, one would expect each color to be flashed with a frequency of approximately 25 times. Assume the following data was obtained: Red = 20 times, Blue = 30 times, Green = 15 times, and Orange = 35 times.
Put the proper data in the following table:

Attributes	Observed Results (O)	Expected Results (E)	O – E	$\frac{(O-E)^2}{E}$
Red				
Blue				
Green				
Orange				

Total = _____ = Chi-Square (X^2)

   Since you have taken data on four attributes, and since the number you refer to in the Degrees of Freedom column of the Critical Values for X^2 (+) Table is the number of attributes minus 1, you refer to the Degrees of Freedom number 3.

   Is the value of chi-square greater or less than the number in the p = 0.05 column of the table? _____

   Do you conclude that the differences between the observed results and the expected results are significant (meaning that the color sequence was not random) or due to chance (meaning that the color sequence was random)? _____

2. Using the page from the phone book provided by your teacher, calculate a chi-square on the frequency of the numbers 0 through 9 used for 100 phone numbers (using only the last four numbers in each seven-digit phone number). This will enable you to determine whether the numbers 0 through 9 were selected randomly for the phone numbers.

Appendix

Materials list for the activities found in this resource book:

A

agar powder
alcohol, ethyl
alcohol, rubbing
aluminum foil
ammonia, household
antacid tablets
apple (or tomato), red
aprons, lab
atomizer (or bottle with spray
 attachment)
autoclave

B

baby powder (Johnson's™)
bacteria, living culture of *B. subtilis*
baking soda
banana
beakers (assorted sizes)
Benedict's solution
binoculars (or telescope)
blindfolds
bread (slices)
bubble gum (Bazooka™)
Bunsen burner

C

cabbage juice (red)
calculators (hand)
caramel
cards (3″ × 5″)
cellophane (red, green, blue)
cheese
cheesecloth
chocolate
clickers (or clothespins that make a snap)
coconut

coffee powder
color wheel, picture of
coins
Congo red solution
construction paper (opaque)
containers with lids
cork
cotton
cotton swabs, sterile
cover slips
crayons
culture dishes
cultures, living, of closterium, desmids,
 spirogyra, diatoms, oscillatoria,
 protococcus, *Bacillus subtilis*
cups, paper

D

darts, safety
dice
disks (antibiotic type), sterile
dissection trays
distilled water
Ditto™ masters
dropper bottles
dung, cow or horse or rabbit

E

elodea (*Anacharis*), living

F

felt-tip marker
filmstrip projector
filter paper
flashlight
flasks

floor cleaners, liquid
food coloring, red and yellow
food wrap, transparent
forceps
funnels

G

glasses (drinking), transparent
globe of Earth, miniature
globe, white
goggles, safety
graduated cylinders, assorted sizes
grape juice, unsweetened
graph paper
guidebook to fresh water algae

H

hydrochloric acid

I

incubator
inoculating loops
iodine solution
iron filings

J

jars (large), wide mouth
Johnson's™ baby powder

L

laboratory balance, triple-beam
lamps, microscope
leaves
lemon
lettuce, head
light bulb (red, green, white)
litmus paper, red and blue
lollipops, assorted colors
Lysol™ disinfectant (or a substitute)

M

magnet
map of surface features of moon

matches
measuring cups
medicine droppers
meter stick
methyl cellulose solution
methyl red solution
methylene blue solution
microscope slides, clean
microscope slides, prepared, of
    Closterium, desmids, spirogyra,
    diatoms, oscillatoria, protococcus
microscope slides, prepared, of the three
    basic types of bacteria, spores, and
    flagella
microscope slides, prepared, of *Rhizopus,
    Aspergillus, Penicillium, Pilobolus*
microscope slides, prepared, of amoeba,
    paramecium, vorticella, euglena,
    euplotes, radiolarians, blepherisma,
    plasmodium
microscope slides, prepared, of the 3 basic
    types of bacteria, bacterial spores,
    and bacterial flagella
microscopes, student type and stereo and
    oil immersion
milk, nonfat powdered and whole and low
    fat
molasses
money, coins and paper
mortar and pestle
mothballs
mushrooms

N

nail polish remover
neutral red solution
newspapers
nutrient agar
nutrient broth

O

oatmeal flakes
onion
opaque projector
orange
overhead projector

P

paper, drawing
paper, lens
paper, pHydrion
paper, PTC
paper clip
paper cups
paper towels
peanut butter
pencils, colored and glass-marking
peptone
Petri dishes, sterile
phone directory
pictures, magazine
pipettes (with rubber bulbs)
pond water
potato
potato chips
prism
product labels
protractors
prune juice
PTC paper

R

razor blades, single-edge safety
rice grains
ring clamps
ring stands
rulers

S

salt
sand
saucepan
scissors
scoops
screen (or shield)
sheep's eyes, preserved
sheep's hearts, preserved

shellac, white
silver nitrate solution
soap, bar of Ivory™
soap (bars for lab)
soda, clear lemon, cola, orange, lemon (yellow)
sodium hydroxide
spoon
star constellation map
starch, nonsoluble
stirring rods, glass
stopwatches (or other time-keeping device)
straw (or hay)
sugar

T

tape, cellophane
tape, masking
target (bull's eye)
test tube clamps
test tubes
thermometers, Centigrade and Fahrenheit
toothpicks, flat
triple-beam balance
tripod (camera)

V

vanilla extract
Vicks VapoRub™
vinegar, white

W

water, distilled and pond
weights, 1 pound

Y

yeast, dry
yogurt containing living cultures